Communicating Ideas

Communicating Ideas

THE CRISIS OF PUBLISHING IN A POST-INDUSTRIAL SOCIETY

Irving Louis Horowitz

New York   Oxford
OXFORD UNIVERSITY PRESS
1986

Oxford University Press

Oxford   New York   Toronto
Delhi   Bombay   Calcutta   Madras   Karachi
Petaling Jaya   Singapore   Hong Kong   Tokyo
Nairobi   Dar es Salaam   Cape Town
Melbourne   Auckland

and associated companies in
Beirut   Berlin   Ibadan   Nicosia

Published by Oxford University Press, Inc.,
200 Madison Avenue, New York, New York 10016

Oxford is a registered trademark of Oxford University Press

Library of Congress Cataloging-in-Publication Data

Horowitz, Irving Louis.
   Communicating ideas.

   1. Scholarly publishing—Technological innovations.
2. Publishers and publishing—Technological innovations.
3. Social science literature—Publishing.   4. Communication in the social sciences.   I. Title.
Z286.S37H67   1986   070.5   86–8381
ISBN 0–19–504120–8 (alk. paper)

9 8 7 6 5 4 3 2 1
Printed in the United States of America
on acid-free paper

Preface

There is, I suppose, a certain redundancy to the title of my book. For what does one *communicate* if not ideas. It is possible to *transmit* gold or illness for that matter, but the word communication already implies a cultural, or at least trans-commodity sense. But such a caveat registered, it remains the case that there are a variety of modes for imparting or exchanging ideas from person to person, generation to generation, nation to nation, and language to language. This act of transmission at its highest level is the responsibility of scholarly communication—the heart and soul of this effort.

While we arc at it, the word "idea" is scarcely less peculiar. For it embraces an extraordinarily wide range of language and speech ranging from raw data to metaphysical speculation. If the word "communication" is troublesome, the word "idea" has been downright nettlesome throughout the long history of philosophical reflection. And to operate, as such a work as mine does, in a taken-for-granted atmosphere that the author and reader have both resolved fundamental issues of both communications and ideas is a piece of hubris that could well disabuse even the sturdiest reader that something of worth is taking place in these pages. Yet, having registered such a pious, albeit necessary, act of establishing the limits of reasoning the need to make a leap of faith in this world of communication also remains transparent. For whether or not inherited issues of epistemology are addressed, much less resolved, we still face the need to examine just how, at the dawn of the aquarian age in technology and a new century in temporal terms, the communication of ideas is to be transformed.

Communicating Ideas has been a unique personal odyssey. On the theoretical side it derives from my thirty-five-year concern with political sociology, the class sources and political consequences of culture. On the practical side the work derives from problems in the organization and institutionalization of Transaction over the past twenty-four years. But lest this be viewed as some sort of effort at riding two horses as they gallop in opposite directions, it is necessary to say that the study of political culture, and the operation of a social scientific press within that culture, have drawn closely together in recent years. It is one of the great joys of this final stage in twentieth-century society that technology has provided a finely meshed bridge between ideas and actions.

The dream of Diderot and the French Enlightenment, a dream driven by the idea that thought is itself the highest specie of action, overcomes and breaks down older dualisms and distinctions. My book is aimed directly at discouraging such metaphysical inheritances. It is no longer feasible to parade forth reification in the name of dialectical analysis; a tradition in which dualisms and contradictions, become the goal rather than instrument of knowledge.

Newer traditions, in both social science and scholarly communication, unburdened by dualisms, dialectical or otherwise, are better able to address issues as part of a unified field of ideas. It has been my great privilege to live in the "two worlds," perhaps the "two cultures," of social science and scholarly publishing, only to find after a long trek that they increasingly represent a unified culture, an integrated environment which takes many forms and shapes but expresses the essential truth of the age: the transformation of a dualist culture in which ideational culture and material production are separated, to a unified culture well along in its formative stages.

I confess to being irritated not only by dualism in general, but also by two tendencies in writings about publishing that strike me as profoundly one-sided and hence erroneous. The first is the tendency within the publishing industry itself toward an excessive pragmatism, a how-to mentality that defines the publishing world in strict "nuts and bolts" terms and defies any analysis of long-run trends. Professional publishing is a strangely anti-intellectual environment dominated by individuals often remote from the publishing product. Publishing leaders too frequently see publishing as an "industry" with creases and wrinkles that distinguish it from other industries, but one that shares a common core of commercial "bottom-line" values summarized by the deadening phrase: "after all, we are a business and must turn a profit like any other business"—as if such pseudo-realism explains anything other than narrating the obvious.

The opposite tendency is the intellectualization of scholarly publishing, the flawed presumption that individuals twice and thrice removed from the daily activities of publishing as such can provide a satisfactory analysis of, or resolution to, its major problems. This specie of literature is too often characterized by an editorialist bias, the presumption that problems connected with decisions to publish or not to publish a book or a journal are uniquely decisive, whilst by implication all other facets of publishing are secondary. This facile approach—one that implicitly downgrades, if not denigrates, customer service, marketing, advertising, promotion, warehousing, systems, design, accounting—derives in considerable measure from the hubris of "the man of knowledge" who sees such everyday publishing issues as peripheral footnotes to the editorial parameters of publishing.

The need to transcend a blind pragmatism at one end and a bland idealism at the other has increasingly been felt by many individuals interested in the world of scholarly communication. I have benefited by their pioneering efforts, and throughout have tried to pay my respects to their work. In retrospect, the publishers themselves of mighty scholarly houses have displayed the greatest vision and the deepest foresight. I have in mind such giant figures as Sir Stanley Unwin, Morris Philipson, Frederick Warburg, Leon Seltzer, Henry Regnery, Herbert Bailey, to name but a few, who because of their unique cross-cutting roles have had to combine practical sense with intellectual fidelity. To these little recognized, albeit much rewarded, figures of the world of ideas and their dissemination, this work is dedicated.

October 25, 1985   Irving Louis Horowitz
Princeton, New Jersey

Acknowledgments

It would be most difficult to express adequate appreciation to the many individuals who have helped me gain a clearer understanding of the publishing world. It is far easier, and probably more exacting, to express my appreciation to the organizational components of this world-wide publishing community, who saw fit to commission papers, addresses and lectures from me in which many (if not most) of these chapters had their origin. In this regard I should like to express my special thanks to the following: UNESCO (United Nations Educational, Scientific and Cultural Organization); Smithsonian Institution; CBR (Center for Book Research); AAP (Association of American Publishers); SSP (Society for Scholarly Publishing); AAUP (American Association of University Publishers); STM (International Group of Scientific, Technical & Medical Publishers); IPA (International Publishers Association); and EEC (European Economic Community, Commission on International Communication). I seriously doubt that without the intellectual encouragement of the leaders and members of these organizations, this volume could have been written; or if it were, have been done so in remotely the same way.

There is one exception to this organizational rather than individual acknowledgment; and that is to Mary Curtis Horowitz. In her role as my loyal partner, most serious and constructive critic, and co-author of no fewer than three of the earlier papers upon which chapters in *Communicating Ideas* were originally offered, her support cannot easily, or even with great difficulty, be repaid. Her own role as a senior executive, publisher, and editor, at such major firms as CBS Publishing and John Wiley & Sons, provided me with insights and outlooks into scientific and social scientific publishing that made me painfully aware of the limitations of the view from the academy; and for that matter, the equally constricted view from the trenches of smaller-sized publishers. Mary's ecumenical spirit also enriched my sense of the positions and perspectives of scholarly authors and professional librarians, communities who help make up, along with publishers, the quintessential triad of information delivery and market receptivity to this loosely defined world of ideas.

I have drawn upon papers of mine which initially appeared in the journal literature. Let me list the publications and the chapters in which extracts or segments appear: *Information Age* (Ch. 1); *Journal of the American Society for Information Science* (Ch. 3); *The Virginia Quarterly Review* (Ch. 4); *Scholarly Publishing* (Ch. 7); *Journal of Information Science* (Ch. 8); *Book Research Quarterly* (Ch. 9); *Knowledge: Creation, Diffusion and Utilization* (Ch. 11); and *The Bookseller* (Ch. 12). I would only emphasize that such earlier pieces have been substantially rewritten, revised, and expanded for this volume; all other chapters are new to this volume.

To the best of my ability, I have tried to make this a book which is responsive in both data and theory to the current situation in the cross-over regions linking publishing, communication, and politics. Given the volatility of the subject matter and the variety of the areas covered, legal, technical, and professional, this has been no easy task. But it is time to leave to the reader the assessment of how properly such matters as are taken up in *Communicating Ideas* have been handled.

May 30, 1986   I. L. H.

Contents

Communicating Ideas

1

Valuational Presuppositions of the New Technology

One of the great unquestioned myths about the new technology is that the area is free of ideological presuppositions. Indeed, for some, it is a pure escape from the dirty world of politics; while for others, it is the higher learning itself, offering the ultimate critique of ideological politics. In this sense, the ideology of the new technology differs little from the old engineering ideology.[1] The difficulty with such suppositions is that they are simply untrue. It is more nearly the case that the politics of the new technologists are extraordinarily naive, even primitive, precisely because political and ideological concerns remain so deeply buried under the surface of platitudes which presume the hygienic status of data. This platitudinous style rivals in form the utopianism of earlier rationalist models: they come packaged with a faith in progress rivaling any nineteenth century romantic notions of evolution, or eighteenth century concepts of revolution.

It is therefore not unexpected, or it should not be unexpected, that there is a rebellion within the ranks of practitioners against the new technology. It is a counter-utopianism which rivals the efforts of Aldous Huxley and George Orwell at debunking and anticipating the sort of dilemmas found amongst earlier advocates of industrialization and urbanization. A long-range view establishes clearly enough that the new technology does not so much resolve as enlarge "classical" problems of power and its distribution, wealth and its concentration, or society and its stratification. The people one meets in this world of new technology have been met before: planners, programmers, and forecasters for whom activities outside or beyond the system represent calamities not distinctions. At the other end of the spectrum are those for whom the new technology is little else than a device to carry on exploitative relations.

That opposition to the new technology would come from old humanists is to be expected, if not entirely welcome. But more intriguing is the disenchantment increasingly felt by a segment of inventors and discoverers in the world of computer hardware and software who expected a brave new world, and who received a myopic narrowing down of a classical culture. For these individuals, the new technology has been reduced to Radio Shack merchandising; the personal computer becomes one more artifact to grace the homes of the middle classes in Western societies. Far from being the liberating tool it has been reduced to a libidinal toy. The very totality of the critique tends to make possible an easy dismissal of the disgruntled "fathers" of this new technology. But to do so is to miss an opportunity to expand our common understanding of the problems of no less than prospects for this new technology.

If Joseph Weizenbaum did not exist, his likeness would have to be invented. He is at once an early pioneer in the logic of electronic computers, a theorist of their utilization, and a philosophical critic of their unbridled expansion. In this sense, his philosophical effort *Computer Power and Human Reason* should be simultaneously understood at three levels: instrumental, theoretical, and ethical.[2] The trouble, however, is that the worth of Weizenbaum's position must be differentially measured at each level. One problem which "fathers" have is an inability to appreciate the work of "sons." And in computer technology this form of denial can prove fatal. Weizenbaum, in his stridency and failure to appreciate the immense changes in this area does little to enhance the reputation of the founder of computer language. The fear that home computers primarily equip the child with a "psychic numbing" that further undermines "whatever little moral authority the schools may have left" only extends the earlier arguments of Weizenbaum without deepening or changing his line of reasoning.

The early chapters of *Computer Power and Human Reason* remain unrivaled in the popular literature on explaining the heuristic properties of the computer, the logical foundations of computer power, how computers actually work, and the designing of universes through computer programming. Anyone starting out in the world of computers would be advised to start with Weizenbaum. There have been many works covering technical concepts of computers in a popular way, but few with the genuine graciousness and modesty which characterize the early chapters of this work. Weizenbaum's distinctions, following as they do the earlier work of Norbert Wiener,[3] are simply marvelous: the passion for certainty in science, philosophy, and religion in contrast to the operational quest for control in technology; rules of languages in contradistinction to ways of knowing; and theories as texts versus models as performances. In an area where mechanistic thinking abounds, Weizenbaum's dialectical explanations provide an impressive guide to those in search of larger meaning in the computer age.

Weizenbaum's work on computer models in psychology, natural language, and artificial intelligence are frequently polemical. Weizenbaum takes on such giants as B. F. Skinner, Jay Forrester, Herbert Simon, with relish. He is frequently on target. The metaphorical rather than empirical definitions of such concepts as artificial intelligence; the arbitrary conversion of artificial intelligence into a general theory of information processing as a whole; the presumption that information processing is identical with the "whole man"; the conversion of machine logic into political and social inevitabilities—each of these, and many more examples, can be adduced in support of Weizenbaum's assault against the "imperialisms of instrumental reason." The corruption of the computer revolution by an "artificial intelligentsia" and the mystification of behavior modifiers and systems' engineers are well taken. In this Weizenbaum is a kind of Dostoevsky-like prototype, an underground man puncturing the myths of those who, by faith rather than research, view the computer age as a relief from uncertainty, and then turn around and mock all traditional models of certitude.

Where the position of Weizenbaum and other interior critics collapses is in its own ideological proclivities. The critique of excess becomes a critique of power as such. The uses of computers by members of the armed forces or by practitioners of psychotherapy are declared to be "simply obscene." Computer science programmers are declared to be intellectually bankrupt, comparable to people learned in a foreign language but with nothing to say. These interior critics do not claim that specialized uses are technically infeasible, only that they are, in their judgment, immoral. The question of whether all uses by the military of computer simulation is immoral, or solely the work dedicated to certain fields or tasks, is not resolved. Nor are we ever told what constitutes the "inherent message" of things and events. In an era of computer-guided satellite missiles (ASATs) Weizenbaum's concerns are both entirely justified and yet sadly misplaced.

The offer of pacifism with a computerized face is attractive, but neglectful of an environment in which "one side" does not retain a monopoly on actual power, not to mention real weapons which are computer-directed. Thus, the interior critics are subject to the same sorts of criticism as are earlier advocates of unilateralism.[4] For what is involved is less an analysis of the efficacy of the uses of the new technology for military ends than a statement about the immorality of such uses. In such circumstances the authority of the computer scientists who argue against further expansion of the military options—i.e., "Star Wars" scenarios—is neither greater nor more compelling than that of those arguing opposite premises.

The "arrogance" of the computer scientist is contrasted to the ambiguous but honest quest by humanists (unarmed) for an (unreachable) moral world. Nothing is said about the failures of humanists to resolve such issues through conventional methods in the past. Indeed, humanism in this ideological milieu is simply equated with pacifism.

The destructive, counter-utopian picture of the world of new technology is not especially unexpected or even innovative. Such a view fails rather thoroughly to show how the human race is worse off with a new technology than with the old one; what mechanisms are available for realizing a better social environment when arbitrary curbs are placed on technology; what types of options exist to achieve economic growth, social stability, and military parity in a world that retreats from computer power. Blaming the machine, like blaming the victim, offers little promise. The technologist turned pacifist is in the typical Luddite position of giving birth to an entity that exceeds expectations, and moves in uncontrolled, unanticipated ways. But there are superior mechanisms of coping rather than standing still or going backward. In short, the better product is still the ultimate critic of the good expectation.

There is another wing to the assault on the new technology—that generated by users rather than inventors, and concerned primarily with the dissemination of the product rather than placing curbs on the usages. The Unesco contributors to *The Right To Communicate* typify this wing of the disenchanted. But unlike the inventors, the users' forum is far more interesting for what they collectively and cacophonously imply than for what is actually said.[5] For what we have is a rather conventional Unesco-type document in which puffery far outweighs substance. Many of the contributions to *The Right To Communicate* emanate from "working groups" established under the auspices of the International Institute of Communications encouraged by Unesco, presumably in response to its medium-term plans for a "new human right—the right to communicate."

In some curious way, the users even more than the inventors strike discordant, counter-utopian themes. The trial balloon has burst, so to speak, on "the right to communicate" thesis even before it emerged from its Unesco closet. No sooner does Sean MacBride, the unique recipient of the Nobel and Lenin Peace prizes, summarize "the history of the world as consisting in the history of the ebb and flow of the tide in the incessant endeavours to secure the protections of liberty," than all sorts of hell break loose. MacBride himself cautiously argues that "governments of socialist and other one-party states should recognize that the right to communicate is a fundamental human right which cannot be denied to their own public without weakening confidence in their own system of government." However, the Soviet contributor to this symposium throws cold water on such a naive approach by noting, and not without telling effect, that the notion of freedom of information as a human right "finds no objective reflection in international law. The right to inform is counterbalanced by specific obligations, which mean that freedom of information cannot be recognized as a principle of public international law."[6] This does not prevent Kolossov of the Soviet Ministry of Foreign Affairs from urging juridical recognition of "a new international order," with what ominous consequences for a free press the innocent victim is left to guess.

Instead of exploring the opportunity provided by such diverse readings of the right to communicate, the users' groups invariably are reduced to a series of statements, platitudes, quasi-resolutions of mixed levels of quality, and views on the subject/theses from a variety of professional perspectives and national prejudices. Every special plan from making Esperanto a language of equality (it might be added, argued forcefully in English—the language of discrimination, domination, and oppression) to making the distinction between "honest information" and "illegal propaganda" central in this brave new world is argued with a sincerity which in the past was reserved by clerical devotees, not information scientists.

This users' group is able to offer, in Unesco-like fashion, optimistic readings on the "democratization of communication," but in its remarkable inability to note any sort of contradictions in the variety or bundle of rights ranging from the right to be informed to the right of privacy, the entire project ultimately becomes an exercise in futility. The counter-utopians soften the very arguments on which a demo-

cratic culture is based. And in so doing they serve only to accommodate communist ideological requirements and nationalist developmental efforts to exclude free enquiry in the name of greater parity in
information dissemination between the First and Third Worlds.

Underlying much of these right to communicate theses is a philosophical failure of nerve in the communications field. The "right" of
every person to a decent meal does not entail a denial of the "right"
of the farmer who grows food to be paid for his labors. By extension,
communication rights involve a series of obligations, apparently a
dirty word except when employed as a defense of socialist legality,
that do not so much limit the human race from accessing information
as it does ensure the donors (presumably also human) from being
paid or otherwise rewarded differentially for their labors based on the
quality and worth of their communications. Amazing as it seems,
scarcely a single line in the bundle of Unesco proclamations offered
pays any attention to the costs involved and hence reimbursement
necessary for scholarly or popular communication to have meaning.

This comes about through the denial, by communist nations and
Third World followers alike, of the autonomous nature of culture as
a fact of life. Indeed, to speak of the autonomy of culture smacks of
the very Kantian belief of "art for art's sake" that is anathema to such
individuals and nations. Here again, we see how in the guise of discussions on scholarly communication and the new technology what
we actually have is a recourse to a very old neo-Platonic and certainly neo-Marxian argument on the need to place culture at the
service of class, or less pleasantly, to make art equivalent to propaganda, and the latter (and by extension the former) defined by the
needs of the ruling hierarchy of the state. Such "rights to communicate" offer a barren fruit, since what is to be communicated is nothing
other than the proclamations of the totalitarian state.[7]

The contradictory character of the information environment is
sharpened by the political demands for making data a free or public
resource, or in other words, a public right like air and water. The
commercial utilization of information has become a central force in
advanced societies, and as a result, a radical view has come to claim
that a "silent struggle is being waged between those who wish to
appropriate the country's information resources for private gain and
those who favor the fullest availability." Needless to say, matters of
copyright infringement simply do not appear on the horizons of this
perspective. Instead dire warnings of "information commercialization" are sounded; with a fear that "proprietary interests take prece-

dence over free scholarly exchanges." The essence of the argument is that corporations erect a "wall" between discoveries and discussions, and as a result, ideas are being diverted and even perverted (for military ends) in place of full disclosure and distribution of data.[8] In this view, arguments about the number of radio stations or newspapers in operation are meaningless, since monopolization creates a standardized package, and the trend toward conglomerate ownership further inhibits the free flow of information. In this way, the robust character of democracy is itself destroyed, along with social accountability and public dissemination.

In this nether world, the only admissible allies of democracy are librarians who unabashedly argue the case for free access to information. Behind such pleasantries is the denial that knowledge is a hard-earned value with costs attached to its promulgation no less than its disbursement. The hidden predicate in this line of argument is that information was once "free" and is becoming less so in the information society. To note that such a presumption of original freedom is as groundless as the notion of original goodness does little to disabuse critics of free-market societies. Nonetheless, it is important to establish ground rules to overcome this current dichotomization between those who insist that every piece of data be paid for and those who argue the free use and disbursement of hard-earned information. Obviously, stretched to their respective limits, both positions represent dangerous exaggerations. The struggle for the control of information is multifaceted. The place of government as a disburser of information is being touted by critics of the open society as a desperate effort to open up the system. But this argument takes no heed of the prospects that solutions proferred may be worse than the problem of information distribution. Government as a single source of "free information" is hardly an improvement over competing networks, agencies, and institutions searching for viable information outlets and markets.

While it may be the case that the costs of generating useful information increase along with the complexity of demands and as the needs of professionals become more exacting, it is also the case that sheer quantity of data outlets or numbers of computer programs in service do not resolve the issue of democratic choice or governmental responsibility. The government serves as a balance-wheel between private sector ownership and citizen rights rather than as advocate of either the private or public sector. In this approach the metaphysical assumption that the free operations of the market are a unique path are no more advantaged than those who argue that only government control of the market is viable. An inventory of relative costs, rather than an ideology of abstracted rights or responsibilities is an urgent order of business for those concerned with communicating ideas.

Thus, we are once more back to the land of reality, a spiritual land to be sure, but one in which obligations co-exist with rights, and in which questions of a modest sort, such as copyright protection become part of the warp and woof of author protection. The recent work by Judy Erola and Francis Fox indicate that bureaucratic and administrative reports need not be turgid, tendentious recitations of official party positions. More important, such emphasis on legal frameworks and normative contexts provides the strongest response to empty slogans and generalizations about national rights.

Every nation has the responsibility to rewrite its copyright legislation in light of the new technology: from the revolution in reprography (happily avoiding the more commonly used phrase Xerography) to the efforts to protect new forms of intellectual property such as computer programs. This act is itself a statement of the ideology of authors and publishers. To the credit of the Canadian approach, it does not in any way seek limits to the communication of information and opinion. However, this Canadian document does seek to define the intricate network of costs and benefits that are brought about by the explosion in communication media (press, radio, television, computers, cable, satellites, recordings, film, theater, home entertainment units, etc.) in a way that will not collapse the very plethora and pluralism of information that characterizes democratic societies.

From Gutenberg to Telidon marks an advance upon copyright reforms in the United States by recognizing explicitly the moral no less than legal claims attaching to the ownership of ideas. It does so without weakening the need for dissemination of information. This clear distinction is made as an essential fabric of the Canadian approach. It provides for a bundle of rights attaching to claims of authorship, integrity of product, length of proprietary interest. The Canadian position also develops a clear-headed set of legal guidelines to remedy infringement. The authors of this document urge relief from violations on both civil and criminal grounds; and in so doing provide a potential basis for prosecutorial activities at international no less than national levels in terms of such problems as privacy of information no less than more shadowy forms of infringement, such as piracy.

If I have one significant area of criticism of the Canadian approach, it is with its acceptance of the American fair-use doctrine, which, as I will outline later in the book, has created such mischief in Western copyright law and traditional copyright in general. The thrust of the Canadian approach, in contrast to the Unesco approach, is to recognize and secure creators' rights in a communications era, and to ensure compensation without needlessly limiting the efficient dissemination of information and ideas. Hence the all-too-bland acceptance of a fair-use doctrine, with its vague, easily violated limits, runs counter to the thrust of this report.

It suffices to say that in my estimate the Canadian report offers an excellent counterweight for nations seeking a model to alter existing copyright legislation. This is no mean-spirited, tight-lipped effort to limit information flows but rather a sophisticated attempt to provide the foundations for a post-industrial legal framework that seeks to balance the rights of a society to knowledge, with the obligations of that same society to protect the wellsprings of its creative talents who produce such knowledge. The presumption of this report is the protection by copyright of creative work and the payment to the creators for providing communication. By extension, the creators of such works are entitled to the same rewards and payments as any other individuals providing goods and services. The Canadian approach strikes a balance between hand work and head work that is too often observed in the breach.

Human rights begin with creative rights. Creations are the work of real individuals, not fictive collectivities. We sometimes, perhaps too easily forget that governments govern, publishers publish, but only individuals create. The protection of copyright is thus a quite new human right as these artifacts are measured in the scale of evolution. It guarantees, or at least seeks to guarantee, to the creator of information and/or ideas a place in the brave new world of bureaucratic demands for order and orthodoxy. Moreover, it does so without eroding the distinction between ideas and powers. The Canadian view is of significance in helping us to move from the anarchical puffing of property as theft to the careful study of the theft of property. Of course, all reports and recommendations rest upon a social structure in which the marketplace freely determines not only protection of information but differential rewards for such information or ideas. In the topsy-turvy world of *The Right To Communicate,* there are few issues of scholarly communication, since the government personally pays communication agents a going protected wage to provide delivery of what the evangelists used to call the good news.

This sort of criticism is less with the work at hand, than an indication of scientific and legal tasks yet to be addressed: specifically, the relationship of communication to property in a whole gradation of social environments extending from free-market systems to command/control systems. A *White Paper* of this sort can at least move us ahead to a consideration of such vexing themes.

In each of these three perspectives what is new is the sense in which the new technology, with its emphasis on communication rather than production, operations in place of ownership, represents fundamental challenges to the inherited ordering of things and people. Yet, in each instance, powerful ideological postures are at stake: the policy uses to which advanced technology is put; the sort of information which is public and how such data become verified; and finally how one can cope with a changing technology without sacrificing democratic principles of dissemination or free market principles of supply and demand.

Surely, one could just as readily locate three other archetypical examples of such ideological tendencies. But the key point is simple enough: the new technological-informational environment does not automatically resolve major dilemmas of our epoch. Indeed, in the very acceleration of data, and speed of transmitting and communicating such data, many "classical" themes are exacerbated. And if this serendipitous finding is not exactly what people are seeking, then at least it provides a bridge between technologism and humanism—a common core of issues that require and deserve cross-fertilization. For the crisis in scholarly communication is not in any particular new discovery or old moral caveat, but in the break-neck speed of technology in contrast to the snails-pace changes in the moral order. This contradiction forms the essence of the next several chapters.

2

New Technologies, Scientific Information, and Democratic Choice

A broad range of literature is now abundantly available about the worth of the new information technology at the level of business and industry. The new information technology has grown sufficiently large to merit its own slogans, the most recent being "the videotext revolution."[1] Even a cursory résumé of events in the past forty years will help to explain the magnitude of this technological revolution, a revolution in the collecting, storing, processing, and transmitting of information. As Tom Forester recently summarized matters:

> The first electronic digital computer built in the United States, ENIAC, was unveiled at the University of Pennsylvania in 1946. It weighed 30 tons, filled the space of a two car garage, and contained 18,000 vacuum tubes, which failed on average at the rate of one every seven minutes. It cost half a million dollars at 1946 prices. Today, the same amount of computing power is contained in a pea-sized silicon chip. Almost any home computer costing as little as $100 can outperform ENIAC. Put another way, if the automobile and airplane businesses had developed like the computer business, a Rolls Royce would cost $2.75 and run for three million miles on one gallon of gas. And a Boeing 767 would cost just $500 and circle the globe in 20 minutes on five gallons of gas . . . This revolution is not confined to the world of science and technology, it is bringing about dramatic changes in the way we live and work, and maybe even think.[2]

But the widespread implications of this new technology for the political prospects of democratic societies has thus far largely been overlooked. In this chapter I intend to address this question of the political impact of the new information technology, not from the vantage point of contending commercial proprietary interests, not to make purely technical distinctions between delivery systems, but rather primarily from the standpoint of political sociology. More exactly, what are the effects of societies upon citizens as a result of developments that come under a variety of labels—from electronic data to information technology, broadcast teletext to interactive videotext? In this chapter I am concerned with the dissemination of information from senders to receivers in formats that do not have the characteristic benefits of hard copy—that is, the printed word.

Scholarly responses to the new information technology seem to fall into two camps. The first is grounded in what might be called the Orwellian or counter-utopian model. The new information technology is feared as inevitably dominated or controlled by a small political clique or power elite, capable of maneuvering and manipulating mass sentiments. In this respect, there have been dire predictions that the new information technology is some awful majesty, a veritable handmaiden of totalitarianism. An entire tradition has, like Orwell himself, come to view with deep concern any control or domination of the masses by electronic media as such.[3] Critiques of the totalitarian potential of the new information technology extend from an established position taken in English scholarly circles from Aldous Huxley to C. P. Snow, no less than from American social and cultural fears by critics from Dwight Macdonald to Marshall McLuhan. The key issue was not and is not, about the quality of the hardware or the data being transmitted, but rather about ownership and control. The new information technology in this context becomes only a larger and more ominous evolution of a long-standing process of centralization of authority.[4]

At the other end of the political spectrum are those who have been critical of the new information technology as a "wholly other" culmination of the imperial capitalist state in which the means of scientific communication is monopolized.[5] Western Marxists see in the new information technology a definite threat to potential for public ownership or popular expression, usually only in Western societies. There is a fear of the new, a mistrust of the potential for the management and manipulation of ideas, not so much by a political elite as by an economic ruling class.[6] If one looks closely at the two main lines of criticism, their conclusions and arguments present striking parallels with inherited moral discourse.

The question for both Orwellians and Marxians is essentially the same: Who will dominate the political order? Their bitter differences reside more over which elites are identified as the main enemy of freedom rather than attitudes toward the significance of new technology as such. In this regard, both those who fear its totalitarian implications and those who fear class domination of the new information technology are very much part of a long-standing difficulty in understanding how an advanced society, in which traditional modes of expression become obsolete, can at the same time hold firm to traditional forms of political rights and obligations. Although the extremes represented by these antipodal positions fuse, the analytic problem remains the same. Those who fear political totalitarianism and those who oppose economic stratification share an assumption that no positive political good can evolve from the new information technology.

The concerns that have been expressed in the scholarly communication environment, which will be most directly affected by a shift of preference from paper print to videotext formats, represent a specific extension of the general premonitions and predispositions shared by political leaders of developed nations. While such concerns are often couched in the rhetoric of business prospects and profits, they are no more and no less the kinds of concerns which have occupied a literary and scientific intelligentsia working in the areas of mass communications throughout the twentieth century, down to the hushed atmosphere of impending doom. There is nothing in the evidence to suggest that the flow of print has contracted under the impact of the new technology. As one report indicates: "In 1950, when the impact of television first began to be felt, 11,022 books were published in the United States. In 1970, when the impact of the computer began to reach major proportions, the number of books had risen to 36,071. In 1979, after almost thirty years of television and ten years of major computer use, 45,182 books were published in the United States. Book publishing revenues in the United States in 1950 were less than $500 million; in 1970 they were more than $2.9 billion; in 1980, more than $7.0 billion."[7] Even with a leveling off in hardware sales and production the multi-tiering of information is now a fact, not a conjecture.

The scope and range of this "revolution"—one that crosses national and systemic barriers—indicate the existence of democratic potential in the new information technology. Although by no stretch of the imagination will these potentialities be automatically realized, the notion of democratic outreach is worth pursuing in at least five components: first, the increased amount of information available in the new technology; second, the necessarily active role of the participant in much of this new technology; third, the corresponding capacity for confirmation and verification of information to an extent previously unavailable; fourth, the public rather than privileged nature of this new information technology; and fifth, a redefinition of the structure of information and cultural climates within advanced societies.

It has been argued in the past that the sheer abundance of information creates the basis for a system overload with such information pollution. There is supposed to be a corresponding acceleration of narcotizing dysfunctions of mass media.[8] While this "drugging" of society has in the past been the most widely identified concern of researchers, the point has too often been made at the cost of any appreciation that the massification of information is by no means an intrinsic evil.[9] So much of the post-World War Two political and sociological literature on information and communication was laden with moral imputations about the risks and dangers of succumbing to the blandishments of bureaucratic or mass society that the explosion of possibilities opened up by radio, television, and satellite communication became strangely converted into threats and predicaments for intellectuals.[10] Even those who dared adopt a more level-headed and realistic appraisal tended to channelize their thinking about information technology into questions of leisure and mass culture.[11] One has to search this earlier generation of social science literature far and wide to come up with a serious analysis of media politics or of information transmission and democracy.[12]

The discussions which are now beginning to take place on the relationship between the new information technology and democracy are, for the most part, not unlike the earlier literature we have been describing. There is the same tendency to perceive recent developments in science as favoring elites, dooming masses, narcotizing recipients, manipulating the poor, and massaging the wealthy. But if we keep in mind the earlier literature and recognize quite frankly that its most dire predictions have not come about, or at least have been counterbalanced by serendipitous aspects of mass communications, we can then move to a higher ground in a discussion of the new information technology as a set of possibilities concerning democracy and free expressions rather than a predetermined unilinear totalitarian outcome.

To start with, a modular, grid-like pattern of information storage and retrievability such as that permitted by videotext allows for a wider level of choice and decision than previous forms of telecommunications. If one takes into account that standard television viewing provides a maximum of 99 channels to be used as separate outlets on two main frequency outlets, and if we multiply that by 99 additional outlets within each of the original channel separations, the outcome is no less than 9,801 possibilities at any given instant of videoviewing. That is to say there are roughly 10,000 active possibilities available through broadcast teletext at any given time. These may range from shopping market lists and updated information on industrial patents, air schedules, to musical concerts and experimental dance. New forms of interactive communication such as videotext permit even higher levels of retrieval, storage, and utilization of data to wide numbers of people who in the past have been largely passive recipients of such information.

To this must also be added the explosive rise of satellite television, which by the end of 1985 reached 2,500,000 people in the United States. "Dish owners" largely in rural areas, currently not served by cable television, can now receive in theory over 650 television stations, and in practice close to 200 outlets within the current "Clarke range" which extends from Alaska in the west to French Canada in the east. Extra-large dishes now bring the morning news broadcasts from Moscow to the Russian Studies department at Columbia University in New York. The evolution of satellite viewing is clearly based on mass demands for amplified choice in viewing. But what starts with mass demands for football and baseball "feeds" has now evolved into class demands for financial news, book review digests, and worldwide weather reports.[13]

Despite the fear that interactive videotext may mean the end of the printed word, the more likely proximate consequences are less pernicious. We are clearly moving toward a multi-tiered system: one based on both hard copy and videotext (or video-disc) information bases. They serve very different but mutually important purposes. The parallel may be radio and television: Television did not replace radio, but it did influence the content disseminated by the older medium. With videotext, we are now at a point where each family, individual, or business unit may have at their disposal 10,000 different "titles" or forms of upgraded information—far more than any average home or office can currently maintain, much less store—and, in addition, hard copy for more abstracted and more portable forms of information. The act of broadening the amount of information accessible through technological devices opens channels of choices and decision-making for individuals that hitherto have been available only to powerful elites within a society.

Citizens in advanced societies are already living in an environment which has a multi-layered media system. The audience which continues to buy a mystery novel or a philosophic treatise in hardcopy form will also insist upon having a personal computer and satellite dish with which to access financial data banks and update their portfolios. The individualization of information and not the collectivization of ideology is what realistically is beginning to occur. Policies to implement an information environment that remains competitive thus becomes part of a democratic imperative. The key is competition and not monopolization of the sources of information. The nature and history of scholarly publishing uniquely equips this dissemination center to act upon such concerns.

The new information technology encourages active rather than passive public involvement. Whatever virtues are possessed by traditional printed materials, the litany extends from ease of use and retrieval to shifting back and forth within a journal or book, the act of reading a given book or periodical remains relatively passive and singular. How information is structured, and moreover what is not revealed, is decided by others. Unless one is dogged and determined, it is difficult to verify data or check possible sources of confusion, misunderstanding, or even downright error outside of comparatively few library compounds. Alternative information sources still go largely unchecked in traditional communication environments.

The new information technology permits a higher level of interactional involvement. One can confirm or disconfirm exact information, test propositions, and develop comparabilities, not envisioned by the author or the original source, in the comfort of one's home. In discussing experiential confirmation we generally are considering factual rather than interpretative information. Even at the level of speculation, there may be possible uses of the new information technology hardly thought about in the past. For example, tracking sources of ideas through space, time, and culture becomes entirely feasible. The paired acts of verification and confirmation may become part of everyday life of ordinary individuals, rather than an exceptional event requiring extraordinary effort and skills by specialized elites. Optimally, in the act of further data specialization, new forms of generalization become possible.

In interactive videotext systems, advanced societies may finally be moving beyond the narcotizing and dysfunctional environment in which the individual passively receives images and signals, as in broadcast teletext. The multiplication of images may lead to higher levels of narcotizing behavior, but more likely, it will stimulate a computer or satellite involvement which will permit not only verification and correction of information but also the capacity to relay information from the individual back to various stations or data banks with which that person is networked. Voting behavior, for illustration purposes, may change dramatically, as it becomes possible to cast ballots through a hookup between a decoder-equipped television receiver and a main system computer. Opinions and votes may be cast on matters of local and parochial interest no less than national interest. One can receive and view the activities of local boards of corporate directors, local courtrooms, federal hearings, or government political offices. Optimally, this will be plugged into a cable access system permitting the individual to see, hear, and register his or her personal points of view and persuasions almost instantaneously. What is being developed is not simply heightened technical complexity but a decline in human passivity; or put more positively, an increase in human activity. This in itself makes for an enlargement in the scope of the democratic process. New communication forms is a process linking not simply individuals but communities and continents as well.

The importance of the publishing process within this context will not necessarily diminish; since with such a massive set of availabilities made possible by electronics, the need to select, screen, and simply search out what is relevant itself becomes a special province of the publisher.[14] The act of making public has been closely identified with the process of marketing. One must surmise that in the new information technology environment marketing activities will both increase and become more focused and segmented. This is especially the case in the short run. High start-up costs in computer information devices mean that they will be more profitable and competitive within a "narrow" rather than "wide" information band. The capacity to retrieve information electronically expands rather than retracts the amount of hard-copy requirements. However active recipients of information may become, the need for intermediary layers of sifting data and ideas will not disappear, but will in all probability expand.

The tendency to exaggerate the consequences of technological innovation, so that its apocalyptical features are enlarged while its cumulative features are negated, has taken on dangerous proportions. The prophets of the new information technology in their emphasis on a transition from a paper-based to a paperless society are invoking a *mysterium trendum*. The idea has taken root that advocates of a continuing role for books and journals are somehow offering obstacles to progress. Arguments have been presented in terms of resistance of the academic community to view publications in electronic form as legitimate: the inadequacy of copyright to deal with a fluid situation in which text can be transferred from creator to user, loss of revenue from advertising sources, and so on. But these fears often rest on the notion that a single-tiered, paperless world is an inevitable outcome of the new technology. A few researchers have come to take for granted the impending "paper-less" society and "book-less" library and are already turning their attention to the social consequences of a world without ideas.

Before accepting such prophecies we should observe the obvious anomaly that such blunt predictions related to the demise of the printed word are invariably registered in conventional books and journals. The larger problem in the single-tiered approach is a failure to reckon with great variety in the structure of thought. Organized rationalized conceptions are of three sorts: information, ideas, and interpretations. While one can readily appreciate how legal documents, government economic statistics, and specialized abstracting services can be designed to displace conventional journals and reference volumes, the need for ideas and, even more important, the play of ideas that permits a range of interpretations is not readily subject to a paper-less environment. The most potent argument against the anti-utopian vision is that a government's frightening power to control life and crush opposition in an abstract sense is in fact restricted by the greater availability of multiple forms of information dissemination, idea construction, and interpretative analysis.

The history of science and technology indicates that the latest and newest modes of communication and transportation do not liquidate the need for earlier forms, but rather become value-added phenomena. While supersonic jet travel may make sense at the level of great global distances, conventional jets at subsonic speeds still work more economically at shorter national-haul levels. Indeed, for distances under five hundred miles, railroad and boat travel may suffice and be most comfortable. Beyond that, surface transportation such as automobiles, buses, and trucks is clearly best for local travel. One of the most disastrous events in American transportation history occurred with efforts to replace the railroad with the airplane. This only created a crisis point at which the costs and convenience of transportation became exorbitant. Railroad travel has been widely re-stored, with stations vastly improved and even new ones built.

There is much in this slice of transportation history that should inform the communications industry. Once again, we are faced with a modest add-on view of the new technology confronting an apocalyptic view that such a technology does away with the need to transmit ideas and interpretations (and even information) in paper form. Those for whom democracy is a central issue would do well to recognize that the value of a multi-tiered approach is a question of ideology no less than empirics, since the multi-tiered approach is also a wide choice approach. Before publishers worry about big brother controlling the big tube, it might be wiser to resist the temptation of exaggerated premises about scientific manipulation of communication and seek to utilize new media for the further promulgation of technical and scholarly materials.

It has long been assumed that the television screen has helped privatize individual life in America, that its widespread use in the home has led to a decline in public participation and an increased willingness to receive images without living a life. The extent of such consequences remain moot. Patterns of public participation can just as readily be stimulated as dulled by screen presentation. Further privatization may be reversed given the magnitude of the new information technology. The signals that individuals are able to send forth by cable or telephone may make for enlarged public and civic participation. It is probably true that such public roles will not take place in the form of street manifestations or public outcries still typical in developing areas. On the other hand, the scope of interactive video-text participation is such as to add rather than subtract meaning to the notion of civic participation. This will become increasingly clear as the new information technology is made more widely available. It may not be possible for everyone to be constantly involved in every phase of decision-making, nor would citizens wish to be so. However, levels of opportunity will certainly be expanded.

The expansion of democracy does not entail any dimunition in specialization. The division of labor goes hand-in-hand with the enlargement of opportunity. In its offer of abundance, the new information technology implies checks upon, no less than reliance upon, the specialist. Just as academic life itself has become increasingly specialized, so too these new developments in information technology will, on a consumer level, move toward the servicing of a highly refined and limited clientele with particular interests and tasks. It will do so in a variety of ways using a plethora of techniques. Hard-copy text will surely remain a primary source for communicating knowledge and innovative ideas.

Traditional critics of the new information technology have ignored the fact that reading is itself a highly private act. One can conjecture at least that as a consequence of reading good literature or listening to good music certain public activities and participations will occur. But whether civic virtue results from high culture has always remained problematic. The act of reading or the act of viewing is still largely a private phenomenon. The forms of such enjoyment will undoubtedly change under the impact of the new information technology. This does not necessarily mean that changes will be toward either greater free expression or greater totalitarian control. There is only hope that the public and private roles may be meshed, and the thin line between entertainment and instruction will be further reduced. For example, for a portion of American youth the mechanisms of videogames already perform mediating roles between science and entertainment.

Less speculative is that the new information technology represents not a dimunition but an addition to what now exists in the way of publishing potential. Such forms of communication provide a definite value-added attribute to the reading of books in hard-copy form. The fears that self-publishing, in effect vanity publishing, will conspire to destroy the foundations of scholarship fail to reckon with the accepted gatekeeper functions assigned to publishers in modern societies.[15] Just as commercial publishing has flourished in an era of widespread photocopiers, so too it can be expected to survive in an age of electronic dissemination of information.

The conversion of the television screen into a key feature in home and office information dissemination has permitted new linkages between instruction and enjoyment in mass culture, everything from television cable to video games—that is, the wide-band—while at the other end there is a promulgation and promotion of scholarship and research in electronic media forms—what has come to be called the narrow-band. At the moment, it is the quantity of new forms rather than their quality that is most obvious. Effective supply and demand ratios have yet to be established. This awaits a sense of the market at one end, and the ability to supply that market in cost-effective means at the other.

It is hard to predict just how people will apportion their time in this new information environment. There is also the problem of how many will be excluded. The new information technology provides so many options that a new paradigm will evolve in terms of how an individual makes decisions about apportioning time and energy, rather than how interests are narrowed down. It might even be the case that democracy will dissolve under the weight of excess choice and decision. In this scenario, there will be a balkanization rather than pluralization effect. A less dramaturgical view of this new pluralism is the emergence and evolution of a knowledge industry infrastructure which will solve the problem of access and delivery of information and ideas it has created, only at a much higher delivery rate and level of abstractive than hitherto possible.

The political problem during the final years of the twentieth century is much less the amount of scientific information and technical material available than the integration and accessibility of the value in that information. Such a plethora of technical options has now been made available that society is threatening to fall behind in the orderly processing of data and information as such. Democracy works best within a set of commonly accepted guidelines and acted-upon procedures. It is not reducible to pure choice within the confines of a normless external environment. If the potential for a near-insoluble problem does exist within the new technology, it is less with its totalitarian capabilities than its anarchical consequences. The multiplication of options may well be responsible for the increased chance of anomie and normlessness, rather than the purely narcotizing dysfunction based upon a supposed information overload.

There is no common computer protocol or language able to synthesize the roughly 200 or 300 databases currently available. The Department of Defense's promulgation of ADA as its routine language is an attempt to impose order within the information recourses of the armed services. But thus far this has simply added one more system capability for specialized users. There are other problems of anarchy; for instance, the definition as to what constitutes bona fide research results when systems such as COMTEX are available in which one can publish work in progress. Problems without precedent are beginning to emerge in evaluating quality, regarding refereeing techniques and gatekeeping groups. Academic gatekeepers may not be adequate to the task of screening such a superabundance of data. These are only some of the enormous problems that information and knowledge industries are going to be confronting in the very near future. These are not simply or even primarily limited to blockage and prevention of access, but include the dilemma of what happens when access becomes more important to a society than ownership, and recompense for producing information becomes more and more the author's responsibility. If proprietary considerations yield to considerations of availability and access to information, issues of a new sort emerge for Western societies as a whole; considerably beyond the hard copy or text paradigm.

If researchers have had a difficult time providing a conceptual map to chart the relationship between the new information technology and political democracy, it is not for lack of data, and not only because much attention has been focused upon the short-run consequences for publishers of hard copy, but because there remains a suspicion deep in Western culture that technology in and of itself creates unanticipated negative outcomes. Theories of a new information technology have made evident a generational gap: an older generation for which hard copy is a symbol of status, achievement, and arrival; and a young generation of people for whom the video cassette, videotext, and video games have become paramount forms of conveying information. The heroes of the young are less the authors of novels and articles than celebrities who dominate television, whether they be in newscasting or commercial entertainment fields.

Many of the presumed weaknesses of the new information technology concern assumptions about the appropriateness of certain formats to deliver data and ideas to precise audiences. But in fact, the multi-tiered approach permits the market to adjust for such shortcomings. For example, the video keyboard may be a dominant force in matters of cultural transition and transformation, but when these same people go to an airport they may still prefer to buy a paperback book rather than carry a videopack in their knapsack. Even with miniaturization, electronic, onprint media may not be a preferred mode for delivering information, certainly not in any foreseeable future. Data systems of the future will be multi-tiered and the costs involved will have to be relative to the benefits expected. In the 1980s it is still cheaper and far easier to put paperback volumes into an airport newsstand than to put video cassettes into the same space. But even at such an obvious level, the researchers should be cautious. Western societies are moving toward a high degree of miniaturization as a result of microscopic-sized computer chips, which are so high-powered that it may soon be possible to consider private screens of a small, portable, battery-powered compact size, and capable of rendering the kind of information currently carried chiefly by hard-copy text. The portable television set already provides a model for such new delivery capabilities and processes.

The relationship between political democracy and the new information technology is by no means either uniform or mechanistic. In rapidly developing areas nationalism may conflict with a wide use of a technology that has foreign or colonial origins. Anti-democratic constraints come masked in hostility to foreign ideas, influences, artifacts, and scientific systems. The intense desire for national autonomy not infrequently spills over into tightly knit controls over the new information technology.[16] As one observer has shrewdly noted about Brazil—a prototypical country in this contradiction between national interests and democratic aims—there are definite limits to such restraints. "There is tremendous demand from all sectors of the economy for computer hardware and software; . . . [where] there is the principle of diminishing the scientific, technological, and economic dependence on the country. Controls on information flow can be justified on the basis of national security, privacy, economics, or nationalism. The restrictions, however, are often a two-edged sword: they may protect the country in one way and injure it in another."[17] In other words, the need for socioeconomic development involves maximum participation in the international exchange of information and ideas, even as the need to protect national interests may seek elites (of both advanced and backward economies alike) to limit such maximal use.

Resources restraining the further distribution and disbursement of information are often viewed as negative—that is, nationalist regimes, military cliques, political elites. But perhaps the greatest impediment to the mass distribution of information are the scientific and professional societies. Such organizations represent groups for which intellectual property is an issue and concern of moment. Without again examining the merits and demerits of the great debate on the right of public access versus the obligation to recognize proprietary claims, it should be appreciated that the notion of confidentiality, when carried to its ultimate logic, is also a powerful restraint on the democratization of culture.[18]

Everything from the statutory protection of privileged data to the development of limited partnership arrangements between universities and industries has a dampening impact on the broad use of information and ideas. Dorothy Nelkin has expressed the current contradictory tendencies within professional life with great persuasion.

She indicates that the response of scientists "rests on a notion that scientists have a 'right' to control their research, that autonomy is necessary in order to maintain integrity, to avert the misinterpretation of premature data, and to protect their 'stock in trade.' Those who request data claim the 'right to know' as an essential condition of democracy. Government agencies claim the right to information as part of their obligation to assure responsible use of federal funds, to meet policy goals, or to maintain national security or law enforcement in the public interest. Contradictions persist, reflecting the deep ambivalence within science about its cognitive and practical dimensions. Is science the pursuit of truth or the pursuit of useful knowledge, a carefully disciplined process or a professional instrumental activity? The ambivalence so apparent in the disputes over the control of research suggests that there have been significant changes in the social role of science and in the importance of research."[19]

These disputes are part of a larger struggle to renegotiate relations between scientist and citizen that were established at a time when science was a very different, more confined, social enterprise. This suggests that the new information technology enlarges the possibilities of both greater access and hence the wider practice of democracy and greater limitations to new data and information and hence narrower opportunities for the practice of democracy. The new electronic technology heightens the awareness of democracy as a problematic. However, and this is critical, it does not in or of itself lead to either democratic or dictatorial outcomes.

Arguments over the present-day feasibility of the electronic, or nonprint, journal often center on whether "garbage" will be displayed on the video terminals; specifically, articles that are not refereed, properly edited, or scientifically worthwhile. In point of fact, most scholars do not share print publishers' concerns. Only 20 percent, by one estimate, view this as an issue. Moreover, the arguments tend to be prima facie spurious.

To referee a journal in electronic format is neither more nor less difficult than for a standard journal. Indeed, the refereed report can much more easily become part of the article being viewed than the article being read. The quality of editing varies so much in printed journals that one can scarcely expect a worse situation to occur in the videotext formats. Finally, the role of technology in defining the quality of scientific research is not so much in contention, as is the early establishment of primacy in the discovery process. In this sense, the new information technology can only speed up the transmission of ideas.[20]

What is likely to take place in the short run at least is the use of microprocessor-based technology as a prelude to hard-copy format. There are still some clumsy aspects of electronic publishing: unavailability of terminals and unreliability of computers. But again, these are short-term considerations. In the larger sense, or at least in the macro-political sense, the new developments clearly presage alterations in the nature of scholarly procedures. But, just as clearly, they do not alter the demands for quality control of research. To be sure, the sophistication of the new technology and advanced data bases provides unheard-of checks upon fraudulent reportings and preliminary findings published in multiple sources that simply have not been available in the past. Through the more active involvement of authors in scholarly communication the new media provide more in the way of service to the scientific community than threats to that community.

These microscopic aspects of the relationship between technology and society should not get lost in the grand theorizing that has become customary. The keyboard itself serves as a device in which parts are purposefully manipulated in a social situation according to a logical scheme in order to create, interpret, send, or receive symbolically meaningful information. In this interactive environment, computers as a class of objects involve continuous feedback, sending and receiving information, egalitarian norms in a controlled environment in which rules must be observed to garner useful ends.[21] In other words, the structure of computer-related products, starting with the keyboard, creates a rational environment that is conducive to both bureaucratic and individualistic decision-making. Again, we must observe the contrary potentials of the new technology even at micro-levels of computer control.

The computer revolution enters into everyday life in a variety of ways: virtually all new machines and procedures for a wide variety of communication possess computer interfaces. Mastery at this level is essential for individual no less than industrial growth. The very nature of bureaucratic rationalization is defined no less than aided by this new technology. Upward mobility at all levels of industry and commerce involves training in and mastery of the new technological equipment; as a result, oral and handwritten skills take on different, probably lesser roles in an advanced environment. As we begin to speak of "generations" of equipment replacing and displacing each other, their equivalences to human patterns of evolution become apparent. Whether we are entitled to assume an isomorphism between bureaucratic rationality and political democracy remains highly problematic. But it is not problematic to appreciate the emergence of new forms that will alter relationship that now prevail.

The plethora of new developments in information dissemination provides a potential for democratic expression hitherto unavailable. I have indicated that problems created by a new information technology are not purely pedestrian but rather exemplify the struggle between economic and educational classes, that is, between those who do and those who do not have the ability to manage, manipulate, and massage the new information technology for their own goals. We may well reach a point where a sophisticated portion of the population capable of managing a new information technology and participating at the highest reaches of democratic participation comes into existence, while an entire other stratum of people is created for whom the new information technology remains an eternal mystery and who are largely unable to master the trends and tendencies of the proximate future. Whether this will be played out into yet another expression of class struggle or become a new way in which society is benignly stratified remains to be seen. But it should be evident that the uneven distribution of hardware and software components make for a special problem in democracy, and, it should be added, a more costly one than the uneven distribution of books.

The issue of computer literacy is nothing other than the issue of literacy and its uses writ large for a future that is rapidly becoming now. Whatever its stage of evolution, technology neither opens nor closes possibilities automatically.[22] It does provide for new options and hence new dangers and opportunities. The new information technology contains potential for self-correction, including ever larger numbers of people who at present are profoundly blocked from the mainstream of democratic participation. These remain political no less than technical challenges. Hopes for future developments in the area of scholarly uses of information technology require a further sense of user needs even more than manufacturer capabilities. We are, in a sense, once more recreating a post-industrial environment in which life and death issues are replicated on a canvas, this time called information rather than environment.

The central problem posed by the new information technology is the possibility of reaching yet more profoundly those capabilities of utilizing, or accessing, available, cumulative knowledge, and reducing the numbers for whom knowledge remains a mystery. The problem of illiteracy now extends beyond words into electronics. The task of democracy is not simply to widen the horizons and opportunities by the new information technology but, more significantly, to greatly increase the number of people involved. Democracy is not exclusively a question of options and choices for elites, but a social responsibility on the part of those elites to the widest number of people for their inclusion into the decision-making framework of society. At this level the problematic of information technology has not begun to receive proper attention; yet it is at this level of mass participation and technical literacy that the issue of democracy in the next century will surely receive its heaviest challenges, and it is hoped, most innovative responses.

We turn next to the area of publishing, in which the causes and consequences of the new information technology can be readily examined as a current issue rather than a future potential.

3

Technological Impacts on Scholarly Publishing

Discussions of the new technology and its impact on publishing have often centered on technical issues, such as the methods of incorporating specific hardware into systems so as to maximize efficiency in the production and dissemination of books and periodicals.[1] Other discussions have been concerned with the implications for traditional book and periodical publishing of such matters as the impact of xerography on copyright and the use of word processing equipment to increase control over costs of composition. This chapter will emphasize the impact of new technologies, not simply on the publishing industry as it now exists, but with respect to its consequences for the social structure of the publishing business. How is the new information technology changing the fundamental character of author-publisher-marketplace relations?[2]

The common consensus, and the source of much concern, is that significant social changes, no less than the technological changes, are under way. The dimensions of these changes can still only be surmised, but the questions are at least becoming clearer. They include these: How will the new technology affect the notion of property rights to intellectual material and the limits of copyright ownership in the publishing enterprise? How will decisions be made in future years about what to publish in print format, what to place in archives, and what is disposable? Are they even now being made wisely? What will be meant by a work being published? Will publishing be limited to mean the production of material in print or will it include the products of the new technology?

The Latin root of the term "publish" is *publicare*—to make public. This simple meaning of publishing has grown more complex. Today, anyone can make anything public simply by affixing words to a piece of paper and photocopying it. The same individual may distribute the paper or add it to a data bank where it may be retrieved by users. Publishing can be performed by anyone who has the opportunity and ability to use the new technology to enter and retrieve information, from librarians to researchers in industry.

The United States Copyright Law of 1978 began to acknowledge the implications of some of the changes imparted by technology by stating that copyright protection exists from the moment an idea is made permanent.[3] Permanence can mean affixing words in print, or transcribing a document into some kind of machine-readable format so that it can be introduced into and extracted from a data base. But the publishing community has yet to confront some of the legal implications of this broader definition of copyright. In fact, the new copyright legislation has moved a long way in the direction of considering ideas in relation to the creator apart from mediating agencies such as publishers. Publishers gain few rights simply by virtue of having transcribed words into print, unless these rights have been explicitly transferred to them by the creator. Permanency can exist apart from any particular format such as type. There is a strong presumption that since the work is now protected from the time of creation in permanent form, the relationship between author and publisher is different from what it was in earlier times. The proprietary presumption, in the absence of a contract, is more heavily weighted on the side of authors than in the past.

As technology influences publishing still further, the definition of what constitutes publishing will become more and more diffuse. There are now many ways to publish and disseminate information.[4] There are formats other than print, or in addition to it. In a high-technology environment, the publisher's traditional "value-added" contributions of selection and evaluation, editing, typesetting, and proofreading may become less important in relation to some products and more important in relation to others. Marketing and promotion may become critical elements distinguishing publication from availability. Certainly marketing has long been a critical factor distinguishing legitimate from so-called vanity press publishers. The latter require the author to assume financial responsibility for production of the work, while the press assumes only limited responsibility for selling the work—and too often makes little or no investment in marketing or promotion.

Publishing has been moving towards greater emphasis on marketing and promotion for more than a decade. These factors have become increasingly critical, even in scholarly publishing, partially because the marketplace has witnessed a proliferation of published material. More books have been published since 1950 than in all the years before, and a great many of them have been scholarly in character. Those who participate in the complex system through which scholarship is produced and disseminated have consequently developed a growing awareness that publishing has commercial determinants. In textbook publishing, market research into consumer capabilities and demands plays an increasingly important role in the development and packaging of new works. In scholarly publishing, the relationship between identifying and communicating with the market and responding to that market is more ambiguous.

Traditionally the publisher runs a certain level of risk in selecting books and periodicals to compose, copy edit, print, bind, and promote, and that risk is compensated by sale of those products beyond the level needed to recoup the investment in those activities. In an environment where writers have increasing access to sophisticated technology such as word processing equipment, and where some responsibility for pre-publication activity can be transferred from publisher to author, the traditional author-publisher relationship may change.[5] As publishers yield certain responsibilities, they also yield control; and as authors invest more time and money in the preparation of copy prior to printing and marketing, their share of risks and rewards is likely to increase commensurately. Traditionally authors take a small share of the return on investment, called a royalty. When a larger share of the initial investment is shared with the publisher, the royalty rates should increase. There are other issues. As we witness more active participation in the pre-publishing process by authors, will publishers accept a decline in standards of editing and proof-reading? Can authors maintain a press's quality standards?

Before the printing press, people with ideas permitted others to copy their spoken words for a fee; human copiers recouped the fee by permitting others to copy their copy. Before commercial publishing, authors simply printed their own work, and tried to recoup their investment by selling that work. Historically, a number of commercial publishers began as printers. When they decided to support their judgment that certain work had commercial potential by investing in marketing and sharing the return on their investment with authors, they became publishers rather than printers. As publishers began performing greater services for authors, advising them how to improve their work and helping them to do so, they indisputably added value to the author's work. It was not the same work that the author had originally presented to them. The value added by a publisher to the work created by an author has mainly taken the form of print-related activity—copy editing, typesetting, proofreading, and so on. But now that the concept of publishing need no longer be restricted to print, the publisher must rethink what value can be added to the work an author creates. Publishers are uniquely positioned to perceive that work presented in one format could be packaged and sold in another; perhaps they can provide the means for transcribing the material into other formats or offer to combine the material with others in a collection in which it would have different applications and could be reformatted.[6]

The possibilities are as limitless as our imagination. Publishers who continue to limit themselves to a concept of print may experience economic difficulties resulting from the new markets created by the new technologies. Certain publishers operating solely in traditional print formats have attempted to reduce their pre-publication costs in the last decade by abdicating some of their traditional responsibilities for authenticating the merit and validity of a work. They will have to rethink those decisions. The publisher serves as a clearing-house for specialized information; he is not simply a passive instrument transmitting ideas and information. If a publisher limits his role to production and dissemination and reduces his pre-publication contribution to the work he publishes, a more limited definition of role, coupled with the new technology, may make him redundant.

Decisions about what to publish and how to publish it will be of increasing rather than decreasing importance, especially in scientific and scholarly publishing. Organizing the decision-making process and incorporating some form of authentication into it must remain one of the publisher's chief responsibilities. A publishing enterprise is known for a particular quality of book or periodical; its reputation rests on its publishing decisions. A publisher's imprint can become a mark of bona fides to prospective authors and customers alike, and reputation will be a key factor ensuring credibility in the developing markets based on the new technology. Specialization within the scientific community has encouraged smaller, more specialized forms of scholarly publishing and the development of specialized units within larger publishing houses. Both have close relationships with subsets of the scholarly community, and their publishing activity both supports and is supported by these subsets. The new technological environment will re-emphasize the role of the publisher in authenticating the work of an author to a select public of users. Even now, in scholarly publishing, publishers do more than select information to make public; they validate it by the act of making it public, enhancing the value of the intellectual effort.

When professional societies are involved in a broad range of publishing activities, why is commercial publishing needed in the same areas? Both the American Chemical Society and the American Sociological Association, for example, are intensively involved in publishing. They publish journals, magazines, even semi-popular periodicals and newsletters. So do many other professional and scientific associations. Paradoxically, such professional agencies find it difficult to innovate. They must develop an internal consensus in order to act, and this is a complex process.

Unlike a commercial organization, a learned society has a presumption of collegiality and sees its responsibility as collective. Consequently, marginal areas of scientific inquiry seldom find expression in society publishing. If all publishing were centralized, or grounded in professional societies, scientific communication could well be hampered. Even if a society representing a disciplinary area did represent every legitimate field addressed by that discipline, emerging fields might not be covered, because a consensus about their merit would not yet have developed. Such intellectual high-risk areas are best served by commercial publishers or independent academic presses. In addition, subjects that are of interest across disciplines can best be exploited by commercial publishers who already have established relationships in more than one discipline. Professional societies are reluctant to put their imprimatur on a work that may not be defined as serious five years hence. They often are minimally aware of the interests of those outside their own disciplines, or disagree about the merit of these interests. They are therefore conservative and reluctant to take intellectual risks. Commercial publishers, on the other hand, define intellectual risk in terms of business risk, and cannot afford to be too conservative.

This suggests a corollary activity. Universities and other large institutions engaged in research activity do not define themselves as responsible for encouraging innovation outside their own institutions. They serve as initiators, places that provide supportive resources so that serious work can be done; they do not propagate such work once it is completed. The publisher of scholarly work in the physical and social sciences serves as a filtering agent—an independent, autonomous factor, able to permeate the university or scholarly environment as a whole, to sift through opinions and evaluations until he perceives a degree of agreement about what work is important. Publishing gives scholars and researchers a way to move beyond parochialism and organizational constraints. It is not only that organizations and universities are unwilling to make publishing decisions; it is that they are ill prepared to propagate pioneering work they have helped to initiate.

Publishing has a peculiar position in the scholarly world: it is a broker of innovation. It cannot stimulate innovation; it can only respond. But without the broker, it would be difficult to verify scientific innovation or intellectual imagination. The publisher's interest in the verification of what he publishes derives from the fact that a publishing house is defined not only by the information it releases but also by what it does not publish. That sifting of information is one of the means by which the scientific endeavor is rationalized. The publisher, as part of the division of intellectual labour, performs unique chores. He is the agent prepared to evaluate and market specialized data and ideas, as well as the agent uniquely equipped to provide a forum for the distillation and synthesis of those data and ideas. The new information technology, as it multiplies mechanisms for scientific communication, will make the mediating role played by the publisher even more important. The classical division of intellectual labour may shift, but the relationship will be enhanced rather than weakened.

Scholarly publishing is itself intended as a legitimating device. It is also a medium through which work can be further authenticated by a scholarly community. As such, publishing facilitates decisions about promotion and rewards. The publisher provides a medium for ideas to which other people can respond; the publisher creates an entity which exists apart from what the author alone creates. A book can be reviewed, receive an award, be cited, etc.; it has a reality that is vouchsafed only by the publishing process. The extent of the resources a publishing house commits to marketing a publication says something about how important it thinks the work is and what kind of financial return it expects the publication to yield. Users perceive that fact, and respond accordingly. As an adjunct to this process, communication among individuals interested in a particular area may be facilitated. For example, if their names and addresses are captured, say, on a subscription list or a list of book-buyers, development of a network may occur as the list becomes an instrument through which the publisher introduces new publications and products. Without such instruments, as the network becomes refined, the difficulty of communicating with that group may increase. Precise, targeted marketing

itself becomes a central publishing function. The new technology
both enhances and complicates this function.

Bibliographic data banks, containing comprehensive information
about the existence (and sometimes the availability) of scholarly
books and periodical articles, enable users to search for everything
on a particular subject that has been published over a defined period
of time. In some cases, the user can scan large amounts of text and
obtain specific pages of a work to determine whether or not they are
relevant to his or her research. With the right equipment, the same
researcher can go one step further and order information visible on
the terminal to be printed on the spot; if a large amount of material
is involved, he may order the material printed off-line and mailed to
him by a document delivery service. The user need never go to the
original printed product.[7] In the United States, on-line services now
permit searches of material published by Dow Jones, Inc., the New
York Times, the Washington Post, and other newspapers. KIT (Key
Issue Tracking) offers a constantly up-to-date index of important
and topical subjects. LEXIS provides searches of legal material. The
Congressional Information Service is available on-line. Acceptance of
these services has been mixed. LEXIS, for example, is a solid success
among attorneys, partially because of an intelligent initial marketing
strategy. Use of such services will expand as faster terminals become
more widely available, and as more scholars become familiar with on-
line searches as a supplement to traditional forms of scholarly research.[8]

The wider acceptance of such technology may also affect traditional ways in which publishers communicate with their customers.
When searching through bibliographic data banks becomes routine,
publishers may no longer need to invest in extensive direct mail to
bring certain categories of scholarly books and periodicals to the attention of a wide spectrum of professionals, particularly if only a
handful of the recipients are likely to care about the work. When the
prospective customers are scientists and businessmen, groups which
still comprise the majority of microcomputer owners, scholarly and
professional publishers may find it cost-effective to set up free access
to information about new products through existing telephone networks such as Telenet. The librarian of the future will be an "information manager" skilled in knowledge of information storage and
retrieval systems and able to provide information about where and
how material of interest to researchers can be obtained.[9] Publishers
may confine their efforts, in some cases, to informing librarian/infor-

mation managers about a work; the latter in turn will direct users to the work. Marketing today customarily involves informing large numbers about the availability of a book or journal but selling to only a small peripheral group in addition to the market core—often less than one per cent of those informed. As the marketplace becomes increasingly segmented, reflecting the development of science and scholarship itself, technology enables publishers to communicate effectively and at acceptable costs within these smaller divisions.

Publishing itself may become redefined. Certain works are now produced in extremely limited editions, perhaps only "on demand" or by means of xerography with loose-leaf binding. It is possible that information centers (libraries) will produce needed material on demand in addition to informing researchers about it, de facto assuming some publishing functions. Availability will then become associated with a given center of research. Aspects of scholarly publishing are already taking place in other non-commercial environments as part of the performance of research. The cost of "publication" is now more frequently built into specific allocations of funds to projects. In such cases, material is prepared for distribution with little attention to any but minimal standards of publication.

As this kind of in-house "publishing" becomes commonplace, and as bibliographic data banks receive information and maintain records about the availability of such material, the "informing" role of the publisher may become less critical to the dissemination of certain kinds of scholarly material. Those who seek specialized information may be required to take a more active and less passive role in its pursuit. As the information manager redefines his role, he will play an important part in this communication process. Conversely, the publisher of such material can become more passive with respect to traditional marketing. In the future, a publisher's decision to commit substantial resources to promote a work may be a key factor distinguishing active from passive publication, and broadly important from technically significant work. The definition of a work's importance may be as simple as the number of direct-mail pieces that are mailed and the response to them, or the number of display advertisements, directed to how many discrete audiences, that are placed in specific periodicals. Promotional and advertising budgets will become a key definition of what constitutes significant publishing; and commitment to a certain level of effort in an area, or clarification of an intent to promote aggressively, will become central to contractual negotiations between authors and publishers. A distinction will continue to be made between self-promotion by an author and promotion by a publisher addressed to the buying public.

The role of the marketing professional within publishing is changing dramatically. Authors have thought about marketing as a routine activity: information about the work is given to a marketing person, and that individual provides generic information to another generic entity known as the public. Increasingly, however, marketing people are becoming involved in publishing decisions at earlier phases. They may point to a need for publication on a particular subject because sales suggest there is demand for such books or journals. They are also ideally positioned to filter information about acceptance of and demand for products based on the new technology. The marketing role, in short, is not limited to the satisfaction of letting people know that a work exists; increasingly it encompasses the interpretation of consumer needs, or the needs of scholars in a particular area, and assistance in defining what kind of products might satisfy those needs. In most businesses, marketing people play a major role in product development, in figuring out how to shape a product that people will want to buy. To some extent, marketers in the business of scholarly information are also going to begin participating in shaping products that their customers will buy, and these products will not be exclusively confined to print.

Historically, producers and consumers of scholarship have been closely identified. In addition, a larger, general audience bought some serious books, particularly those dealing with history, politics, and social issues. This market still exists and an occasional book taps it, but such successes usually result from serendipity rather than careful planning. Certainly, the general audience is much smaller than in the past, when it ranged from dilettantes to people who were simply curious about a particular subject. Our private and business lives increasingly require such a high level of specialization of interests, tastes, and skills that the curious onlooker, the person interested in serious work in an avocational way, is disappearing. Few book or journal buyers are seekers after truth, in a general non-heuristic non-utilitarian sense. The marketplace is radically different from what it was even ten years ago. At the end of the twentieth century, everyone is part of a market. Even the buyer of antiquarian books is a distinct market. As the general-interest audience has declined, the market is increasingly limited solely to producers and consumers of information, who are fast becoming one and the same collectivity. The publisher, therefore, rarely can expand sales by innovative marketing techniques; success resides in identifying, with utmost precision, the actual potential of the market, and achieving results in that scaled-down universe.

The market for scholarly and professional material is highly educated and technically specialized. When it is interested in a problem, this population wants to know everything that has been written about that problem, and may be willing to pay a high price to avoid the possibility of missing even a small part of the available information about the particular question. In some areas—patent research, for example—the cost of overlooking even one item is unacceptably high. Unless a data bank is complete and current, patent researchers will not bother to search it. When the stakes are high in time and reputation, consumers will pay a great deal and take the information any way they can get it. They may even be willing to pay for the same information twice. Many subscribers to on-line systems now subscribe to a back-up system carrying the same data banks, to ensure that if one system goes down they can get at the data through the other system. Users of on-line systems are even more likely to use them when someone else ultimately will be paying the bill: this truism may in part account for attorneys' acceptance of LEXIS. The prices charged for scholarly and professional information in print have gone far beyond what general-interest readers are prepared to pay. Publishers price books and journals for the specialized rather than the general reader. Scholars write for their peers, not intelligent laymen. This has come operationally to define what we mean by scholarly publishing. Books dealing with serious issues are no less plentiful than they were in previous decades, but they are rarely picked up by the general reader. Journals, too, are directed to segmented audiences.

The new technology may accelerate this process, which can be likened to a type of modern feudalism. The scholarly publishing world is one of limited numbers, limited players, and searchers for legitimation with an extremely high personal investment in the results of the game. Authors and publishers share an interest in the same outcomes, although for different reasons. Both hope to reach their target audiences so as to allow the information they have generated to be more widely used. Generally, the pay-off for authors is recognition and the emoluments that accompany publishing. They are less concerned with general impact than with specific impact. Both author and publisher realize that they cannot effectively communicate with the entire universe of persons who may be marginally interested in a work. It costs too much, and ninety-nine percent of those reached may not be interested. Funds that are spent in reaching the ten percent of the world that may be marginally interested in an author's work will be money better spent to reach those people who are known to be eager to know about it. Resources are finite. Authors are being encouraged to become more realistic about the limited number of potentially interested people, and to become active supporters of specialized marketing. Increasingly, publishers' questionnaires require authors to provide relatively sophisticated marketing information. Publishers know that probably no one in their firms can define the specific audience they want to reach better than the author. Certainly questions about target audiences, major outlets, and primary sources assume (and encourage) a high degree of sophistication on the part of authors. Publishers thus compel authors to accept the notion of the specialized marketplace; the questions evoke that awareness.

If the post-printing press environment, like the pre-printing press environment, permits more direct interaction between the author and the marketplace, the scale will be different. Publishers exist and they are large. The modern scholarly world is diverse and geographically dispersed. Authors still need the resources publishers offer, but publishers must rethink their role and figure out exactly what they will do for authors in order to retain their value to them. We return to the medieval notion of the author, who is not only involved in the production of his work, but with its dissemination. How the involvement of authors in marketing will evolve in relation to publishing as we now know it, and how it will interact with the new technology, are fascinating questions. How they are answered may define conditions for success for scholars and other professionals and the survival of some publishers.

Scholarly publishing addresses specialized audiences, and it will be heavily affected by the new technology. Products even now can be delivered in microfiche, microfilm, diskettes, in looseleaf, updates, and on demand—as well as in the form of traditional books and journals. By the late 1980s, on-line access to vast quantities of full-text material will become widespread as optical disks reduce the costs of storing on-line data, as computers become faster, and as software becomes more sophisticated.[10] The inherent value of the information and ideas, rather than the cost of manufacturing the package, will increasingly determine pricing. The new information technology, at least in its interim phases, may also compel us to move away from the notion of risk and liability as the sole province of publishers, to risk and liability as a shared responsibility of the community of scholarship.

Technology does not mechanically resolve itself into new social systems. A fully articulated post-print publishing world awaits the resolution of a number of complex issues. These issues are as fundamental as the form of presentation of information we will define as publishing. Will saddle-stitched reports prepared by an agency or a university with which a scholar is affiliated constitute publication? What about the entering of information into a data bank available to subscribers to an on-line system, when no hard copy at all is created unless the subscriber requests it? There may be works for which no physical inventory is ever created, and other works that are published solely to satisfy an institutional need and receive no reviewing attention. Are these to be considered publications? Even now, a myriad of post-publication issues exists. The complexity of these issues will be intensified by the possibilities inherent in the new technology.

The scholarly environment has a number of feudal elements, and publishing has taken on some of the characteristics of the scholarly world it serves. If scholarly publishers as we now know them are to maintain a primary role in this world of rapidly accelerating technological development, they must get beyond a kind of cottage industry approach to the way in which information is prepared, distributed, and evaluated. The new technology offers the possibility of extraordinarily rapid accumulation and dissemination of information. Yet, curiously, word-processing and even information-retrieval systems share characteristics of cottage industries. For example, composition, until the past decade, was performed almost exclusively in large typesetting shops and factory settings. Increasingly factory settings are being replaced by composition units in private dwellings, perhaps controlled by a central management that allocates work and processes magnetic or paper tapes on computers to create camera-ready material. Entering typeset material into data bases at acceptable levels of cost requires capture of the typeset material in machine-readable format and knowledgeable people who can work with the on-line service to translate the composition codes and appropriately structure the format of the electronic product.[11] Publishers may have to make a short-term choice between goals. They may have to choose between buying composition at the lowest possible price, which will be especially important as the market for print material declines, or positioning themselves to create an electronic product by using full-service (and usually more expensive) compositors who have programming staffs committed to help develop an electronic version of the product.

Technology is already affecting publishing. In mass-market pub-

lishing, tie-ins have been important for some time. The appearance of
a television show or movie alongside the first appearance or a reissue
of a paperback can ensure its success. What comes first is often transformed: sometimes the paperback is derived from the television show.
Diskette or video-cassette versions of print stories may become more
frequent, as packaging the same entertainment in multiple forms for
the mass market becomes common.[12] Educational publishers are developing software that will enable students to apply what they have
learned from textbooks in simulations of real-life problem solving.
Similarly, scholarly publishing is developing new products in response
to markets opened by the new technology. Consumers of information
as well as entertainment may have a variety of ways of receiving the
same content.

Those who are trying to develop and disseminate on-line data
bases are at something of a crossroads in developing new products.
The general consumer market is clearly going to be a major user of
the new technology, but so far data bases directed toward the consumer market, such as the Source, have not been particularly successful. Data bases that are designed for specific professions or industries
with a major commitment to R & D have been far more successful.
More than half of the many thousands of data bases now available are
source bases, containing raw data, summarized data, or data in manipulated formats. Source data bases may be exclusively numerical
(financial and stock quotation), textual/numeric (such as Disclosure,
which manipulates data provided by the U.S. Securities and Exchange
Commission), and full-text (such as LEXIS, offered by Mead Data,
and Weslaw, offered by West). As terminals can more rapidly screen
large amounts of material, and as graphic terminals become available
at a price users can afford, we may expect widespread acceptance of
full-text delivery. Some products formerly produced in print may be
constructed solely for on-line distribution, such as newsletters or fact
and answer data bases. Video disks hooked up with on-line services
may enable people to retrieve visual as well as textual information on
any subject without delay. Encyclopaedias and catalogues are prime
candidates for this kind of electronic product.

This is a new publishing environment. According to the American
Association of Publishers, nearly thirty publishing houses are trying
to develop electronic versions of book products.[13] Bibliographic data
bases now provide mechanisms for managing an incredible amount of
information, especially technical information, that our society gener-

ates.[14] One can define through use of "key terms" what kind of information one wants to know about and immediately find out where work on that subject has been printed, screening out in the process a great deal of information "noise." Information-retrieval systems based on the computer afford researchers instant access to what is pertinent to their interests. The researcher's sophistication in defining key terms is a critical factor in the usefulness of on-line services, of course. Access to on-line terminals is still restricted, too, and use of on-line services can be expensive. But as scholars become familiar with using terminals to reach on-line data bases, the manner in which much research is conducted may be transformed. Depending on the kind of study and who is paying for it, research can be performed on terminals at home, much as some authors now work at home on word-processing units. Of course, people will need to come together in public forums for certain purposes, but these occasions will be supplemented by work at home. We are moving into an era when people will be able to control and obtain directly the large quantities of information generated as direct and indirect by-products of business and scholarship.

Access will not be automatic. There will be a struggle to define who is allowed access to what kind of information. The nineteenth century was largely defined by the struggle for control of the means of production; the twentieth century is being defined as a struggle over the means of communication and information. The new technology forces us to come to terms with the social content of ideas; who controls the hardware, software, and marketing, or information about the information, may ultimately control the information itself. What is released, and in what quantity, will itself come to define what me mean by big words like "democracy." In totalitarian societies the struggle is clearly on to limit all possible access to the means of communication. We may begin to talk about democracy in terms of how widely a society permits access to information, to computers, to photocopying equipment. Thus, while there may be threatening or uncertain aspects to the new information technology, there are undoubtedly liberating aspects as well.

Potentially, every person is both a producer and a transmitter of information. In the past, information was the monopoly of the few. As access to control of the delivery of information itself becomes democratized, as more persons become involved in the publishing process, there is an opportunity to maximize information as a liberating, democratizing activity.[15] Authoritarian regimes restrict access to information, while at the same time they are plagued by the need to use advanced information. Whatever the short-term difficulties, democratic societies will benefit from the new technology and its openness to all. These are, after all, problems of abundance and affluence—issues that an open society can more readily cope with than a totalitarian one.

4

The Political Economy of Database Technology

The rapid evolution of the new information technology has brought about a revolution in how we perceive data. We have acquired a positive perspective of the actual and potential uses of computer-manipulated information to reach higher standards in the assessment, evaluation, and use of social science products and activities. Such a perspective generates, if only indirectly, high expectations for improved control of decision-making and evaluation of the consequences of policy-making. How realistic these expectations are, given the state of the art in new information technology, is the subject of this chapter.[1]

Technological developments have served to highlight central questions about information in general: What data are critical? How accurate do they need to be if we are to draw conclusions? How can limited resources be used efficiently? How should data be collected and disseminated? Who should pay for the gathering and use of statistics?[2] While these are pressing matters, my focus here is on the specific issues generated by a socioeconomic environment in which computerized databases have become common. It is sufficiently challenging to identify the central contradictions between a databased statistical environment and a socioeconomic marketplace that is still evolving in its responses.

In the publishing industry, electronic databases were initially seen in a unilinear economic fashion—that is, as a product transferred from seller to buyer—and as a mechanism for moving beyond hard copy to diskette or cassette rendering of basic information. The revolution in software came with optimal scenarios extended to include a shift from a "hard-copy" society to the "automated office." When such ultimate expectations turned out to be, more or less, exercises in hyperbole, floundering on the limited market demands for such a total overhaul in conventional modes of information delivery, the thrust of databasing shifted to a more user-specific framework: how to use high information availability to develop better policy, management, and evaluation procedures.

There is nothing qualitatively new in the creation of databases as such. Indeed, databases and online searching has come to be viewed as analogous to scientific inquiry in general.[3] Excellent files on a wide variety of subjects have been collected and maintained for many years in manual, hard-copy form. Even the storage and updating of materials maintained in hard-copy and disk form cannot be viewed as particularly revolutionary; microfilming has been with us for some time. What the computer gives us is multi-tiered and multi-tracked access to information maintained in databases: the ability to rapidly process and select large quantities of information from a given database in various ways. From a single online database, a business organization can produce printed items such as catalogues and product announcements, specialized newsletters, editorial and planning lists, checking documents, and order lists and create advertising materials and output magnetic tape for both in-house use and external systems. Additionally, dial-up, online searches of central databases can be performed from communicating terminals, using logical search commands similar to those of online host database systems. This networking is no small step in the integration and rationalization of business functions formerly thought of as separate and discrete.[4]

In the publishing area, for example, databasing can be used to rationalize production and marketing functions, providing coordination with the full cycle of reviews, promotions, advertisements, etc. Databasing rationalizes the following prototypical functions: selection of book titles in production, logging of appearances of books in newsletters and exhibits, retrieval of lists and copy for other uses, production of planning lists for direct-mail efforts, production of output in specialized formats to serve as input to other systems, and finally, generation of formatted output to substitute for forms previously completed clerically.

The technical foundation of any system is a well-defined database. The engineering principle behind the new vision of the database is that nothing is recorded more than once, and the purpose of databasing is to bring the entire processing function into a unified field or frame of reference. But, again, it must be emphasized that what is new is not the notion of the database but rather the concepts of multiple access and use coupled with database comprehensiveness.

Computer manipulation of databases has profound consequences for the academic workplace, no less than for knowledge systems in general. Social scientific information systems will change traditional hierarchical arrangements within academic culture. Traditional distinctions between top "theorists" and middle-level data gatherers are becoming blurred as information experts perform decision-making tasks. How databases are set up may define the kinds of questions one can ask and the information they will yield. In some fields, especially economics and psychology, top scholars have helped develop principal databases to ensure control of the information they contain.[5] The behavior of social scientists toward one another in all probability will still be dictated by personal power relationships; but just what constitutes power may itself be largely determined by the ability to access and utilize databases.

Electronic access to databases also permits the use of data to back up long-range economic planning in a systematic, logical way, displacing seat-of-the-pants intuition. Better control of statistics may reduce creativity and risk-taking. But whether databasing increases or decreases creativity, it will lead to more control of numbers, ease modeling, and permit use of "what if" scenarios, thus giving us correspondingly more confidence in decision-making. In business, complete data on impact of changes in sales volume, inventory, or commissions are easily maintained with databases, which is why economists have so readily adapted to the new technology. Today the researcher can access information from commercial databases like Standard & Poor, Dow Jones, and Dun & Bradstreet, which means better ability to predict both specific and general economic trends. While the ability to draw policy implications from such databases is far from self-evident, they do support the rationale of such decisions and clarify who implements them.

Individuals seeking policy-making roles will increasingly be required to understand how information is gathered as well as how it is used. No longer residing in bound folders or manuals, data in computers provide easier access and facilitate use by decision-makers. Different spending levels for marketing activities can be modeled against variations in sales and prices. The validation is done by use of computer-programmed historical data from a wide variety of sources. But, again, the same problems remain. In validating common sense with computer analysis, does one maximize profits or minimize risks? Historical trends may or may not be an accurate gauge of future trends. Unaccounted-for larger environmental variables, which are seemingly endless, like Brownian movement, limit the predictive potentials of any database, however thoroughgoing. While theoretical generalizations will sometimes be informed by a data-rich environment, the place of specialization and even the role of speculation will hardly dissolve.[6]

Demographers work with population sizes and shifts, political scientists work with voting patterns, sociologists with stratification networks, and, of course, economists have the monetary system as a touchstone to guide them. Whether databases in each of these areas will be structured with sufficient flexibility to be "plugged into" other bodies of data, gathered and filtered in different ways, will become a major challenge for those working with the new technology. If we only multiply databases as self-contained monads without "windows," linking databases to other databases, resulting in a larger world, then we will simply compound the problem of determining what constitutes knowledge by providing a systems overload of information, without the synthetic framework to make the new data broadly useful. Indeed, the risk is that theory construction will itself be dismissed as idle chatter.

Although significant technical developments continue to take place with software development (notably, the ability to retrieve systematically and rapidly great amounts of information formerly thought to be disparate and unrelated), the major changes affecting computerized databases will largely depend upon developments in technology as such. The era in which creating, reproducing, storing, and retrieving data each stood alone as distinct activities is now past. New trends of technological convergence have led to a more encompassing field of information management. The convergence of databases is really an aspect of the new technology, which in turn is part and parcel of revolutionary changes now customarily referred to as post-industrial society.

Computerized bases as a specific subfield of information services have added to, rather than displaced, traditional reference works. Once again, we witness the phenomenon I have described earlier as multi-tiering; that is, tracking information in a variety of forms that manage to co-exist much more neatly than the advocates of hard copy might have predicted. To be sure, databases have introduced new wrinkles to the knowledge world, i.e., the value of information is estimated by the time spent linked to the database, or by whether one orders an offline print; but such matters must be seen within a larger context in which the expense of storage and retrieval is still far greater than in print media. Even when hard-copy, inexpensive formats exist, the speed, convenience, and timeliness of databased information delivered electronically may overcome price resistance; this of course will depend on the value ascribed to rapid access to the information.

Databased publication has raised demands for standardization of information presentation, rationalization of the way such information is delivered, and, above all, consistency in what one receives. If a reader depends on Dow Jones coverage of financial performance of public corporations, statistics on location, sales product lines, number of employees, and such, coverage is adequate for only 50 percent of U.S. public corporations. The information purchased is subject to the same criticisms of incompleteness or shoddiness as information delivered in hard-copy book form. The difference is that information is corrected more rapidly in the online form than in hard-copy form. One keeps returning to the obvious but elusive truth: the form in which information is delivered does not absolve one from analyzing the substance of what is delivered. One must evaluate the cost of electronic information services in terms of return on investment. And these are empirical, not a priori, matters.

The evolution of databases is highly instructive on a number of counts: First, technological push can operate in the absence of economic pull. That is to say, even without broad market demands for electronic databases, the innovative impulses of high technology have plunged forward. Second, the costs of this plunging forward may bear little relationship to cost-benefit efficiencies. The economic costs of databased products are more excessive than one might have either predicted or expected to the point where wide-band databases, such as newspapers, are so inefficient as to be just about priced out of the market. Third, the current situation of excessive supply for inadequate demand is not likely to be easily reversed; quite the contrary, new technological pushes are such that computer databases are moving into areas where economic inefficiencies are simply taken for granted rather than reduced.

The political economy of the new information technology is such as to maintain rather than replace older modes of delivering systematic information in hard-copy form. The increasing costs of transmitting information over telephone lines, the relatively small amount of databased information actually used with respect to the amounts created, and the institutional rather than personal uses of computer databases will add new labor costs rather than reduce old costs. All of this adds up to a political economy of information that is going to remain multi-tiered; i.e., to be delivered in both print and electronic forms for many years to come, much as radio and television co-exist. For while it is correct to note that the economic constraints on high technology may not stem innovation, such constraints may be quite significant in containing levels of use.

While electronic publishing as a whole is not a natural monopoly, specific software or databases may be. But such databased forms are "monopolies" in such a narrow band of information that the ever present fears of a master database seem remote and exaggerated. Ithiel de Sola Pool has provided a realistic appraisal of the actual economies of databased publishing: "Once an organization has compiled a bibliography of all the chemical journal articles of the past 20 years, no other sane entrepreneur will attempt to duplicate that massive effort . . . The chemical bibliography may have both too much and too little information for biochemical engineers; there may be room for a specialized bibliography for them."[7] Depending on the cost of creating the database, the same may be true in a wide variety of areas: real estate agents may not cover rooming houses or hunting lodges; consumer compilations may be good on prices but weak on quality tests.

Once the question of monopoly is introduced, then the role of government also becomes evident. For just as the Sherman anti-trust legislation aimed at preventing an undue concentration of industrial power in one firm, so too are mechanisms required to inhibit similar forces of technological concentration in the area of information gathering and diffusion. For the moment, the government (i.e., the state) seems more intent on the rational bureaucratic potentials of such databases, rather than their potential for mischief and/or malice.

What makes this a matter of importance is the need to see databased information as providing an opportunity and a challenge, and not just a mechanism of conspiracy or repression by the all powerful forces of the state. Once again, it becomes apparent that changes in technology do not necessarily represent an automatic change in the marketplace. For the present and immediately foreseeable future, databased delivery of information is an additional resource, but while it may alter, it will not eliminate the system of publishing and exchanging ideas, much less fundamentally transform the social order in any generalized sense.

The purpose of these remarks is not to disparage or discredit innovation in information technology. Such an exercise would be futile at best and idiosyncratic at worst. The forms of technological innovation in this area must continue to amaze even the most hardbitten skeptic; would that the power of the market were viewed with equal appreciation by technologists for whom the brave new world carries few tremors or doubts.

The rapid acceptance electronic formats inspire is in part a function of a behavioral transformation in which the information comes to the user rather than the user going to the information (as is the case in conventional hard-copy formats). There is no need to move from drawer to drawer or search from volume to volume of an index; no need for physical movement about a library. The cost of this behavioral *immobilisme* may be the reduction of serendipitous findings, and sometimes it may not occur to the user to consult alternative sources if they are not entered into the database. On the other hand, sometimes, desired information may only be retrievable electronically. We are in a transitional psychological mood, one in which we take for granted a multi-tiered information environment, instead of approaching knowledge needs in a unidimensional mood. Electronic databases are value-added media rather than alien intrusions aiming at the destruction of other, more conventional, forms of delivering information.

It is entirely understandable that technical scientists would emphasize what computerized databases can do for potential users rather than what these human beings can do for databasing. Nonetheless, it must be appreciated that some quite real imbalances need to be redressed. There is now an entire negative literature on databasing, expressing everything from generalized fears of the computerized society to particularized fears about violations of the privacy of individuals and new sources of class polarization. The more sophisticated the information technology becomes the louder will become the concerns expressed by a variety of critics—often drawn from the social sciences and humanities—until we have a virtual crescendo of assault. It would be risky to think that because databasing is a more benign activity than genetic engineering, we will be able to avoid entirely the same impulses to foreclose aspects of the new technology.

The multiple relationships among those who create, diffuse, and use information are entirely germane to databasing. The need in the next phase of the new technology is to search out the psychological and sociological dynamics underwriting the assumptions of information technology. We must acknowledge the profound differences between information and knowledge and, no less significantly, how potential for the misutilization of information and misunderstanding of what constitutes knowledge comes about because of inaccurate evaluation and dissemination of unwarranted interpretations of computer-derived research results.

Databases have logical components, and using them sometimes requires specialized training. Many databases are highly sophisticated, including controlled vocabularies, concept codes, and hierarchical tree structures. Beyond that, user guides and database manuals must also be collected and updated. If one takes as a task the study of social stress, one is often led to data on divorces, abortions, illegitimate births, infant deaths, fetal deaths, disaster assistance, school dropouts, etc. But of course such easily quantifiable information assumes rather than proves the existence of social stress. Beyond that, such indicators do not properly indicate, as any good social scientific approach would, that certain stress levels are functional and not dysfunctional with respect to economic development and industrial expansion. And while it might be pleasant to speak of integrating databases and systems analysis, the raw fact remains that the sophisticated rendering of scientific ideas extends far beyond databasing; and, at times, can even be falsified by the arbitrary and premature narrowing down of research fields.[8]

Let me further illumine some of these differences between raw data and refined knowledge by a small-scale example rather than a large-scale metaphor. If one wants to determine who publishes the largest number of scholarly journals, those data are available through an online search of *Ulrich's Guide*. A first count shows that Pergamon is first and Elsevier a distant second. But it does violence to what we know about the publishing world in common-sense terms: namely, that Elsevier is the largest publisher of journals worldwide. The reason our search tells us differently is that all Pergamon's journals are published under the Pergamon imprint; whereas Elsevier publishes its journals under six to eight different imprints in accordance with general research areas and in several countries. As a result, unless we know this a priori, we may ask the question in such a way that we derive false results at the holistic level. It takes a certain qualitative type of knowledge to ask the right question, or to ask it in such a way that we get results in keeping with what we know to be the general contours of real-world experience. The answers one gets from electronic databases may be limited by the requirement that users define their terms and ask their questions properly. Every user has been frustrated by not knowing how to ask the question that will yield the evidence common sense dictates is there.

Quantitative measurement of scholarly output has become a widely employed application of databasing. Coding data in terms of the names of key actors in the world of scientific and quasi-scientific productivity is both a natural consequence of the systematic storage of information and presumably a technique for assessing the quality of research. The hidden assumption of citation analyses national or worldwide in a given area of research is that they yield a true sense of the worth of a particular publication, and since citations may be disproportionate to the actual levels of individual productivity, the assumption would seem to have some credibility. However, here too one must exercise the greatest caution: citations rarely if ever disaggregate approbation or disapprobation with a point of view taken; citations are often a function of extrascholarly values, i.e., high numbers of citations are given to departmental chairmen who have the power of appointment and dismissal. At times, too, citations are subject to a contagion effect, i.e., once an article is established as important or seminal it continues to be cited long after such seminal values have been absorbed into the common wisdom. The electronic database phenomenon has changed our notions of scientific and scholarly value, but too rarely has it given us an appreciation of the distinction between the quantitative and qualitative, or even the negative and the positive.

To illustrate this point further, one even closer to home: the same database inquiry that inverts the relative size of Elsevier and Pergamon also reports only 19 journals within the Transaction Periodicals Consortium. But Transaction has 32 journals in its Consortium. The discrepancy results from the assumptions made by the inquirer who defined a journal as a serial publication that appears regularly at least four times or more per annum. Transaction has a number of journals that appear only three times annually, others that appear semiannually, and still others, serially. The way the question was asked distorted the results. It takes a peculiar kind of special knowledge to know how to structure criteria for inclusion and exclusion.

One may also get inaccurate information by questioning the wrong database. If one inquires of the United Airlines flight information system what connecting flights there are from Newark to Jacksonville, the information derived from the "Apollo System" may not include flights scheduled by People's Express (and other regional carriers as well) between these two terminals. There may be valid or at least understandable commercial reasons for failure to report all connecting flights within a computerized system that has the capacity to do so. Nonetheless, one must again have a certain amount of a priori knowledge of the limitations of a database to ask the right questions of the system: specifically, what are the criteria of inclusion and exclusion of information. Problems in the use of computerized databases for scholarly research deserve and are receiving serious attention.[9] Still, we do not yet have reviewing mediums for databases. These perplexing and frustrating microscopic examples of limitations in the new informational environment should not be lost sight of in our search for larger macroscopic issues.

We must broaden our understanding of information and its retrieval. At the same time, we must also be in a position to extend the economic infrastructure of knowledge. If we fail in that critical task we will indeed end up with what the late C. Wright Mills referred to as "crackpot research," a form of research in which the only questions permitted are those that the hardware and software as currently defined can logically handle. Rather than function as a handmaiden for economic innovation, such limitations can frustrate research and innovation. In a worst-case scenario, a broad range of questions may not be permitted; further, no social actions will be permitted that are not sanctioned by existing data or information.

We must broaden the conception of political economy to include those aspects of the new technology that involve considerably more than market factors and their expansion. Indeed, the least malleable and most difficult to pinpoint aspects involve social benefit rather than economic cost items. Computer intelligence is, after all, part of organized intelligence as such, and hence involves educational questions: What should be the appropriate community expenditures in this area? How should appropriations be made—from new taxes or taking away from other ongoing activities? To what extent, if any, should considerations of reducing existing racial, gender, ethnic, etc., inequalities be invoked? We can see quite dramatically that the political economy of databasing is nothing short of questions of political economy at a time of technical innovation.

What we have then is a need to respond to dangers from quite opposite sources: a fast-moving technology that threatens to leave many behind and create ever new varieties of uneven social stratification, and a slow-moving normative foundation that is severely challenged by the imposition of anomie and atomization of the valuational base of society as a whole, i.e., the reduction of ethical and aesthetic issues to possibilities of gain and loss on one side and sound and noise on the other.

Computerized databases are an enormous resource, a significant development heralding the twenty-first century. They finally shift emphasis from the means of production as a critical variable in the social order to one based on means of communication.[10] At the same time, they fail to do away with long-standing problems of good and evil, right and wrong, beauty and ugliness. One can hope that knowledge, and here we mean specifically the knowledge gained from hard work in the sciences, social sciences, and humanities, will fuel the revolution in information technology. If information and knowledge move in tandem, this will comprise a revolutionary step toward solving larger normative and distributive concerns. However, if either is permitted to subvert the other, in the name of a crude empiricism or an even cruder moralism, we have the capacity for an equally gigantic reaction: a darkness born of modernity.

Beyond the issue of inverting economic costs and educational opportunities through databased technology lies the question of whether a constituency exists that can move beyond considerations of market demand and consumer supply. Innovation in databased technology has been so rapid that in many areas informational needs have not caught up. In many fields of scholarship, traditional indexing and abstracting services may be quite ample to meet current needs. If the sales of conventional informational sources are any indication, this narrow view is fully confirmed. Yet while the new technology is focusing upon the finer points of information retrieval, with sophisticated techniques of term weighing and relevance judgment, many fields of learning still operate in a parochial and gross fashion.[11] Nothing could prove more dangerous than a dizzy-with-success attitude to technical developments in computer-related technology. There is little evidence that technological innovation marches lock-step with economic change into a brave new world. The present databasing environment confirms the need to study the past and plan for the future as we examine the present. I turn now to one such present issue: copyright.

5

Copyright Legislation
and Its Consequences

The purpose of this chapter is to examine the ramifications of legislative recognition of the concept of fair use in the Copyright Act of 1976. The fair-use concept, while of small consequence in its normative origins, has turned out to be the foundation of the most perplexing and divisive issues in the new legislative guidelines governing copyright. Legislative recognition of the concept of fair use, coupled with enormous growth of a new technology—extending from Xerography to on-line database systems—creates de facto exemptions to both the intent and content of new copyright guidelines. The issue is not one of limiting use or suppressing information but of mechanisms for safeguarding the rights of copyright holders, be they authors or publishers, and ensuring the free flow of information by providing a proper return on both intellectual creativity and capital expenditures. The authors argue that the elimination, or at least curtailment of fair-use doctrine, coupled with an increase in technological approaches to reporting of secondary use of copyrighted material, will benefit all sections of the knowledge industry. Authors will receive proper royalties on use; publishers will be able to sell more books and journals at lower prices; and librarians will be liberated from extensive chores such as monitoring usage or determining fee schedules and transferences. The issue is one of fair return—an issue obscured and ultimately subverted by fair use.

Prior to the Copyright Act of 1976, the law had never given explicit statutory recognition to the concept of "fair use." The courts had recognized the concept in decisions extending back more than a century, but in practice fair use generally had to do with the brief quotation by a second author of a first author's work. Insofar as fair use had any broader definition, that definition had emerged from litigation and legal precedent. When a copyright holder chose to challenge a use as improper, judicial "rule of reason" was employed, and a body of legal precedent thus developed that provided guidelines for both user and copyright holder in questionable situations. However, in no instance did fair use mean reproduction of a work to use it for its own sake.

The doctrine of fair use as presently evolved stemmed from a wide variety of exceptional circumstances not related to intrinsic use of the work, ranging from quoting materials for review purposes to reproducing excerpts from books, magazines, and films for pedagogic purposes. Such uses simply could not easily be regulated or monitored. Those who sought secondary use for the reproduction of copyright materials usually asked permission for such uses. The decision about whether use fell within commonly accepted bounds of fair use was made by copyright owners. If a user used material without seeking permission of a copyright owner, it was done with foreknowledge that the use might be challenged, and if so the judicial rule of reason ("would the reasonable copyright owner have consented to such use?") would be applied.

Earlier periods of discussion concerning possible revision of the 1909 Copyright Law devoted much attention to the doctrine of fair use. Broadly, there were two schools of thought. One group argued for explicit recognition of the concept of fair use in the law, and wanted the law to list instances in which the fair use concept might limit copyright prerogatives. A second gorup argued, as it turned out without ultimate success, for general recognition of the concept, but wanted no specific mention of particular uses that constituted fair use. This group felt that any definition of fair use in the law would inevitably erode copyright prerogatives. "Any attempt by statute to define fair use or to clarify it would probably expand its scope."[1]

The 1976 Copyright Law revision gives specific recognition to fair use, and since then, the concept has been transformed from a rule of reason into a loophole for unreason, a rationale for unrestricted use of copyright materials. The Report of the Register of Copyrights on Library Reproduction of Copyrighted Words, charged with assessing the extent to which an appropriate balance between creators' rights and users' needs has been achieved, concludes that the balance has not been achieved. I agree with this interpretation, but believe that the problem resides with the attempt to define fair use legislatively. Using "fair use" to defend the loophole, and locating the odd event not explicitly covered by legislation threatens to negate copyright as a whole. The judicial doctrine is being transformed into the injudicious doctrine of free use.

Allan Wittman, onetime chairman of the Association of American Publishers Copyright Committee, has underscored the unintended consequences of this broadened use of fair use: "The principle of fair use arose out of the legal concept that the law does not deal with trivia. When that doctrine was developed, small amounts of copying were trivia. However, modern technology changed all that. One work can be subjected to thousands of so-called "trivial" transactions and the result is no longer trivial."[2]

Prior to the 1976 Copyright Law, the copyright owner determined whether or not to require payment for a secondary use or reproduction of a copyrighted work. If a copier took the time and trouble to copy even an entire book by hand, no penalty was exacted because there was no way it could be known that a copy had been made. If a copier reproduced a hand-copied document, however, he probably would be discovered, and of course he would be liable. The 1976 Copyright Law exempts certain reproductions as instances of fair use; by extending the concept of fair use it rendered it ambiguous. It also restricted copyright holders from collecting payments for some reproductions the law defines as "fair uses."

One intention of the 1976 definition of fair use was to ease certain uses of copyrighted materials. The law permits a teacher to make and use a single copy without seeking permission; for example; under certain circumstances, multiple copies if they do not exceed more than one copy per pupil for classroom use. Within this broad framework clear limits are put forth concerning the brevity of an abstract cited, the spontaneity of copying purposes, and the prevention of a cumulative effect so that such fair use is not employed to repress or inhibit the production of new anthologies or collected works. In practice, pedagogic "fair use" has been extended, as argued by a group of publishers in the recent legal action against New York University. Certainly some interpretations of the notion of fair use by teachers have become so broad as to be eccentric, as indicated by the interpretation of the fair-use doctrine "in terms of constructive teaching and the extent to which photocopying needs to be used.[3] This unusual statement, made by Robert Gorman, professor of law at the University of Pennsylvania and onetime president of the American Association of University Professors, reveals not simply a personal idiosyncratic view of fair use but a widespread belief that it is the statute of exemption and entitlement rather than a judicial doctrine of reasonableness. Operationally, pedagogic copyright exemptions have not only inhibited anthologies and collections, but have seriously eroded use of whole journals or books. And because copyright holders have been slow to defend their rights, small infringements have simply passed into the realm of social norms—legal abuses have become quite acceptable.

Nine commercial publishers, as members of the Association of American Publishers, brought suit in December 1982 against New York University and select members of its faculty, alleging that photocopying and distribution of course materials without permission of the copyright holders violated the federal Copyright Act. The litigants reached a settlement in June 1983 under which the University agreed to adopt, implement, and honor the terms of an Agreement reached in March 1976 by the Ad Hoc Committee on Copyright Law Revision, representing the Association of American Publishers and the Authors' League of America. The Agreement, which brought together author and publisher groups, covered a broad spectrum of issues ranging from single copying for teachers to multiple copying for classroom use. However, this Agreement is also noteworthy for the absence of any mechanism for exact payment for photoduplication, and by the absence of librarian support for the document as a whole.

Copyright holders have little control over social practice. Users and their agents such as libraries have tended to interpret the guidelines contained in the 1976 law very broadly. Robert Wedgeworth of the American Library Association has forcefully stated this position: "The law permits a number of uses for photocopies without fees and the copyright owner cannot demand payment for these fair uses and other possible uses under Section 108."[4] Just how broadly fair use has come to be viewed is reflected in another librarian's position that "one of the traditional foundations of librarianship is ownership of information sources in order to make them accessible to library patrons." The auteur of this position, Jeanne G. Howard, fearful of publishers disservices, goes on to argue that "another basic tenet of librarianship is the guardianship of informational sources for archival purposes."[5] It is easy enough to see that underneath the question of fair use is nothing less than the proprietary claims to the published word itself—whatever its form.

There can no longer be any question that for one group, the Copyright Subcommittee of the American Library Association, fair use has become the essential vehicle with which to confound and

confront the publishing and author associations' demands for a fair
return alike. The Copyright Clearance Center, which, as its title suggests, is an independent entity aimed at providing a mechanism of
payment for the use of copyrighted materials, is opposed "for the
most important reason of all . . . only a small percentage of library
copying falls outside the limits of fair use." But since a "model policy"
for fair use may involve reproducing materials at the behest of a faculty member for reserve use, "a reasonable number of copies" which
"will in most instances be less than six" the intent of the new copyright legislation is clearly and intentionally to be circumvented.[6]

Clearly, the librarian leadership perceives itself as providing
"balance" between the rights of creators and the needs of library
patrons. Ignoring the presumption that such a balancing role is
uniquely the charge of librarians, or whether they even welcome such
a discretionary role, the fact is that it is the doctrine of fair use which
provides the legitimizing role for insisting, contrary to the Register of
Copyright, David Ladd, that a balance has been achieved between
owners and users of information. Again, under the banner of rights
of fair use granted under Section 107 of the 1976 Copyright legislation, the librarian would presume to be the unique interpreter of such
legislation—and in so doing, thoroughly subvert the consensual aims
of the legislation to begin with.

This is not intended as a denial of a central role to librarians,
nor as a refutation of specific empirical points about the extent of
copyright violations—not even research reports intended to resolve
such an issue have satisfactorily done so. Indeed, not until a sense of
vestedness exists whereby the library community properly shares in
the proceeds from copyright use will the critical participation and
support of that community be ensured. But the point from my perspective is simply to note that the notion of fair use is increasingly
being invoked, not to broaden the basis of library use, but to subvert
the foundations of copyright itself; that is, to hold acquisition by any
means and without payment to the copyright holder no less than
access to copyright materials as essential and legitimate functions of
a librarian.

Some early critics of the 1976 law argued that it is fundamentally flawed because it tampers with copyright in a fundamental way.
Because the notion of copyright itself balances the rights of creators
and the needs of users, exemptions interfere with its internal work-
ings. In his analysis of fair use in copyright, Leon Seltzer observed
that the photocopying problem was dealt with in the 1976 law by

creating exemptions to the copyright holder's exclusive right to make and sell copies. Although the exemptions are held not to disturb the essential dynamics of copyright, the distinctions outlined in the 1976 copyright law are difficult to enforce and almost impossible to administer. "It is unreasonable to expect a user to distinguish between what is fair use, what is exempted use, and what is neither. And when Congress itself has failed to do so with a precision in which it has much confidence, courts will not find it easy to bring a photocopying excess about which there is any doubt at all within the reach of the enforcement provisions of the liability clause, Section 504."[7] Seltzer's predictions proved correct.

Writing in 1978, Seltzer pointed out that Congress had essentially two options: (1) to narrow the range of the author's exclusive rights by permitting the broadest range of photocopying, or (2) to require a full and complete accounting of photocopying. Choosing the first option would mean that Congress believed that the interests of users and producers could be balanced outside of the copyright scheme. The second option relies on the internal efficiency of copyright as it has traditionally existed, to balance these interests. Seltzer's analysis led him to favor the second option, but Congress attempted to chart an ambiguous middle course between the two in the 1976 revision.

Ambiguities in law are usually clarified through subsequent litigation. In the case of the 1976 Copyright Act, these clarifications have been slow to come, for a number of reasons. Those who argued for maximum liberalization of the copyright law have simply behaved as if the new law gives them all that they had demanded. Librarian groups, for example, issued explanations and clarifications of the law to their membership that go far beyond the limited guidelines given in the law. Technological developments carry their own momentum. Library automation and networking involving reproduction of copyrighted material have become widespread. As the Register's Report indicates, the role of libraries has been profoundly changed by the existence and use of photocopying. Some libraries have become relatively efficient document delivery centers, competing with legitimate centers that compensate copyright holders. Because some believe any copying that takes place within a library to be exempt, they do not compensate copyright owners. Because interlibrary loans traditionally were made without compensation to copyright owners, libraries argue that "loans" that involve photocopying require no compensation.

Publishers, for their part, have been slow to respond to the implications of the revised law. Those engaged in kinds of publishing most vulnerable to any decline in unit sales by broadening the definition of fair use were those primarily serving small, segmented markets—scientific, scholarly, and medical publishers. These publishers were poorly organized. In 1976 the Technical, Scientific, and Medical Publishing Division of the Association of American Publishers (AAP) was relatively small. Many publishers of specialized materials did not even participate in publishers' trade associations, and others were affiliated with professional societies and therefore had mixed allegiances. Many major scholarly and professional publishers were outside the United States—Elsevier, Pergamon, and Springer-Verlag, for example. With some notable exceptions, large U.S. publishers with major commitments to specialized publishing, such as McGraw-Hill, were divided on how and whether to act. Only as other categories of publishing, such as textbook publishing, began to suffer the impact of the erosion of regard for copyright, did publishers begin to develop a united front in regard to unauthorized reproductions.

Publisher-initiated attempts to clarify ambiguities in the 1976 Copyright Act through litigation did not begin until the 1980s. It is interesting to speculate about what may have finally mobilized publishers to take legal action to defend further erosion of copyright. In part, it was undoubtedly awareness that other technological developments were, without any doubt, going to affect dramatically their role as primary disseminators of information, in ways they could not anticipate and could not control unless there was clear-cut certainty about their copyright prerogatives. In part, it was increasingly segmentation and specialization in all of the markets served by publishers—educational and professional as well as scholarly. In part, it was growing awareness that new technological developments were having severe impact on other segments of the information industry: on movies, television, and record industries, for example. Some of these were responding to technological challenges to their own copyright prerogatives with aggressive legal action.

Demands by copyright owners for protection of their rights have almost uniformly been challenged by arguments that any such protection would erode "fair use." What was intended as a modest series of pragmatic exemptions is now itself highly inhibiting to resolution of issues of concern to copyright holders, because the concept of fair use has been broadened to signify limitations on the exclusivity of copyright holders' claims. Since the definition of circumstances in which use may constitute fair use (Section 107) has been codified, it has in effect been linked with Section 108, permitting reproduction by libraries and archives of copyrighted material from one publisher to another, and secondary transmission of the same copyrighted material. The American Library Association critique of the Register's Report explicitly argues for the interrelationship of these two sections, challenging the Register's interpretation of Congressional intent. The cumulative impact has been an erosion of copyright. Social practice is taking us a long distance beyond the narrow exemptions articulated in the 1976 law.

The 1976 Copyright Act does attempt to address the question of copying by individuals for activities connected with teaching and research, but as with the guidelines for photocopying by libraries, they are ambiguous and unenforceable. It does not even begin to address copying by an individual for his personal needs and convenience, which has been fundamentally transformed by photocopying technology. Copying by hand was time-consuming and laborious. Machine photocopying is not. While it gives the copier physical possession of a personal copy, the copier pays a negligible amount for the privilege of ownership of a photocopy, essentially only the cost of the copy. No record, no accounting, and no compensation to the copyright holder is made.

The economic aspect of the information user's decision about how he wants to receive his information is more complicated than it used to be, because the user now has multiple options.[8] Before the development of technological capabilities such as photocopying, the economic decision of the user boiled down to a choice between expenditure of time and effort (in copying by hand) versus money (to purchase the printed product). Consciously or not, the user now makes a more complex choice. Today the user may spend time scanning a document and order a copy, or make one personally. The user may first wish to scan a screen, but then prefer the convenience of a hard copy. He often would have to spend more time and money to purchase the original product, even if he could find it, than a photocopy.[9] Consequently, the economic decision is more heavily weighted in favor of machine copying than it was when hand copying was the sole option. Purchase of the entire journal or an entire book may even be economically unsound. Machine copying is fast and relatively inexpensive versus the per page price of a printed product. As interests have become more specialized, and personal storage space more limited, users may want only a portion of a journal or even a book. As library sharing becomes more sophisticated, the printed product may rarely be readily available even if the user wants to go directly to it or to buy a personal copy.

The economic issue, as defined in the fair use guidelines, is too narrowly stated. Congress could not foresee the rapid explosion of the body of scholarly knowledge coupled with the need for sophisticated technology to control and manage that body of literature. Thus, the question of whether making a machine copy substitutes for buying a subscription or a book is much too narrow. Library spokesmen assert that their collections are no longer title (journal or book)-related, but article-related. Online electronic access to abstracting services has accelerated this shift. If access, control, and use of scholarly literature are no longer title-related, what meaning do copyright guidelines have that assume a title basis of use?

Congress clearly did not intend to suppress or weaken the distribution system by which scholarly literature is made available to the public. Its concern was further not to make it impossible or difficult for that user to access and use the literature. Congressional intent, coupled with advances in technology, has certainly benefited the user. The originator of scholarly literature, the copyright holder, has fared less well. Despite dramatic growth in use of scholarly literature, and despite data that the number of journals and the total number of subscriptions to all journals have increased, subscriptions to individual journals have not increased in the United States. In recent years, under the pressure of library networking and resource sharing, subscriptions to established journals have declined by 2 or 3 percent a year.[10] Users are now confident that they can obtain any literature they require from libraries. They are frustrated by the escalating prices of books and journals, which have been accelerated by declines in unit sales, and they have cut back their personal subscriptions or purchases of books. Publishers are caught in a classic economic double-bind. They must increase prices to continue their publishing activities. Further price increases drive down unit sales and make individuals and libraries feel justified in obtaining photocopies from a central source. While Congress certainly did not intend to encourage this dynamic, it has been intensified by the post-1976 erosion of copyright. Even information centers or libraries that would like to maintain their physical collections have been forced, by escalating prices, to cut back. The only non-loser, the end user, may eventually suffer if economic factors force publishers to change the nature of their publishing programs, fundamentally eroding the delicate mechanism by which scholarship and other forms of specialized publishing are disseminated.

Most discussions of copyright and fair use have become hung up on the mechanism for a full and complete accounting at a reasonable cost. Initially, the problem was conceptualized as a licensing problem, and the debate was over whether licensing should be voluntary or compulsory. In cooperation with the Authors' Guild and publisher's associations, the Copyright Clearance Center was formed as a voluntary licensing body similar to the American Society of Composers, Authors and Publishers (ASCAP). After that point, the problem shifted to accounting: how to provide a simple, cost-effective mechanism for accounting for photocopying. As with off-the-air videotaping, the problem was made more complex by the widespread and uncontrollable amount of reproduction by individuals. While institutions, essentially libraries, complained about the expense and difficulty of record keeping and reporting under the licensing scheme of the Copyright Clearance Center, no one even addressed the economic dilemma of unaccounted-for photocopying by individuals.

It has become increasingly clear that licensing is not, after all, the key issue. The real problem is accounting for copying, including the large amount of copying by individuals for purposes ranging from teaching to research to convenience. It is unreasonable and unworkable to expect individuals to report on copying activity, or to expect that copying machines can be restricted only to those who participate in such accounting. Such restrictions would seem, properly, to be an erosion of individual rights to free access. However, if accounting could be achieved passively, without requiring an individual to take some action, but "automatically," the compensation problem would be more easily addressed. If, for example, a record was made of items photocopied, by means of an ISBN, ISSN, or a bar code such as is used on products sold in retail outlets, and if these records were used to report on reproduction by item (or even by publisher) to a central body on a regular basis, compensation to the publisher could be made according to reasonable terms. The issue is similar but not identical to the videotaping issue. Home videotaping takes place in a private, personal situation. Most photocopying, at present, takes place in an institutional context, but at unsupervised machines. If copying was passively recorded and subsequently recorded, publishers would have other problems. They would have to establish equitable procedures for sharing revenues from copying with authors. Institutions, particularly libraries which traditionally would not have charged fees for photocopying, would have to decide who should pay for secondary uses of materials they archive. Just as some libraries and institutions ask users to pay a portion of the costs of online bibliographic searches of data banks, they may decide to ask photocopiers to pay a surcharge for photocopying privileges. Alternatively, they might decide to absorb such costs in their materials budgets, although few have budgets that could absorb such costs.

Legitimate photocopying per se cannot and should not be constrained; the right to use photocopying machines has been established by technological development no less than by social precedents. The right to reproduce copyrighted material without compensation is an unqualified right. Ambiguities and unwarranted exemptions in the 1976 law, above all the assertion of the concept of "fair use," have impeded recognition of this fact and impeded technological solutions to a technologically induced imbalance between the rights of copyright proprietors and the needs of users.

Another fundamental problem, one that was not properly understood by the publishing community at the time the 1976 statutes came into force, is that the fair-use exemptions operationally turn out to mean exemption of the first copy, or the right to reproduce a single copy of a copyrighted work without compensation. But very often the first copy is the most important copy, if not the decisive copy. If there were a strict economic correlation between value and price, the first copy would be the most expensive and the tenth copy the least expensive, rather than the current situation in which the first copy is free to users, and succeeding copies are compensated for at a predetermined amount. The fair-use exemptions inhibit any possibility of compensation whereby the first copy produced is reimbursed as the first order of magnitude.

The notion of fair use is sufficiently ambiguous and confusing as to vitiate any protection provided by other clauses. For example, not only can copying of an extract, a chart, or a graph be considered fair use, but also a chapter from a book, an article from a periodical, a short story, or an essay. Who is to say how much material from a book or journal is fair use and how much is gratuitous use? That single article lifted from an anthology or a book may make the difference between a sale and a nonsale. De facto the burden of proof that a use is not a fair use now rests with the copyright holder. To take one example, the cause of multiple copies, while presumably safeguarding publishers who insist on notice of copyright, leaves wide open the use of multiple copies in multiple classes. To take another, without an enforceable proviso on length, the core of a book may well be extracted to the detriment of the author and publisher. Ultimately, books and journals will not be published because a market contraction of such magnitude cannot readily sustain the costs of publication.

Publishers who have argued for a narrow interpretation of the fair-use doctrine have ended up having to defend themselves by proving that economic harm has been brought about by the application of the doctrine. Economic analyses have concluded that publishers suffer no economic hardships as a consequence of photocopying exemptions—that they are still receiving an "adequate return"—whatever that means. A CONTU-sponsored study by the Public Interest Economics Center reached this somewhat presumptuous conclusion, one which reflected the anti-business climate of the early 1970s, and one which certainly revealed little understanding of how business actually operates.[11] In any case, it is extremely difficult to demonstrate the existence of economic harm, and since publishers tend to increase prices to offset unit declines, fair-use-driven corrective actions by publishers may have prejudiced the public against the copyright holder, as well as distorted the marketplace. The consequence has been public perception of copyright in an older and essentially illicit view, as mere privilege, as a favor to publishers rather than an instrument to encourage broad-scale production and distribution of creative works. This position is forcefully stated in the ALA's response to the Register's Report. As Nancy Marshall states the case: "The CONTU Guidelines are useful guides, but they do not carry the force of law."[12]

Copyright has never simply been a property right. Its underlying intent since the Act of Queen Anne of 1709 has been to encourage dissemination of literary, scientific, and artistic works.[13] It recognizes that a creator requires some period of exclusive control of that work and protection of that creation to enjoy sufficient fruits of his labor to permit him to continue to produce. This aspect of protection has been turned against copyright holders, who are now asked to demonstrate economic harm as a condition of protection of copyright prerogatives. This demand has occurred as a response to fair-use guidelines, which stipulate that permission to copy is not intended to reduce purchases of primary materials.[14] It does not follow that copying is permissible when a copyright holder cannot prove economic harm, but that is essentially how those arguing for minimal protection have put the issue.

The fair-use doctrine has divided the consumer from copyright holders. It has juxtaposed entrepreneurs, investors, artists, and shopkeepers against consumers and their agents, librarians. Fair use has served as an ideological vehicle to argue that the copyright holders want to restrain trade and information in seeking to protect their literary property. The publishing community has been characterized as restraining knowledge and information rather than simply claiming their right to protect their property and derive some return from secondary uses thereof. This position is a difficult one for publishers, for both historical and moral reasons.

Perhaps the most serious short-term consequence of the 1976 fair-use doctrine is its effect on inhibiting development and use of technological and/or mechanical devices that could account for what is copied. Proponents of the 1976 fair-use doctrines assert that exemptions preclude any use of present technology to record the number of reproductions. The available technology, such as mechanical devices activating a reproduction machine, calculate from the first copy forward. The argument goes that because the fair-use doctrine inhibits chargeback for the first copy, no known technology is appropriate. While this does not have to be so—that is to say, while equipment could be designed in such a way as to accommodate these objections—there is no doubt that the 1976 fair-use doctrine forestalls a universal form of payment to authors of copyrighted materials. Use of the new technology to resolve dilemmas in accounting for copying has been thwarted by legislative safeguards that have no real status in tradition and even less meaning in fact.

Recent landmark developments in the fair-use exemptions concern the settlement reached between the Association of American Publishers and E. R. Squibb, the pharmaceutical giant. In an effort to keep the momentum going for some sort of general recognition of copyright prerogatives, certain specific exemptions have been registered. The pharmaceutical firm negotiated an arrangement whereby a 6 percent exclusion—in effect an exemption of payment for "fair uses" in this amount—was agreed upon. While this clause undoubtedly was agreed to reluctantly by the AAP, it does contravene the essential principle that all materials copyrighted by a publisher are protected, and not a percentage thereof. It establishes a contrary notion: that reproduction of an entire article and/or book may be permitted if it can be included in the permissible 6 percent. It should be noted that the Squibb agreement provides for an exemption of 6 percent of the material copied over and above material in which copyright has expired and government documents in the public domain.

The principle of fair return—i.e., of proprietary claim—may be critically weakened in the very act of securing compliance with established legislation. Quite apart from requiring consent to monitor photocopying, instead of encouraging manufacturer's installation of simple mechanical devices, the foundations of copyright prerogatives may become subject to endless bilateral bartering arrangements as to what amount of copying is permissible. If the judicial notion of fair-use exemptions becomes operationally a percentage of total material photocopied, there is no reason to expect that a 6 percent guideline will not turn into a 7 percent solution, i.e., an opiate to the publishers. Herein lies the great weakness of any wide-ranging notion of fair-use exemptions from fair return on investments.

Fair use is legally significant, but only in severely restricted circumstances. It protects the owner of a physical text much more than the owner of the ideas. However, in so doing the fair-use doctrine helps to subvert one of the original purposes of copyright, which was to make findings widely known in the areas of science and humanities. We need to reach a point where copyright is protected not from the second copy forward, but from the first copy. Only in this way can serious objections raised by librarians and academics to the dangers of information control be appropriately met. Ambiguities of the present situation will be salvaged only by recognition that no use is fair use; and parenthetically, that no kind of mechanical reproduction of a copyrighted work is exempt. All copyright materials deserve protection from random forms of copying. No possible resolution of the copyright dilemma is feasible if the ambiguities inherent in the 1976 doctrine of fair use inhibit the use of technology to recognize problems created by the new information technology.[15]

Fair use has been uncritically linked with democratic ideals as part of a free marketplace of ideas; whereas fair return has with equal casuistry been linked to bourgeois avarice. For some commentators, demands for copyright protection as such have come to be labeled a kind of conspiracy against democratic rights to access. In fact, the early termination of 1976 fair-use doctrine would enhance, not detract from, free inquiry. As copyright traditionally acknowledged, the replication of data, charts, or tables, for example, like the duplication of films or television shows, can better be monitored in an environment which recognizes both originating and continuing costs, and does not make presumptions of exemptions. The right to live does not entail a denial of payment for food. By the same token, the right to knowledge does not entail a denial of payment for information. There is an expectation, perhaps overly optimistic, that the elimination of fair-use exemptions would permit publishers to return to marginally lower prices for copyrighted works, especially journals. Publishers can also afford to be liberal and generous in granting permission to reproduce materials for scholarly and educational use. But that generosity can only be forthcoming when 97 percent of reproductions of copyright material is acknowledged; and not as in present circumstances, where less than 3 percent of the reproductions of copyrighted materials is acknowledged—much less paid for.

The ambiguities of the 1976 fair-use doctrine have led to legal confusion and moral ambiguity. They have also helped create middlemen operating on all sides who profit from this climate of confusion and ambiguity. That is the burden of traditional copyright law. Beyond that, it also happens to be the essence of the Western political system and its checks and balances against abuses of trust and privilege.

In its larger sense, the issue of fair use does not concern use at all, but ownership. The 1976 law has been structured in such a way as to satisfy public requirements for access to information and ideas in an entirely unencumbered manner. And while those public requirements are entirely worthy and require societal protection, any method of ensuring the public right to know that results in a frontal assault on the right to property or the proprietary claims of authors and publishers is dangerous. To the extent that the struggle to enlarge the fair-use concept into a blanket endorsement of free use, one might even argue that systemic considerations of "socialism" and "capitalism" are at stake. But to pursue such a line of reasoning would open a Pandora's box of ideology and postpone resolution of the issues within the context of the present social and legal order of Western societies.

However, the passions with which the issue of fair use have been debated on all sides, in all manner of media from video to software to books, would indicate that these larger issues are indeed lurking in the near background. Perhaps as long as actual social-economic formations are increasingly "mixed" rather than "pure," the problems raised by fair use will remain with us. However, a more realistic approach would be to accept the mixed character of our political economy, one which acknowledges a fair return, and hence the need to accommodate specific author-publisher-user demands for information in such terms. This chapter has been an effort to address fair use within the parameters of fair return, and to do so by noting that the right to universal access to information is protected as are the proprietary claims of authors, publishers, and citizens. In short, the issue of collection runs parallel to the issue of information.

6

The Reproduction of Knowledge and the Maintenance of Property

From the *Williams and Wilkins versus the Department of Health, Education and Welfare* decision of 1972, until *Harper & Row versus The Nation* in 1985, it has been clear that the issue of copyright in the United States has essentially brought into play two relatively large-scale principles.[1] The first is the right of the citizen to have, unimpeded, without artificial restraints, and with the exception of areas of national and military security, as much information as he/she deems appropriate. Underwriting this principle are recent executive orders which have extended to individuals the right to know the contents of any private dossiers maintained about them. These rights are intended to combat the capacities of a society to gather and maintain privileged information.[2]

On the other end of the information spectrum is the right to compensation or payment for work done. This right to compensation for copyrighted material is not some selfish effort to create payments for a priestly class, but quite the contrary: to establish the principle that intellectual or creative work deserves the same consideration as manual labor. It dates back to the founding of the American Republic, and it has come to symbolize personal responsibility for intellectual work.

Critics of copyright have sometimes claimed that its provisions entail the restraint of information. But in point of historical fact, the reverse is more nearly the case. Following passage of the first International Copyright Act of 1891, which eliminated cheap reprint competition from foreign sources, publishing entrepeneurs in the United States were able to promote native talent without fear of being "ripped off." These newer publishers initiated an aggressive sale orientation. They commissioned articles, offered advance payment to authors, engaged in innovative promotional campaigns; all of which was made possible by copyright protection. As one historian of the period noted, "International Copyright passage was hailed as a professional Declaration of Independence from the dominance of European tastes. Indeed, the new financial resources made available to American writers by book publishers, syndication agencies, newspapers and magazines were viewed as the means with which American authors could transcend the supposedly stale, academic elitism of the Gilded Age and create a more realistic and democratic literature.[3] In short, copyright protection may constrain free usage, but it also enhances democratic potential.

The disjunction between knowledge and property is exemplified by both public librarians and information agencies who are plagued by present dilemmas as to the limits of property rights and public rights; and on the other, publishers and authors who are usually found on the proprietary side of any argument concerning author rights. The copyright reform legislation of the mid-1970s, however significant in bringing some balance into the situation, failed to solve the dilemmas. It tried to adjudicate the claims of those who believe in the rights of compensation at the expense of easy access to information. The upshot has been that neither side to this deviate of principles has been made content. Librarians and publishers, two groups that desperately require each other's cooperation and assistance, have been placed at extraordinary loggerheads. Neither interest group quite knows how to assuage the sentiments and sensibilities of the other; much less the general concerns of the public.

Librarians have argued, for the most part, that copyright legislation has restricted access to information. At the extreme, librarians claim that they must engage in policy activities to determine what is and what is not proper or fair use of copyright materials. Furthermore, they have had to engage in expensive bookkeeping and auditing to keep records of such use. Above all, they have had to go back in time to an older library concept, when the lion at the gate meant preventing access to available information, rather than encouraging broader employment of library facilities. Specific queries concerning revisions in the U.S. copyright legislation have introduced concepts few librarians can accept with equanimity. How should librarians interpret fair use? How should periodicals more than five years old be treated? How should payment schedules be recorded and deposited? Such current questions suggest procedures that require an unacceptable bureaucratic manipulation of people and massaging of events that librarians find unacceptable.

From their point of view, publishers are equally frustrated by what they see as copyright abuses. They tend to be suspicious of highly ambiguous aspects of current copyright legislation, such as "fair use" exemptions. They point out unmistakable evidence of the near total collapse of the school market for special journal issues or special articles for educational purposes as a whole. There has been a growing tendency to purchase one copy of a periodical or book for a master file, which is then photocopied in multiples and dispersed to libraries in a wider city, county, or state system. There is further the wholesale random extraction of data, tabular material, and technical information from copyright material and the use of this material in data banks without regard to the cost of composition, authorship, or any of the processes involved in the initial creation of the material. This is often promulgated in the name of a doctrine of fair use which new copying technology has made obsolete. That this fact was not recognized in the congressional legislation of the mid-1970s has opened up an area of intolerable ambiguity for publishers and librarians alike in the mid-1980s.

American law, as well as law in general, frowns upon the kind of ambiguity which increases rather than decreases the abuses intended to be removed by legislation. Present copyright law must, at the level of cognition, be put into the category of metaphysics rather than pragmatics. Fair use mandates that as a rule do not permit the making of multiple copies of the same material, nonetheless go on to list a series of exceptions that can only be characterized as wide ranging loopholes which clever entrepreneurs without scruples have found to their liking. At the same time, current copyright guidelines require an extensive amount of record-keeping on the part of librarians. For instance, no more than five orders for copies of a given periodical can be filled during a calendar year for articles less than five years old; yet legislation permits different responses for light and heavy use at the discretion of a library clerk. The Association of American Publishers, or at least some of its more powerful members, helped establish a Copyright Clearance Center which has no uniform rules for granting permission, since each publisher sets their own fees for copying.

Current legislation makes participation in such a center entirely optional with no penalty for nonmembership and no particular rewards for participation. Indeed, given the amount of funds supplied by the major publishers to buoy such an ostensibly autonomous agency, it might well be argued that there are greater penalties for membership than non-membership in the Copyright Clearance Center. The reasoning behind this is that copyright owners believe they have the right to assess the value of their materials, but should not be subject to mandatory licensing.

Any fundamental solution to the two principles—the right to know versus the right of property—would have two elements: one technical, the other corporate. At the technical level, several copier controller systems are already in place. They have the capacity to provide the name of the person using the particular document, and the number of copies being made. All this information can be recorded individually and summarized. Several such systems are programmed to record and print out data for billing clients such as lawyers, advertisers, public relations officers, management, and consulting and professional organizations of all kinds.

Several advanced models of copier controllers have the capacity to prepare summaries in computer printout for auditing purposes by project, department, division, and ultimately by periodical to the copier. The librarian need only insert his or her coded card and the ISBN or ISSN numbers borne by the book or periodical into a small terminal attached to the copier. If the card is valid and the information accurate, a central recorder can transmit this information to the photocopying machine, which is instantly activated, permitting the user to make copies. As those copies are being made, the equipment can record a fee (or no-fee) to be transmitted either to a copyright collection agency or to the owners of these materials directly. Many copying machines have a special document button which automatically charges the user for the reproduction of bulk matter, such as books or journals, at a different rate. So we are not discussing future technological potentials, such as compact disk, read-only memory, but rather, ongoing systems in the mid-1980s.

The technology clearly exists that would audit the use of copyright materials, encouraging maximum usage, and satisfy the librarian's concern for the unimpeded flow of information, while permitting simple, accurate record-keeping and procedures for compensating copyright holders. ISBN and ISSN systems are in place that provide exact identification of material in copyright, permitting compensation to publishers and authors. Let me emphasize that bar coding scanning technology is fully available and in place. Supermarkets and other stores use such systems to determine everything from consumer demand to inventory requirements.

The most vexing and troubling issue is what can best be called the corporate ghost in the photocopying machines. Librarians and publishers have confronted each other as adversaries, although in reality each needs the other to survive. In this situation, manufacturers of reproducing equipment have intelligently stayed out of the conflict and walked away with enormous profits from the reproduction of copyrighted materials without compensating owners. Xerox, Minolta, IBM, and other manufacturers currently have the capacity to install controlling scanners, but choose not to do so in order to encourage wider numbers of individuals and agencies to install their equipment unencumbered. This posture also permits the major reproduction/ equipment firms to escape possible litigation by staying an arm's length from the contentious issue of property and knowledge.

The weakening of copyright that has resulted from uncontrolled copying occurs to the greater loss of the community of knowledge as a whole. It is an odd situation in which the manufacturers of photocopiers can take relatively low risks and reap relatively high profits. They can ignore with impunity an industry called publishing which takes relatively high risks for relatively low profits.[4] This dichotomy is untenable, and the remoteness of manufacturers hard to maintain. It is ludicrous that these parties to the copying of copyright material have thus far been largely successful in avoiding responsibility for the current confusion about copyright legislation. The claim of remoteness for infraction is weakened by the frequent installations of devices which add to profits, which could just as readily provide limits to illicit use of coyprighted materials.

There remain serious legal problems involved in holding manufacturers accountable for unrestricted copying. Many of the photocopying manufacturers both sell and lease their equipment: What should be the relationship between proceeds generated as a result of leased versus sold equipment? Manufacturers have no direct control over licit or illicit use of their equipment. How then can they be expected to be liable in situations of copyright abuse? Further, how can one legislate that abuse should be corrected by a manufacturer? Is this tantamount to charging a gun manufacturer rather than the user with manslaughter? The role of the corporate ghosts in the photocopying machine is not parallel with a defective product, since it is not malfunctioning but perfect functioning that is the problem. In this period when such relationships of manufacturer to consumer are being widely debated in both law and custom, in one industry after another, photocopier manufacturers may nonetheless share culpability for illicit copying not on the basis of the merits of a product so much as the unintended consequences of its unlicensed use.

These remain questions to be addressed, and not glossed over to avoid shared responsibility. To further complicate issues, both IBM and (until recently) Xerox were directly involved in the world of publishing. This places them on the "publishers' side" of this debate. Further, their patent rights have been illegally reproduced, stolen is a better term, by foreign firms. They have subsidiary organizations with vital concerns for the protection of copyright. If these interests are to be served in a healthy way, without creating an unintended monopoly of information, then the major photocopying agents must become cooperative in the most intimate meaning of that word. They might begin by modifying their hardware to permit users to compensate copyright owners and to permit the widest dissemination of information while reimbursing authors and publishers for their materials.

At present, each copying machine is provided with an easily violated copyright notice based on the new legislation which can be either ignored or peeled off. Such notices have absolutely no binding value, only a vague moral force and are affixed (if at all) at the user rather than manufacturer end. Photocopier manufacturers might be required under law to supply their machines with copyright controllers to permit systematic recording of the name of the user, client, ISBN or ISSN number, number of copies, amount to be billed, where payments are to be automatically rendered, and any other requested information for later computer printout. Such equipment might also have automatic clearance, so that no copies will be improperly billed to the next user. The ISBN and ISSN system is now clearly universally used and recognized in publishing. The Copyright Clearance Center, with all of its imperfections and crudities, could well serve as collection agent. And even if it is ineffectual at the pragmatic level, CCC does provide a repository of legal claims to copyright at the moral level.

The technology that both makes possible and delimits copyright devices exists and is being marketed.[5] Thus, the issue has shifted from legal objections to copyright infraction to technological corrections. One serious weakness in publisher and author approaches to date is to seek restitution from legal actions without any corresponding attention to technical developments that would alleviate, if not obviate, such a recourse. If the problem is technological, the strong likelihood is that the solution too will be technological.

The basic weakness remaining is the sloth of tradition, the reluctance of major copier manufacturers to provide a point of sale or rental for the controlling equipment which comes with the proper copyright controller devices. Agencies considering copyright revision in the mid-1980s have now moved the discussion from a futile fratricidal struggle between professional publishers and professional librarians, to a common and concerted effort to make photocopier manufacturers aware of the magnitude of the problem, and to make them legally responsible to the needs of users and owners of information alike. Only when responsibility for fair compensation for use of copyright materials is accepted by the manufacturers of copiers no less than by librarians and publishers will the present inadequacies of most current copyright law be resolved in a manner acceptable to all interested parties. And only when publishers appreciate the fact that technological infractions require technological solutions, will the present litigious environment give way to a clear appreciation that great principles are not destroyed, but simply modulated.

Former Commissioner James F. Davis, who found in favor of Williams and Wilkins and against the Department of Health, Education and Welfare, put the matter most succinctly in noting that "the issues raised by this case are but part of a larger problem which continues to plague our institutions with ever-increasing complexity—how best to reconcile, on the one hand, the rights of authors and publishers under the copyright laws with, on the other hand, the technological improvements in copying techniques and the legitimate public need for rapid dissemination of scientific and technical literature." This formulation has not been improved upon over the years. We must keep in mind that the essential purpose of copyright is not to restrict use, but to benefit the arts and sciences—presumably society at large—by compensating people who create. In this sense, the appeal of the publishers and authors has been to the free market; whilst the appeal of hardware manufacturers has been to make machines that provide something for nothing. This transvaluation of commercial values is not likely to go unnoticed.

The rise of a new technology, the dawn of an era when information is electronically stored and transmitted rather than recorded solely on printed paper, requires that librarians and publishers, in their quest to serve users and creators alike, must confront the realities of this new technology. This further means publishers, librarians, and authors must deal directly with industries and manufacturers in this new world of copiers and computers. Ignoring these facts will ensure that, whatever solutions now are found, several years hence, further revisions will have to be considered perhaps at a period when the balance of forces will weigh yet more heavily against those who believe that copyright encourages creativity no less than protects those who create.

The fears and alarms that photocopying would destroy publishing have proven unfounded. For the most part, large-scale print publishers, especially in trade paperback and mass periodicals, remain virtually impervious to photocopying infractions. But the specialized services, from musical publishers to scientific journals have been profoundly affected. Initial page costs can be more than one hundred times that of the reproduced product. Thus, the corporate ghost haunts scholarly and scientific productivity far more than it does mass culture as a whole. This disparity may help explain why the issue of copyright remains unresolved; and why communicating ideas is not some abstract, undifferentiated activity, but a highly stratified, segmented struggle between the knowledge industry, serving an affluent segment of the literate public, and a communications industry, serving broad masses, rather than between publishers and librarians.

Thus far we have dealt essentially with direct methods for compensating copyright or proprietary holders. As the costs of litigation have increased, and as the range of infractions has extended to nontext modes of information delivery, efforts at indirect means for protecting copyright have come into sharper focus. But far from easing debates on the right to knowledge versus the right to compensation, these new modes have only served to deepen debate.

One approach, pioneered by the Copyright Clearance Center, and largely endorsed by the Association of American Publishers, is a blanket agreement for large corporations to pay an average annual fee based upon average annual use (after a direct on-site monitoring service) with a "fair use exemption of anywhere from six to ten percent." Fair use becomes, in effect, a discount on volume use. In almost every case, this agreement between a major corporation and the CCC publishing spin-off, is a consequence either of litigation or the threat thereof.

The obstacles to this approach have proven considerable. First, averaging is a profoundly imperfect mechanism for determining fees. Second, the fair-use exemption enshrines a doctrine of widespread abuse, one which places the publishing community on record as supporting a legislative loophole they should seek to close. Third, very few industrial firms, major or minor, have accepted this blanket-fee arrangement; and the costs of monitoring much less litigating each firm (at least until a precedent becomes apparent) is large enough to cancel the fees generated by the program. Fourth, large corporations tend to reproduce scientific journal articles only. Hence book publishers, and for that matter publishers of humanistic, popular, or social scientific materials in no way benefit from these essentially "sweetheart" arrangements between large corporations and large publishers—which are essentially corporations of some substance in their own right.

These severe shortcomings registered, the very existence of a Copyright Clearance Center provides a significant mechanism for adherence to the new copyright rules and regulations. Without such a mechanism, an argument can be made that compliance is not possible since no mechanism for processing materials and money exists. Further, however slow the process of litigation may be, its very potential for correction sets up precedents for adherence on a voluntary basis, and on an involuntary basis if necessary. Finally, the CCC, or its equivalent elsewhere, provides lobbying functions for improving legislation, and also for providing a bridge between hitherto antagonistic scholarly communities, i.e., publishers, librarians, authors, and researchers. For these reasons, the thin reed of the CCC, however cracked, continues to be played.

I have already drawn attention to the fact that the Copyright Clearance Center approach to copyright infringement emphasizes the actions of major corporations against scientific and technical publishers. But this does not much help the scholarly or for that matter trade authors and publishers. The European nations, starting first with Denmark in 1946 and most recently including the United Kingdom in 1979, have developed a Public Lending Right, or more realistically an author's fee for the use in libraries of copyrighted works.[6]

The system involves a borrower of library materials paying a fee for reading a text while it is still private property. It is a quantitative system, with no particular judgment on the moral worth or intellectual peerage of the author. It is a payment for use, in such modest sums, as to supplement and augment wages, royalties, or other forms of income. The English system starts with a floor of £1 and extends to £5000. The principle of payment for library copies is relatively simple to monitor, certainly it is far less cumbersome than the direct or indirect payment systems devised by the CCC thus far.

The main opposition to incorporating Public Lending Right legislation in the United States has come from the library community. Its arguments are not unlike those leveled at the new copyright measures in general: first, the expenses would be largely borne by librarians and staff; second, local administrative burdens would readily become abusive, spilling over into police functions; third, payment schedules introduce an elitist function into an essentially egalitarian environment. These arguments clearly have prima facie merit; but the precedent set by Western Europe, the relative ease with which the system works in other democratic societies, does serve to weaken arguments against such payment for the "right to knowledge."

Between 1973 and 1983 there was a great deal of agitation for Public Lending Right legislation in the United States, concluding with a bill calling for the establishment of a national commission to study the merits of such a PLR measure. While it died in committee the first time around, it has been reintroduced in 1985 in the 99th Congress. While author sentiment in favor is high, and librarian opposition is equally firm, public reaction remains hard to gauge. Interestingly, the Association of American Publishers has taken no public position. While its sentiments are clearly to establish proprietary measures over copyrighted materials it does not want to further estrange a library community with whom it is already at loggerheads over such items as fair use and registration with the CCC.

But in the long pull of time, some form of PLR is bound to be institutionalized. The emergence of payments for video cassettes, indeed the mergency of film libraries in nearly every shopping mall in the United States, makes this development in the borrowing of books and journals more than likely. Indeed, what is becoming increasingly plain is that the book or the journal represents a form of scholarly or popular communication. Its properties physically are different, but its intellectual properties are similar to other forms of disbursing knowledge and information. In the past it was the very uniqueness that inhibited the recognition of the printed word as a private property no less than a public service. In the future it will be the very isomorphism of the book and journal to other modes of information/knowledge presentation that will enhance this recognition that property and service are not necessarily at odds.

The lines are being redrawn in the class struggles over the control of information and knowledge. It is not between an intractable bourgeoisie who own the means of production and an inscrutable proletariat in search of a new ownership and distribution. Rather, it is a struggle between property owners and populist users. It hardly matters whether the merchandise is called information or entertainment, another remnant of the early twentieth century. What does matter is the owners right to compensation versus the users right to choice. Owners marshall new umbrella organizations like the American Copyright Council whilst users counter with "groups" organized about the unrestricted use of everything from computer software to space satellites.

What is intriguing in this evolutionary process from the struggle to control production (nineteenth century), consumption (twentieth century), and communication (twenty-first century) is how reality outstrips rhetoric. Academic scholarship has barely mastered its Marxian and Weberian lessons when along comes a new reality, with new relationships of forces, in search of a new way to describe events and explain realities. What saves the situation "theoretically" is less political economy than moral philosophy. For what we witness is not just a "new" technology but an "old" morality—in which control over information is not only access to power, it is the definition of power.

Question of piracy or illegal infringement upon copyrighted materials, for instance, are by no means open and shut matters. For example, it has been reported that between 1981 and 1984, close to 700 book titles, including a number of translations from Western literature, were illegally published in Poland.[7] Clearly, if the overriding concern is the liberalization and eventual liberation of Poland from military communism, then the issues of copyright infringement in that country must be placed within a geo-political context. On the other hand, if copyright is the central issue, whatever the nobility of a cause or movement, then one establishes a different set of legal and political parameters. Admittedly, the Polish situation is quite different from the Taiwanese situation, where crass commercial concerns prevail. But to raise this sort of issue is at once to be confronted by a world inhabited by people other than and perhaps more important than, authors, publishers and pirates.

To summarize this extraordinary bundle of issues: The widespread acceptance of copyright principles does not automatically resolve long-standing disputes. It only accentuates these intra-copyright issues. Among these issues of law are the ability to copyright art or architectural items in the same way as written words. Is an original work of any kind, in any medium, subject to copyright restraint, or are they to be treated like ideas, i.e., entities operating largely in the public domain. What have come to be identified as "threshold questions" are even more contentious in the mid-1980s: Is a piece of sculpture copyrightable matter, whether copyright protections obtain whether or not media objects are actually copyrighted; and how it is even possible to determine whether actual copying takes place in a world of images where variations on select themes are widespread?[8]

What we are now witnessing is a concrete evolution of these new forms of alliance and misalliance that reached a crescendo in the past decades. In a multi-media no less than multi-tiered informational environment proprietary issues will become increasingly complex and important. In an older environment in which the disjunction between material goods and spiritual services was taken for granted, it was relatively easy to assess the ownership of artifacts and books. But now, in an era of dissolution of such dualisms, the issue of copyright can be seen as wrapped up in larger concerns about property and identity as such. The fine line between words and things, ideas and artifacts, is becoming ever finer. In such an environment the relationships between knowledge and property inevitably link up with classic concerns of knowledge and power.

7

From Computer Revolution to Intellectual Counter-revolution

This is an effort to assay the consequences of a dangerously widening breach between information and knowledge. Information applies to facts told, read, or communicated that may be unorganized and even unrelated. One speaks of "picking up useful information" as a rather casual, limited activity. In contrast, knowledge is an organized body of information, or the comprehension and understanding which is the consequence of having acquired an organized body of facts and theories. One speaks of "a knowledge of" physics or economics. There is a strong implication of holism in knowledge, a sense of working to create an integrated framework that permits the production of judgment and insight.

In order to avoid confusion, a few caveats are in order. One should not identify the word "quantitative" with information or the word "qualitative" with knowledge. While it may be correct to note the parallelisms between quantitatively arrived at materials and information, and qualitative narrative and knowledge, yet mathematical formulae or musical notation systems are very much part of the knowledge environment. Indeed, symbolization is the highest form available for expressing a data-rich environment. Still, some rough-hewn distinctions are called for in describing the rise of information and the decline of knowledge as socially defined goals for a new age.

I begin by taking recourse in this elementary vision of information and knowledge not to engage in a specious form of nit-picking, but as a reflection of a growing confusion in the publishing community as to its essential tasks; and no less, a widening gap in the world of scholarly communication that beckons to cut more deeply than the inherited dualism between applied and pure research, and more broadly than the presumed two cultures of science and humanism. More is at stake than sheer linguistic niceties. At its core this issue concerns the status of human intellect in the world of advanced technical culture.

A paradox will become readily apparent, even at the outset. On one hand, I draw sharp attention to the differences between information and knowledge, while on the other, I inveigh against the dualistic tradition which lives off of concept reification. One person's distinction is another's dualism. That as the case may be, the need to examine older, well-established distinctions may of necessity proceed through an awareness of newer, less recognized ambitions. While this is hardly a satisfactory answer to paradox on epistemological grounds, it will have to make do on sociological grounds.

Without an unduly elaborate linguistic excursion, it remains worthwhile to distinguish information and knowledge in terms of their respective social implications. Information is to policy what knowledge is to wisdom. That is to say, the ultimate value of information is to provide a series of options for human behavior that will maximize satisfactory or optimal outcomes; whereas the function of knowledge is to provide some form of human wisdom that admits of limits to success even when capabilities are eminently available. Hence, we must distinguish between policy and wisdom, between choices based on optimal scenarios for future success, and those based on acceptable normative standards of past performance.

At some level, the question of knowledge shades over into a question of ethics; or if one prefers, the normative structure of human society, the capacity of information for use in solving problems does little to answer whether particular problems are deserving of solutions. As Jonathan Swift once noted, the problem of famine in Ireland could be resolved by recourse to cannibalism, by serving the starving children of tenant farmers as table meat for the absentee landlords who had already devoured their parents. We dismiss such "solutions" because of their immorality, not inefficiency. One can readily design situations of surprise attack to annihilate a potential enemy, but the actual implementation is something else again. Indeed, everything from surprise attacks at Pearl Harbor to unanticipated atomic bombings at Hiroshima are debated not only on pragmatic grounds of workability but no less on normative grounds of morality. This then is an essential distinction between information and knowledge, a ground which is blurred only at great peril to useful communication as a whole.

A more contemporary way to illustrate this distinction, one which is crucial to my text, is to differentiate between game theoretical circumstances for fighting a war, and the practicality of whether such a war will prove so costly in human lives, or the loss thereof, that such victory in combat will prove phyrric. One can readily design a winning scenario by considering elements of surprise (the time of day or evening, holidays or workdays) with elements of tactical superiority (types of weapons available, manpower backups). However, it is the realm of *both* unanticipated consequences and predetermined values, that is empirical and moral judgments alike, which provides inhibitions to the unfettered recourse to information-based only actions.[1]

One other mode of distinction may be called for: information has properly been identified, since the age of Francis Bacon, as the source of power. However, knowledge, since the time of Immanuel Kant, has with equal force been viewed as the source of authority. This distinction between power and authority need not be reified to assess its worth. All individuals and systems have the power to perform acts they dare not do for fear of destroying a delicate social fabric. Crimes of regicide, deicide, infanticide, and a host of taboos come readily to mind. This realm, whether enshrined in custom or law, is called authority. But clearly, the basis of authority is a form of knowledge quite beyond ego gratification or personal satisfaction.[2]

Arguments can be adduced on how and under what conditions information and knowledge shade into each other. There is no purpose in reifying two concepts. However, distinction is not reification. In an information-rich and knowledge-poor environment it would be risky, even foolhardy, to blur distinctions. To be frank, the limits of information technology—or if one prefers, the information society—are much more its successes than its failures. In an environment of increasing application of computers and robots in the organization of social problems, the role of knowledge increases, taking on the chores of negotiating the foundations of moral conduct—critical reason in Kantian terms—along with the traditional role of knowledge in determining the truth functions of experience. That more sophisticated techniques of information are included is doubtless the case, but this simply means that the information technology throws up more issues in the very process of dismissing pseudo-problems. The brave new world of logical positivism anticipated and understood well the place of technology in discarding pseudo-problems, where it failed miserably was in any understanding that beneath the debris of metaphysics, there still remained the hard core of the problem of defining knowledge as such.

The amorphous nature of knowledge in contrast to the specificity of information or data makes it easier to market the latter and denigrate the values of the former. Basic information can be massaged and manipulated by large numbers of people with diverse views. This is the case whether that information is in video-disk or hard copy form, or whether that information pertains to the location of museums in travel guides or statistics on employment segmented by race or age or sex. This sort of approach leads directly from data to application, without due regard for issues of relevance, validity, worth, or selective impact. In this way, knowledge is reduced to methodology, to testing data rather than analyzing data. It serves little purpose to add, as positivist defenders of networking information claim, that this is a function of the marketplace, or of supply and demand, since the demand for a certain type of data may at once be adequately supplied and yet hugely lacking in merit. One can supply a great deal of information on types of crimes and neatly break out such data into usable components for everything from law enforcement to tax abatement purposes, and yet never ask the question why, i.e., causal questions about the functions of crime, or even socially importuned redefinitions of criminal behavior. To be sure, the "qualitative indicators" movement came upon hard times precisely because it was transformed subtly into a quantitative indicators movement.[3] It addressed issues such as the number of homes wired for television or for cable television, without any corresponding capacity to deal with the contents of what is being viewed. Similarly, many claims are gratuitously made for the correlation of social revolution with a rise in literacy, without any corresponding analysis of the propagandistic or tendentious contents of such newfound literacy.

The merits of the so-called "market orientation" to information are clear, starting with finding out what people actually want in the way of data and supplying those needs. Nonetheless, the demerits too often go unexamined, namely, the presumption of a bottom-up environment in real discovery; when in fact, real discoveries are more often than not top-down. Another way of making the same point is that the pure theory of democracy is not the same as the practice of knowledge acquisition. Satisfying marketplaces, however large or small, is not quenching the thirst to know things and events truthfully. One could satisfy the need for maps of the world while presuming a flat planet earth. Indeed, for small distances, such an assumption was entirely viable. Still, a larger impulse to satisfy rather than ignore monumental discrepancies took place amongst a narrow band of researchers who were somewhat removed from the marketplace of ship captains and cartographers.

Democratic doctrine is so widely ingrained into advanced post-industrial environments that the peculiar features of knowledge-building and knowledge-creation are easily overlooked. The Aristotelian environment in which a class of knowledge-builders was segregated and held to higher account (and no less advantaged life-styles) over all other classes cuts against the American grain in particular. As a result, filling the needs of a marketplace becomes the information world's equivalence to every person counting as one, and no more or less than one. If in fact the acquisition of knowledge were isomorphic with the maintenance of democratic order such equiva-lencies would work fine. It is, however, precisely the discontinuity be-tween the marketplace and the idea, between the democratic order and the scientific order, that remains the uncomfortable bedrock upon which such presumptions of synergy founder and flounder.

The tradition of publishing is powerfully linked historically with the discoveries of science and technology. Indeed, the early printed books, other than the biblical texts, were extensions of scientific and technological speculations. That is why the book industry, such as it was, became the focus of critique and attack by established authori-ties in Western nations.

As Andrew H. Neilly recently summarized the matter, while sci-entific publishing as an industry is as old as publishing itself, its accel-erated growth is structurally linked to the technification of publishing.

> It probably began with the early dictionaries of the Greeks and Romans. Plato's *Republic* was written in the fifth century B.C. *The Censure and Judgement* of Erasmus was published in 1550. Galileo published *Dialogues on the Two Principal Systems of the World* in 1632, for which he was censured by the Church and placed under house arrest. His *Dialogues on the Two Sciences* appeared in 1638. Lavoisier's *Elements of Chemistry* appeared in 1789, and Darwin's *Voyage of the Beagle* and *Origin of the Species* in the 1850's, by which time England, as a function of the Industrial Revolution and its flow of new ideas and developments, became a center of publishing—as did France, Germany, and Holland. In the United States, Lea and Febiger was founded in 1785, J. B. Lippin-cott in 1792, and John Wiley 1807 . . . Most U.S. publications were then based on the practical sciences—civil engineering, me-chanics, agriculture, railroad engineering and many came from the

faculties of the land-grant colleges that later became our state universities.[4]

The new absorption by the publication world of a theory of information, predicated on a doctrine of pure service to a market, in effect limits that traditional role, abdicating the search for knowledge in favor of commercial criteria of success as measured by profitability or sheer longevity. Nor does it quite solve the puzzle by assigning knowledge activities to an entity known as scholarly communication or university press publishing. Indeed, doing so, only insinuates the largely irresponsibilities of the publishing worlds to deal seriously with its traditional concerns, i.e., the search for the dissemination of knowledge. The stratification of publishing converts knowledge itself into a portion of the hierarchical mosaic of information. And in so doing, the relationship between information and knowledge is itself distorted. Instead of information's being tested by its knowledge functions, knowledge is tested by its marketability, i.e., information functions.

A peculiar development is taking place in American publishing, which for want of a better expression I shall refer to as the internalization of anti-intellectualism. By that I mean the shift on the part of publishers and scholars alike to an information mode in place of a knowledge search. In part, this is the inevitable outcome of the computer revolution.

The social sciences reveal this shift from knowledge to information in a dramatic fashion. One recent report pointed out that, whereas in 1946, some 50 percent of the articles employed statistics, by 1976, some 87 percent of the articles in the *American Sociological Review* did so. Furthermore, in the earlier postwar period 62 percent used simple statistics of totals, percentages, or cross-tabulation. Thirty years later, these simple measures were essentially displaced by multiple regression, matrix and path analysis, and other measures demanding extensive computations. Psychometrics, econometrics, cliometrics were key manifestations of a positivist trend. Quantitative data held out prospects for non-ideological solutions to vexing problems.[5]

The rise of microcomputers allowed for yet higher control and massage of data. Numerous commercial statistical programs for microcomputers, by the mid-1980s, handled data sets of 20 variables for 100 cases, and newer models could handle 72 variables for 750 cases. Microcomputer statistics also permitted easier editing of vari-

ables and data. This also permits researcher response to new measures whose relevance could not have been anticipated before seeing
initial results. Finally, a division of labor between microcomputers
and mainframes takes place in the transfer of heavy computational
tasks and massive storage needs.[6] But the computer revolution—
whatever its level of penetration to the individual scholar—sets in
motion a trust of data, i.e., information; and a declining use, if not
outright mistrust, of knowledge, i.e., speculation, generalization, and
rationalization.

The publishing industry, no less than the social science industry,
has quickly come to appreciate the historic significance of this shift
from knowledge to information. For not only is it easier to sell information, it is easier to command a much higher price for goods and
services, i.e., books and journals, based upon information. The social
world is no longer carved up taxonomically in categories of economics, sociology, psychology, political science, and anthropology. The
carving up, in less than one hundred years, shifts to financial services,
management studies, communications, decision-making, evaluation research, artificial intelligence, etc.

This came to be seen in publishing terms as a shift from product
delivery to market orientation. McGraw-Hill, perhaps the most aggressive and advanced publisher to link social research to computer
technology, put the matter starkly and accurately in its recent annual
report. An extract from its report is well worth pondering:

> McGraw-Hill's historic shift from product to market orientation
> comes as major developments in the information industry itself—
> the rapid changes in computer and communications technology and
> in the new ways in which customers can obtain information—dic-
> tate bold moves to help ensure the corporation's reaching its goals
> of market power and increased profits. With market-centered
> operations, each of McGraw-Hill's strategic units becomes a multi-
> media information provider, capable of serving customers by what-
> ever medium best suits their needs—by print in magazines, news-
> letters, books and loose-leaf files or electronically through software
> and interactive and broadcast communications facilities. Restructur-
> ing its operations this way reinforces McGraw-Hill's long-standing
> objective: to capture, store and sort the millions of items and in-
> formation that the company's worldwide staff collects daily, then
> segment the data into whatever forms and increments are most
> suitable for customers served by each market focus business unit.
> Organizing around markets has been described by some observers
> as one of the most significant advances in business thinking since

Alfred Sloan introduced his decentralization philosophy at General Motors and Procter & Gamble developed the brand management system.[7]

Looking behind this "historic" shift from product to market is a philosophical shift from science to economy. Doubtless, there will be cries of denial, with the invocation of the caveat that it is the scientists who define the market needs. But if that indeed be the case, just what does the shift from product to market entail? The organization of knowledge around the marketplace is in fact a displacement of traditional scientific taxonomies in the name of delivering information in a variety of convenient modes and forms. In this case, the "product" is not, never was, simply the book or the journal; rather it is the contents of science as such. The historic shift then is not simply the packaging of science, but its redefinition as a pure commodity apart from an intrinsic merit.

Before proceeding further with an analysis of this historic shift from product to market, it is significant to point out that giant publishers are scarcely alone in this reorientation process. We may take a minuscule book publisher, one directly plugged into international relations and social-science orientation generally, as illustrative of the scope and substance of this theoretical shift from naturalism to positivism; from a knowledge orientation to an information retrieval network. Frederick A. Praeger, in his Spring 1985 statement to buyers of Westview titles, speaks of a "knowledge supermarket" and "brain food," an approach that is separated from McGraw-Hill in size but not in purpose:

> We see our future as a sort of *knowledge supermarket,* where service is enthusiastic, efficient, fast, and highly professional, handling knowledge and information produced by the scholarly and scientific community. *We want to provide the most advanced brain food available in the frontier areas of scholarship with specialty shelves abundantly stocked,* quality control stations strategically located, and on every aisle, cheerful, supportive service teams ready to intervene with commitment and affection whenever there are problems.[8]

It is disconcerting to see the library community provide a similar rationale to its new approach to technology. It starts with a concept of the "Electronic Library" and ends with one of the "Electronic Scholar." In this "vision of the future" (short term at that—the gay 1990s) outlined by the Office of Scholarly Communication and Technology, we are inexorably moved from the promise of "on-line gateway access to the universe of knowledge" to "information on order and circulation status of documents." What proves so disturbing is the seamless manner in which reductionism and positivism are insinuated as the unique approaches to knowledge-seeking. Boolean logic, call-number searching, backward and forward browsing become essential characteristics of the Electronic Library in the service of the Electronic Scholar.[9] The endorsement of such a position by the American Council of Learned Societies does little to assuage fears that knowledge itself has been sacrificed to information-searching.

It is easy enough to detect in a variety of professional activities, and in clear, bold strokes, the outlines of a frontal assault against traditional modes of intellectual speculation, not to mention a growing suspicion that speculation as such, insofar as it is non-quantifiable, does not deserve more than short-shrift. How the computer revolution has become central to the rise of a technological counter-revolution has itself become a core problem; i.e., what sorts of social and political processes generate quantitative data as a rhetorical tool.

A recent study has indicated the dangers in the quantification approach to information by noting that: (a) There are no real rates of a phenomena and no true measures of outcomes of social intervention. (b) Singling out categories of people, objects, or events for purposes of quantification changes their meaning. (c) Counting, be it the number of people in a particular category or success rates in particular social intervention programs, has a temporal dimension. (d) Counting releases social processes within the setting where the counting takes place in addition to and beyond the activities directly tied to counting. (e) People who produce data in organizational settings are subject to social processes and structural forces similar to those touching other work groups. (d) Enumeration and its products have strong affective and ritualistic properties.[10] This sort of analysis goes to the heart of the new information society, both in its critical assessments, and in a positive sense, the effort to impose a knowledgeable incorporation of quantitative data into a larger set of social processes.

Recent research tends to indicate that the impact of the computer revolution, at least at the level of general concepts, has been highly differentiated. Its impact on the broad population stratum has been less pervasive or dramatic than initially heralded. But its impact on the orientations, interactions, capabilities, and distribution among specialized elites like social scientists has been considerable.

To be sure, there is a sense in which knowledge is organized by other than the knowledge-maker. Publishers organize knowledge into a set of marketing characteristics, i.e., trade, text, and scholarly publications; or by fields that may or may not correspond to academic environments, i.e., "international relations." Likewise, librarians perform similar exercises by installing downloading capacities and local interactive manipulation of archive materials, or in the capacity to order off-line prints of machine readable text. But this is ultimately to confuse who organizes information with what is being organized, and by whom. The relative simplicity of ordering a data base or a factual search, in contrast to the far more complex and at times "illogical" nature of ordering ideas, leads to a strong, but unhealthy bias in favor of the former and at the expense of not simply knowledge in the abstract but innovation in the concrete.

As one researcher has acutely pointed out, the social impact of computer technology has not been entirely beneficial. Computing tends to increase the importance for decision and action of quantitative, technical criteria. Computing use tends to isolate individuals, reducing their interaction with other people in both work and leisure settings. Computing increases organizational control available to central authorities. Computing has become a major source of productivity gains for individuals and organizations. Computing increases social control and monitoring, reducing the privacy of individuals and small groups. The current impacts of computing tend primarily to serve the interests of the more dominant groups in a given setting, thus reinforcing existing power distributions.[11]

While this approach may exaggerate the extent to which the new technology stimulates rather than resolves problems in social stratification, it does at least have the merit of making plain the potentials to cut in both directions. Utopian tendencies have tended to overwhelm more cautious voices, especially in an environment where sales remain substantial, although uneven from the "class" point of view. To deal candidly with stratification issues is not the same as arguing the case for the revolt against modernity. It is to note properly that just as moral issues tend to be highlighted rather than diluted by the new technology, so too has a similar phenomenon taken place in the social world of stratification.

Future research will determine just how strong or weak such tendencies are. Certainly, the explosion of microcomputing, with its free-wheeling, stand-alone systems, will open matters up considerably.

But the point here is less one of rival hypotheses—of which there is no end in sight—but how to explain the shift from knowledge factory to information industry.

We require no cataloguing of deviance to appreciate the irony of a condition in which the computers urge rationality, logic, and exact positive science; whilst a social world reveals tatters of organization: global terrorism, personal disorders, social disorganizations, a variety of malaises documented fully and richly in the sociological literature. Nor is it adequate to say that the function of the new computer environment provides rational information on the social environment. The idea that the rationality of irrationality somehow takes care of matters omits neither the emergence of new forms of deviance and destruction, nor the causal basis of such "irrationalities" to begin with. In other words, the functions of knowledge remain very much alive, albeit buried beneath the rhetoric of reductionism.

We remain haunted by the position of the Grand Inquisitor in Dostoevsky's *Brothers Karamazov:* the freedom of choice, to be left alone to grope our way in the dark. The notion of a computer technology, free of a knowledge search lifts the responsibility from the shoulders of humans, making them willing, grateful, and happy slaves to the information environment. Isaiah Berlin, in his essay *Political Ideas in the Twentieth Century,* properly appreciated the historical irony of the situation. Only the names change, not the substance of his charge.

> The Grand Inquisitor stood for the dogmatic organization of the life of the spirit: Bazarov for its theoretical opposite—free scientific inquiry, the facing of the "hard" facts, the acceptance of the truth however brutal or upsetting. By an irony of history (not unforeseen by Dostoevsky) they have formed a pact, they are allies, and today are often indistinguishable. Buridan's ass, we are told, unable to choose between two equidistant bundles of hay, starved to death. Against this fate the only remedy is blind obedience and faith. Whether the refuge is a dogmatic religious faith or a dogmatic faith in social or natural science matters relatively little: for without such obedience and faith there is no confidence and no hope, no optimistic, "constructive," "positive" form of life.[12]

That the new technological disciples of those who exposed the religious idolatry of ideas should become the most ferocious supporters of new forms of reductionism and reification may be ironical, but surely not a surprising irony. For the demand for certainty, implicit in the reduction of knowledge to information, is the historical *cri de couer* of the anti-intellectual, of those for whom choice and abundance is itself an enemy of the march of civilization.

In point of fact, the empirical shifts brought about by the new technology, the post-industrial environment, call it what one will, have only reinforced the normative condition of the search for reason. The "realms" of information (facts) and of knowledge (truths) remain very much intact. Beyond that, the need for an additional "realm" of judgment (morals) in which the ethical and aesthetic status of facts and truths alike becomes increasingly important. The enormous increase in the amount of available sound information may serve to reduce speculative room for error, but it also has the effect of increasing the speculative element as to the nature of truth.

In publishing terms this leads to a sharpening of differences between types of publication. What the industry refers to as market segmentation is only the formalized expression of differences between these abstract realms played out in concrete arenas. "How to" books are after all pedestrian expressions of the pragmatic ethic in which the way things are manipulated is equivalent to what they are. Data-rich texts or print-outs are likewise part of a deepening demand for the sort of facts which presumably speak for themselves. That facts rarely do provide little deterrent for the holy grail of information. "Scholarly lists," in this sense, are expressions of a realm of generalization which, whether warranted by extant data or the ability to manipulate an environment, are deemed of importance in putting together a world, an environment, that gives a society a sense of the whole—called variously a *Geist, esprit, soul,* whatever makes sense of the very welter of facts and operations that are appealed to in the first place because of the inconclusiveness of the speculative realm or scholarly ideal.

If such an analysis is correct, the speed with which new facts are integrated with or supplemental to existing data banks requires an increasing use of flexible, non-print media which render such information accurately and quickly. Expense is secondary to speed, aesthetic sensibility is equally secondary to the functional malleability of data. At the same time, the realm of knowledge, the systematic rendering of information in general propositions, will continue to be placed in hard copy form. This will be so because the print media continue to serve as a relatively inexpensive mechanism for rendering holistic ideas in an aesthetically pleasing form.

In this sense the information explosion, the emergence of Dow-Jones, Mead, Quotron Systems, A. C. Nielson, the Dun & Bradstreet

Corporation as major forces in the information world, represent an add-on to the world of publishing. They reflect an explosive new information environment, but one to which traditional scholarly publishing, while not exactly remaining impervious to, is at the same time relatively independent of.[13] The continuing growth of scholarly publishing remains quantitative in character; an incremental expansion of the world of higher learning as it were. This dual track—slow growth in scholarship and fast growth in information—is precisely what confirms the above analysis. For the structure of normative thinking is clearly less volatile than the explosion of information capabilities of the new technology. This interaction of factual and normative components of knowledge is key to understanding the present state of both publishing and scholarship.

This should confirm the multiple tracking systems, not only within the domain of publishing but within the domain of knowledge as such. Information has always been on a fast track, since it yields data of an ephemeral or immediate need. Knowledge, likewise, tends to be on a slow track, since it yields ideas at a level of abstraction and normative import more subject to erosion over time than obsolescence in short bursts of time. The co-existence between information and knowledge is not, and need not, always be peaceful. But a world of positive data only would be flat, unimaginative; whereas a world of critical theory, uninformed by data, would be vague, abstract, and ultimately a huge step backward. Inherited dualistic "warfares" between quantitative and qualitative, the concrete and the abstract, the factual and the moral ought finally to be put to rest. That is the essential message of the new technological environment advanced societies are now in the midst of bringing into existence.

8

Scholarly Communication and Academic Publishing

For many individuals in academic life, the entire publishing process is confusing, often reduced to a combination of printing and distribution. The tendency toward conglomeration, with small publishers merging with larger publishers and large publishers merging with each other and with non-publishing firms, has added to this confusion. Size and consequent specialization within firms are intimidating. As Arthur Rosenthal, director of Harvard University Press, recently pointed out, the facts are different. "A primary purpose of a university press is to function as a natural outlet for information, theory, speculation, and methodology that will influence human endeavor and enrich understanding in generations to come."[1]

Academic authors identify a publishing house they hope will want to publish their work by approaching one that has published books they admire and respect. If the model title they have in mind is more than five years old, they may find that the house has shifted its emphasis since the book was published, particularly if the publisher has been subject to major changes in personnel. It is often hard to locate what division of a publishing house to approach, and certainly which individual in that division they should contact. Editors leave one publishing house for another, or they assume other responsibilities within the same company. Added to the confusion are mistaken assumptions about the publishing process that disappoint many authors, even those who succeed in finding a publisher. For the post-publication process is as complex as the pre-publication process.

The publishing industry in the United States divides its activities into a number of categories in which books written by scholars can be located. These categorizations are not absolute, and they are less fixed in smaller firms. Understanding the meaning of these categorizations can provide a basis for deciding what kind of book one has written and what can be expected from the publishing process.

Trade publishing is the first category. This is what most people, and individuals in academic life are no exception, think about when they ruminate about how they would like their book published. Trade books usually are sold to the ultimate purchaser through third parties, i.e., bookstores. Hardcover trade books are primarily sold through such public outlets. Mass market paperback houses sell inexpensive paperbacks through distributors which place books in such outlets as bookstores, newsstands, variety stores, airports, supermarkets, and drugstores. These giant paperback houses, many of which are owned by larger, cash-rich companies, publish a large number of titles. They have the resources to pay huge sums (the current record is $2.5 million) for paperback rights to a book that is, or that they anticipate will become, a best seller. Trade paperbacks are sold through bookstores, but rarely in the additional paperback outlets described above. Trade paperbacks include serious novels by authors who are thought not to be commercial enough to warrant mass market editions but who possess enough name-recognition to sell roughly 10,000 copies in paperback. They tend to be serious books that potentially appeal to identifiable audiences. Trade paperbacks sell at higher average prices than do mass market paperbacks. They do not receive anywhere near the level of advertising and promotion received by mass market paperbacks. Most books in the United States still appear first in hardcover, and only later do the "winners" appear in paperback. Occasionally simultaneous hardcover and paperback editions are published; but for the most part, this simultaneity is restricted to the scholarly area.

A second category in which academic market books are found is in textbook publishing. The nature of what constitutes a textbook has undergone dramatic changes since the 1950s and 1960s. Many college textbooks in the mid-1980s are written by academics with the active participation of the publishing house. Indeed this is the way in which elementary education texts have always been prepared. Large publishers in particular are acutely aware of reading levels of competing texts, of what teachers want from a textbook and what students can derive from a textbook. Publishers invest significant resources in pre-publication reviewing and analysis after which the professor takes a first stab at responding to reviews and criticism; internal staff often make further efforts to rewrite the text. Increasingly, the academic author has a professional writer as co-author or assistant author. This is how major textbook publishers such as Prentice-Hall, McGraw-Hill, and Holt, Rinehart and Winston go about their business. Smaller textbook houses sometimes emulate these procedures. But often they do not. They are either satisfied with publishing books for smaller courses, or willing to publish books embodying a minority point of view toward a profession, which presumably translates into lesser sales potential. Some smaller publishers have developed innovative approaches to the development or marketing of introductory college texts, and apply these to a small list; for example, publishing very few titles in select areas and marketing them extensively and intensively.

A major difference between large textbook publishers and smaller publishers is how they sell their books. Houses publishing a large number of titles for the introductory and required courses have massive field sales forces that a smaller publisher clearly cannot afford to maintain. Smaller publishers tend to rely on direct mail and commissioned sales staffs. With few exceptions, smaller publishers have been most successful when they have concentrated on smaller courses or when they have developed a small number of titles to which they dedicate all their resources.

In the postwar "baby boom" period of the 1950s–1960s, all manner of books were published as textbooks with little development to fulfill course or professional needs. This overpublishing in part resulted from a tremendous, one-time infusion of capital and a desire for a quick return on investment. Many old-line publishers had been purchased by large, cash-rich conglomerates, which attempted to double profits by mechanistically doubling the number of titles produced. In part too, overpublishing occurred because university enrollments were spiraling, due to affluence, the Vietnam War, and the aforementioned demographic explosion.

The end result of this process of overpublishing for the education market was that many books failed in the early 1970s, many editors in publishing companies lost their jobs, and decision-making about how to publish became more conservative, conventional, and scientific. By the early 1980s textbooks no longer just happened, they were designed packages, with accompanying films, test banks, and other supplemental material. At first faculty missed having a diverse choice of paperback books to assign to their students, but they quickly began to expect textbooks that exactly matched their course requirements. Faculty teaching loads became smaller. Upper-level courses and seminars began to appreciate that it was not feasible to use texts in the same way. Hardcover editions were placed on reserve at the university library, or quality paperbacks became the "texts" of these upper division courses.

A third category of publishing, into which most of the books that scholarly research falls, is commonly identified within commercial houses as business and professional publishing, or scientific, technical, and medical publishing. Commercial houses lacking this kind of publishing expertise often identify these titles simply as university press books. This is not altogether amiss, since in fact, 90 percent of scholarly books are still published by university presses. But increasingly, professional publishing is a sub-division in its own right.

A major difference between scholarly publishing and trade and text publishing is the amount of investment capital required to publish a single title. Professional social science books can be published with a much smaller investment of risk capital than is required for a trade or textbook. The expensive support systems required in text and trade publishing is not required in professional scientific publishing. But whether an investment in a title or a series is large or small, there is every reason to insist upon a publishing program to be operated in business-like fashion. But beyond commerce is science itself. Marsh Jeanneret, former director of the University of Toronto Press, put the issues well:

> The scholarly press's function is to produce works which in the main may not be published elsewhere. It must be able to investigate which of such manuscripts are likely to be most valuable to the scholars for whom they have been written, it must prepare them for publication and produce them in appropriate editions and runs, and it has the further duty of ensuring that they are brought to the attention of potential users throughout the academic world and catalogued and distributed through the most efficient channels there are.[2]

The potential returns for academic publishing are smaller than the profit margins on other forms of publication. For example, a social science book might sell 1500 copies at $18.95 ($28,425), compared with a similar textbook that might sell 8000 at $12.95 ($103,600), and a trade book that might sell 7500 copies at $11.95 ($89,625). The potential for a trade book or textbook is much more elastic: each could sell as many as 50,000 copies if it was successful, while a successful professional social science book rarely sells more than 6000 copies. The percentage increments may be similar but the dollar amounts clearly vary.[3] But the number quoted as the average sale for professional books is more certain than is the average quoted for text or trade books. The bottom-line profitability of most textbook and trade book lists is carried by a few very successful titles rather than spread evenly across the list, as it tends to be in professional book publishing.

As English has become the dominant scientific and commercial lingua franca, English-language professional books have found a world market which is not easily available to either text or trade publishers. Professional publishers have found that books in the natural and physical sciences travel best, the behavioral sciences less well, and the social sciences least well. This may be because it is difficult to separate social scientific research from its political implications or ideological proclivities. The social sciences have been among the first curricula to be eliminated or reduced in universities when an authoritarian regime comes into power, and they are the last to be reinstated when that regime feels secure. When they are reinstated, the kinds of social science taught tend to be "safe." Demographic and methodological studies tend to prevail. The slow acceptance of social research in the communist bloc nations typifies this "positivistic" pattern.

Why does the publishing industry divide itself into these big categories? In part, these categories are simply a convenient shorthand for defining how books will be sold, although there are undeniable differences in the characteristics of books from category to category. Small publishers rarely bother to categorize themselves. But if they are questioned about how they plan to produce and sell a particular book, their methods or approaches serve to identify them as predominantly one or another type of publisher.

In trade publishing, unlike textbook or professional publishing, interest in a book is stimulated by the publisher through a variety of devices, such as talk show appearances by an author, interviews, excerpting of a book in a popular magazine or newspaper, advertisements in major media, and displays in bookstores. The purpose of this activity is to communicate to the public that the book is a "must," either for its entertainment value or its self-help value. Self-help publishing by trade houses often addresses leisure-time interests that are widely shared among broad sectors of the buying public—sailing, tennis, jogging, cooking, photography, and so on. These self-help books have market potential comparable to large circulation special interest magazines such as *Field and Stream, Tennis,* and *Modern Photogra-*

phy. Here the trade publisher identifies groups that will find the book of particular interest. Instead of stimulating excitement, the publisher is presumably market-driven. The publisher is selling entertainment value. The appeal is to the individual who is deciding how to use his leisure time, who must be made to want to read the book.

Textbooks sales are achieved by direct appeal to professors, who decide what books to adopt as required reading for students who will take their course. If the book is not visually as well as textually appealing, students may complain and sometimes a professor will decide against adopting a book a second time. But the initial decision belongs to the professor. This sometimes places the text publisher in a unique quandary: whether the appeal should be made to the chooser (professors) or users (students).

Professional books are sold differently from books in either of the preceding two categories. The publication of a scholarly book must be communicated to all the segmented audiences who are likely to find the book useful or of interest. The majority of professional books are read because their audience believes that the book is important and will enable them to perform their work better. In order to make such a decision, the potential audience has to be informed that the book exists. This is no mean task given the abundance of books published in a particular scholarly field in any year. Interest can be stimulated to some degree; reviews and comments can convince academic buyers that even if they are not interested in a particular subject, the book will be influential and must be read. But in general, professionals are more impervious than any other group to stimulation of interest through artificial techniques.

What does convince a professional to purchase a book or to ask his library or institution to purchase in the absence of advanced reviews, is that significance and immediacy of data are of particular importance. If the later reviews or comments say the information in the book is reliable or significant, so much the better. The author of the volume is a factor; it is especially helpful if work is known to the potential purchaser, and if the purchaser has preconceived notions about the merits of the scholar's previous work. If the publisher has handled the author's previous book, and it achieved positive acclaim, there can sometimes be a "halo effect"—but again, only within a confined universe of scholars.

Organizational identification with a book can add to its credibility. But in general, the decision to purchase or not depends on a simple decision that individuals make when they receive a direct-mail promotional piece or see space advertising for a book. That decision is made on the basis of whether they think the information in the book will help them to do their work better, whether the work is teaching, research, or business, and whether it will help them keep abreast of developments in their profession, or help them to be competent even if the information is not required at the particular moment of purchase. In short, a book written by a scholar or a scientific professional is rarely read for its entertainment value. With few exceptions, the writing is not exciting, easily accessible, or stimulating. The ideas contained are generally too subtle or complex to be appreciated by anyone other than a specialist.[4] This, of course, lends credence to charges of elitism in content and jargon in form.

There are exceptions, of course. Michael Maccoby's book, *The Gamesman* was touted as the successor to *The Organization Man* and had modest trade success. C. Wright Mills consciously targeted the general public as his audience in *White Collar*. Alvin Toffler, although not himself a social scientist, has successfully translated social science thinking into language the general public could appreciate in *Future Shock* and parlayed this into a successful trade book through an ingenious promotional campign which he executed. Vance Packard has been perennially successful in translating social science thinking for mass consumption. And James Watson popularized *The Double Helix* by references to personality conflicts uncharacteristic of scientific texts. But these are exceptions. Whether it is a commercial organization or a university press, the object of the professional publisher is to bring a book to the attention of individuals who need the use of the knowledge base or the stimulation of the ideas in the book to do their own work better.

General bookstores will rarely carry a book unless they receive a publisher's maximum trade discount, which, on volume purchases can reach almost 50 percent off its list price. Discounts must be maintained across all categories of customers. The usual discount for scholarly books ranges from 20 to 30 percent, or a short discount. If publishers want to place the book in general bookstores, they must support it by investing a significant sum of money in promotion and advertising, have a delivery system to place it in the stores, and be prepared to give away 20 to 30 percent more in total sales dollars than they would if the book would otherwise be published as a short discount book. Publishers must assume that the book will be bought and sold by general bookstores in sufficient quantities to justify that decision, for they must maintain the discount in any case. It is a difficult decision to make, and usually a publisher will decide against publishing a professional or scholarly book as a trade discount book. For every professional book that has potential appeal to a general audience, there are one hundred cookbooks which a conservative publisher perceives as a sure thing. As a result, professional books are usually given short discounts and only specialty bookstores will carry them. The primary means of selling these books continues to be direct mail, whether it takes the form of catalogs, packaged direct mail, or self-mailers (flyers). Reviews are important in their unique capacity to legitimize a work within the tight little island known as scholarly communication.

The design and production of books differ from category to category. Books intended to entertain, such as trade books, must appeal visually as well as in contents—perhaps more so. A book cannot be printed in type too small to read. The jacket should be attractive. The book competes with other titles for attention on a bookstore's shelves. In mass market paperbacks, there is great emphasis on covers and space advertising: colors are tested and enormous expense is incurred in book design. Design may play a role in sales; Erica Jong's *Fear of Flying* sold modestly in hardcover, but it became a bestseller when an extremely sexually provocative cover was used for the mass market paperback; even hardcover sales picked up. Helen Hooven Santmyer's best-selling 1,176 page novel, *And Ladies of the Club* started life as a University-press book.

Books intended to serve as pedagogical tools—textbooks—must provide visual appeal. Students often have to be motivated by the teacher and by the appearance of the book, rather than by inherent interest in or of the subject. To see how textbooks' appearance has changed, one need simply compare introductory texts published in the 1950s with those of the 1980s: four color pages in place of black and white; greater use of charts, graphs, and photographs. Art may imitate life, but texts imitate *Time*.

In professional publishing, the packaging of the book may or may not be inconsequential, depending on the profession for which the book is written. A book for architects must be visually appealing. Medical books have to be illustrated with precision, and that usually means expensively. However, if a cover looks "too artistic" the book may not be treated seriously by physicians. Norms vary from profession to profession. In general, the more immediate the information, the less is expected in terms of composition, binding, and design. Some publishers charge high prices that bear more relationship to the promotion expended to reach the 700 or so potential buyers than to the expense of acquiring, developing, or producing such books (often these are spiral bound items). In the social sciences, data are rarely indisputable, and ideas and concepts may be as important, if not more so than the raw information.

Often social science authors write in the tradition of the humanities, striving for timelessness rather than topicality. Unlike the natural and physical sciences, where journals have traditionally been the primary medium for new findings, in the social sciences, findings are less concrete and books have greater importance; although this has been changing in recent years. In professional social science publishing, the question of how books are best presented is not yet settled. In part the answer depends on how a publisher evaluates the demands of the potential audience of the author. Are they concerned with immediacy or aesthetics? Is price more important than appearance?

By the standards of trade or textbook publishing, professional or scholarly books have significantly smaller market potential. Yet many social science professionals believe that their books have potential general audience appeal. The problem is the confusion of specific interest in the ideas, findings, or conclusions in the research with general interest in reading the book. Social science findings have an impact far beyond what one would predict on the basis of the absolute number of copies such titles command in sales. Their ideas are picked up in reviews; expressed in popular articles based on the research. Sometimes an outright translation of the research into terms that a general audience finds appealing is undertaken by a professional writer; Gail Sheehy successfully popularized the field of developmental psychology in *Passages*. If a professional-book publisher elects to persuade an author to accept publication of the work as a trade book, that publisher has a major undertaking. Someone has to examine, restructure, and rewrite the manuscript. An author must occasionally be persuaded to abandon scholarly language and to accept the everyday language that journalists aim for. In the end, an expensive, time-consuming rewrite, with which an academic author may remain uneasy, may not translate into sales that will justify the investment. As a result, the option of minor editorial changes and small market penetration is the best policy.

Editorial judgment is always a major factor in the success or failure of a publisher. In trade publishing, the editor must balance a sense of mass taste against an anticipation of elite judgment. Making entertainment value a primary criteria does not exclude serious writers. Many books that appear on best seller lists are not works that will endure; still, some are.

The editor's judgment in text publishing is often supported by information about sales patterns of similar books, or previous editions of the same book, that is rarely available to trade editors. A work designed to entertain has to be original in some respect, even though it may mainly represent a new application of a tried and true formula—the gothic romance, for example. Textbooks are designed around the best information the editor can muster about the contents of courses in the subject and careful study of competing texts. A successful text represents a compendium of accepted information and wisdom about a discipline; it is rarely planned to be an intellectual contribution to a field, an original conception, or an innovative statement.

The editorial decision in professional publishing is different from trade/entertainment or text/educational publishing. There can be little guidance from computer-based information sources, although it is possible to obtain some sense of potential interest from the number of scholars identified with a particular subsegment of a discipline. Prepublication reviews solicited from the author's peers also provide some guidance, depending on the editor's skill in selecting appropriate reviewers. As in post-publication reviewing, one can sometimes elicit a self-fulfilling prophecy in selecting a reviewer.

University and scholarly presses nominally have as their mission the publication of books representing "contributions to knowledge." University presses' decision-making processes are designed to ensure that the best scholarship possible is published, given finite resources. Commercial publishers of scholarly materials review more selectively. Editors seek outside review when they feel unable to make a fair assessment of the merit of a potentially publishable book solely on the basis of its subject. Secondary measures such as author background and previous publishing history, and the editor's own knowledge of the discipline are not always an adequate basis for a publishing decision. Some publishing houses accept an editor's recommendation to publish supported by a single review plus the marketing department's assessment of sales potential. Others discount critical reviews for various reasons. Because of the mandatory reviewing process at university presses, publication at a commercial house is sometimes held in less repute by a profession, although its members usually appreciate the fact that a commercial house makes a decision much more quickly than does a university press. A scrutiny of post-publication reviews indicates that commercial scholarly presses do not publish fewer important books than do university-based scholarly presses. University presses may publish fewer inferior books, but this would be difficult to prove. Suffice it to say that the spillover from profit to not-for-profit is increasingly seamless and difficult to detect.

A dilemma encountered by publishers of professional scientific books can be succinctly stated: Those who can best tell you if the information a manuscript contains is needed are inundated by requests for pre- and post-publication reviews of scholarly materials. They are rarely able to respond quickly to a request. As a result, information in a book can become dated before it is published, and published books are not reviewed as quickly as they should be. It is a balancing act, particularly for commercial houses, which worry more about the information value of their books than do university presses.[5] But increasingly, the time-lag is becoming a shared concern of the scholarly community as a whole.

The market for a professional book cannot be artificially created, it must be identified and informed. In addition to professional pre-publication reviews, computerized information can provide useful sales histories of similar books, providing the publisher with guidance in making a decision.

Commercial publishers make the assumption that all things being equal how well a book sells is an indication of how good it is. But all things are never equal. A definitive book may sell only 500 copies if the audience to whom it is important is extremely small. An assessment of market potential plays an important role in the scholarly publishing decision for a commercial house and for more successful university presses. The level of marketing activity contemplated is a major consideration for the commercial publisher of professional social science books. How many potential subgroups may be interested in the books, and can they be reached through the publisher's normal marketing procedures? If the answer is "not all," will the expense necessary to reach additional subgroups generate enough sales to justify the expenditure? What kind of track record does the editor proposing the book have? Some editors have high credibility within a publishing house because they have a record of publishing successful books; they are greeted with less skepticism when they propose an unusual book than are editors with less successful track records. Thus editorial stability is a hidden, albeit, important element in building a list of scholarly titles in a given area.

There are additional differences between publishers who specialize in entertainment and education and those who produce information and knowledge for specialists. Scholarly publishers infrequently sign contracts for books as ideas or authors who create books from scratch. Only an author who has a substantial track record with a firm can successfully present a proposal, no matter how solid, that elicits a contract, unless he has an unimpeachable record elsewhere. Some authors are major figures in their profession, so publishers are obviously more willing to take publishing risks; often reaching a decision on the basis of a prospectus or an outline. Would-be-trade authors without agents often find obtaining a publisher difficult, although the professional publishers in the sciences deal with authors directly and almost all respond to authors who submit unsolicited manuscripts—unlike many major trade publishers, who prefer to work through agents.

The object of the aggressive professional publisher of scientific materials is to get to the best potential authors first. This is achieved through numerous techniques. An editor, for example, maintains indirect contact with a discipline by following journals, attending conferences (or examining their programs), reviewing lists of dissertations in progress, and reviewing the subjects and individuals receiving research grants from foundations and government agencies. The editor contacts academics who are working in areas of interest, particularly if the individual is someone whose work the editor knows and holds in regard. The editor uses all these methods to identify prospective subjects where interest appears to be on the incline and where a paucity of published material exists. Authors send letters inquiring about interest in their work; scholarly publishers sift through such letters, obtaining the majority of their books "over the transom." Editors often solicit advice from advisers who are contractually tied to a particular scientific publishing organization. Some rely extensively on consulting editors who have direct contact with a discipline.

The role of the editor with a commercial publisher or university press emphasizing a scientific list is to provide the firm with macroinformation about the direction and trends of a discipline. The editor can be characterized as a buyer and developer of products that will be sold by the firm. Few professional-book editors work hand in glove with an author to shape a book. The most an author can reasonably expect is competent reviewing of his work by outside and in-house reviewers, who may provide useful insights about ways the book can be improved, and professional copy editing, limited to correcting the manuscript for grammatical errors, placing into the style of the publishing house, and asking questions about missing information or apparent errors. The editor is the author's representative within the publishing house, the person who makes certain that the book is produced and marketed in accordance with the plan that has been presented to the author. Marketing people can provide micro information to support the publishing decision: how well similar books have sold, how they were sold, comparison of how similar books published by other houses are said to have sold. The marketing department considers every possible way a book can be sold and evaluates the relative merits and costs of each approach.

Scholarly communication and academic publishing has herein been described as if it is a unitary world. In fact, it is not. It can be divided into two camps of publishers, usually characterized by emphasis rather than the absolute content of their lists. One emphasizes the publication of data in which the potential of a book is assessed primarily in terms of its information value. These books are often expensive—all professional books are these days—but not if they are measured against the potential value of the information they contain. That is the kind of evaluation potential buyers must make as they weigh a decision to purchase.

There is a second camp into which professional scholarly publishers fall; these emphasize the publication of ideas or knowledge. These are books primarily distinguished not by the specific information they contain but by the ideas they present. They may represent a synthesis of earlier databased books, or they may simply expand upon existing theory in the discipline in which the author works.[6] One cannot be absolute about dividing scholarship into empirics or theory; good scientific research is uniformly based upon a combination of the empirical and the theoretical. In general it is fair to say that university presses have tended to concentrate on the publication of works of theory, and commercial houses have tended to concentrate on empirical state of the art works.

Major practitioner groups are appealed to by specialized academic publishers. Thus the publisher of a social science sub-list will aim to reach criminologists, educators, clinicians (social workers, psychologists), urban planners, lawyers, policy advisers on the local and especially the state and federal levels, special-interest groups of all kinds, and people in business. Practitioners are less interested in ideas and concepts and more interested in what they can learn and apply in their professional work. Their concerns are usually specific and frequently result from immediate concerns—often from changes in the policy or regulatory apparatus. But in the effort to gain outreach beyond "core" audiences, such proximate "peripheral" audiences may be critical to the survival of a program, if not the firm as such.

The future of professional publishing is as important to the scientific scholar as it is to university presses and commercial publishers. Publishers make decisions affecting the direction of disciplines and the future of individual careers. Those universities which have presses are readily identifiable. Less visible are those commercial firms involved in professional publishing.

Many of them are large companies involved in multiple publishing activities cutting across the three categories of publishing activity which have been described. In terms of the number of titles produced in any given year, they appear to overwhelm smaller publishers—the thirty largest publishers produced over 50 percent of the professional titles published in 1983, and this industry concentration has remained firm.

Companies employing more than fifty employees in professional publishing produce more scholarly titles in any given year, but their real strength is the variety of publishing services they are able to offer under one roof, and the cross-fertilization between these divisions. Smaller publishers make up for an absence of variety in their delivery systems by publishing with imagination and a flexibility that larger publishers often lack; or if they possess, are inhibited from implementing by virtue of economic "bottom-line" constraints.

Smaller publishers' works are often distributed by large publishers. While the distributors do not directly control editorial policy and the smaller houses intend eventually to become full-fledged publishers, distributors may indirectly influence editorial policy. If the distributor elects not to make the inventory commitment, the small publisher is free to proceed with its own distribution. In practice, without the support of the larger distributor, the smaller scholarly publisher is tempted to drop the project.

Smaller publishers emulate the contract terms offered by large publishers, whereas larger publishers are acutely aware of the policies of their major competitors. Long-run industry trends in scientific publishing are higher prices, no better than acceptable production quality, shorter active life of backlist, and selling primarily through direct mail, with some limited effort to place books in specialty stores in metropolitan centers. The importance of international sales increases as average domestic unit sales decline. In the physical and biological sciences, it is not unusual for overseas sales to exceed domestic sales;

and even some social science titles may sell up to 40 percent overseas. Most larger publishers have extremely efficient overseas operations, which is one reason their distribution services are attractive to smaller publishers. But the internationalization of scholarly publishing is clearly part and parcel of the internationalization of scientific information.[7]

What is the future of professional publishing? On the negative side, several university presses have foundered in recent years: Case Western Reserve, Vanderbilt, and the University of Miami presses amongst them. Northwestern was closed in the 1970s and reemerged in the 1980s. Catholic University Press and Duquesne have arranged for commercial distribution, and half a dozen others are perennially "on the brink" of disaster. About 375 universities offer doctoral programs; but only eighty have active university presses. University press sales are less than 10 percent of the net sales of professional publishing in the current era.

On the positive side, professional publishing has been a growth area in commercial publishing. Net sales have increased by over 50 percent from 1971 to 1980. Not only have major publishing houses expanded by increasing the number of professional titles they publish in existing areas of publication, and by moving into new professional areas, but smaller publishers have proliferated. Many of these publishers are distributed by large houses, and some may eventually merge with the larger houses. However, the number of presses publishing in the physical and social sciences now exceeds 300. Many of these presses are engaged in other activities in addition to book and monograph publishing, including journal publishing, reference publishing, and information services. Private associations or societies which would once have been published by major publishers are now self-sufficient. The Institute for Social Research, Hoover Institution, and the American Enterprise Institute are examples of autonomous units emerging from organizations rather than professions.

The publication of professional information is growing by leaps and bounds. Expansion of commercial publishing may be a measure of the competitive failure of university press publishing. It is hard to measure the number of professional books published in any single year, because mainly larger, member firms report their sales to the Association of American Publishers, and the information is expressed in terms of dollars and units sold rather than numbers of titles. It is probably fair to say the absolute number of titles has increased despite certain imbalances from discipline to discipline: It is generally agreed that publishing in the humanities remains troubled, while the hard sciences are expanding. The social sciences occupy a mid-ground, depending largely on current fads, fashions, and funds.

The pressure on librarians, who are the major purchasers of professional and scholarly books, will intensify. How decisions to purchase are made will become an even larger factor in the success and failure of publishers. In the 1960s library budgets were large and librarians bought generously. The 1970s witnessed a return to selective patterns of library purchases, while the 1980s have witnessed tendencies to specialist collections. At many colleges and universities a large portion of the budget is simply divided among various departments, which recommend the purchase of what they consider the most important books. This represents a return to earlier hard-money patterns, when money was less free and it was important to enforce a degree of equity from department to department, maintaining balance among the disciplines that should be represented in library acquisitions. Again, the key change is the rise of specialization within libraries and among librarians. They tend to counterbalance this return to faculty decision-making. Librarians have in fact become a big part of selective faculties.

The information function in professional publishing is under severe pressure from technological developments. Computerized data banks now provide primary information on demand and can be processed by terminals or by telephone. Information from a number of sources is made available to the user who requests specific information. The *New York Times* operates such a service. The Information Bank provides access to over 1.4 million online items, drawn from 70 world-wide publications, and accessed by telephone communication in 70 points across the United States, Canada, Latin America, and Europe. Lockheed has an online abstract and bibliographic service. The Prestel service, emphasizing news, weather reports, commercial data, and sporting events which became operational in the late 1970s, devised and brought to market in Britain by the British Post Office in collaboration with the electronics industry, television manufacturers, and the British Broadcasting Service, may create a totally new market or it may compete directly with existing media.

Many people feel that databased services, which are now $1.5 billion worldwide, will soon supplant conventional information resources such as directories, dictionaries, indexes, and technical manuals. Databased publishing combines the management of information systems and files of information with computer typesetting systems to produce primary and multiple by-product publications using structured data files and information-based sources. But in fact, what seems to have happened is the evolution of parallel "hard copy" and "software" systems, rather than the displacement of one by the other. This confirms a "two cultures" approach within publishing that distinguishes information from knowledge.

The book may become less important as a source of primary data and information. It will probably fail in competition with new information resources. Still, the book will maintain its more traditional knowledge role, which to some extent it had abandoned under pressure from the information explosion of recent decades. The scholarly work remains the source of informed thinking about new information and is a source of secondary information carefully analyzed and digested. In short, the successful scholar will provide a forum for thinking about data drawn from multiple information resources, not only in a purely philosophical sense, but by digesting and synthesizing information that is readily available. What such data suggest, how they should be integrated, what their policy import might be—not simply computer models of the future, but models tempered with human judgment—these issues will be addressed by authors of successful books. In short, books of the 1980s are now less concerned with the presentation of raw information—for better information is available from less traditional sources—and more concerned with an author's capacity to produce substantial knowledge. Doubtless, this dualism, this "two cultures" based on information and knowledge, will create its own dynamic. But for the present, predictions about the death of scholarly communication are widely and wildly off the mark.

This life cycle of the scholarly communication process has scarcely dwelt upon the "gate-keeping" functions of publishing.[8] It is not for want of appreciation of this phase. Rather, I have tried to emphasize those phases of communication involving author, editor, publisher relationships that occur after a decision to publish has been reached. It might be argued that since gate-keeping is often recycled through the very academic community from whence a manuscript originally emanates, that it remains more a part of the pre-publication history of scholarly communication rather than its publication phases. Publishers survive by the avoidance of wrong judgments, but they thrive by the performance of sound judgments.

This disjunction, or rather, distinction is so little appreciated by the scholarly community that it is important to reiterate the goal orientations which distinguish author and publisher: the critical copy for the scholar is often the first copy, the proof that a book is warranted as physically in print. The critical copy for the publisher is the break-even copy, be it 800, 1000, or 1500, at which point a title has paid for itself and begins to provide a return on investment. Scholarly publishers sometimes operate in a world of subventions and underwriters. But these investments on a per-title basis do not alter the need to "earn out." This is not said in a disparaging manner, a lack of appreciation that certain books deserve publication whether or not they "earn out." Such determinations, to be sure, do commence with gate-keeping decisions. In the long, secular pull of time, the process of communication is isomorphic with the process of publishing: for the outreach as defined by copies sold of a particular work remains, in considerable measure, the common touchstone of success for all parties concerned with the structure of scholarship.

9

Expropiating Ideas—
The Politics of Global Publishing

I

A struggle is shaping up in scholarly and scientific circles that goes right to the heart of global publishing. The struggles are political, just the sort of framework that most publishers and editors would prefer to shy away from. The issue is the status or the condition of publishing in the Third World. The stakes are high, in both commercial and intellectual terms. What is at issue is nothing short of political responsibility for the present imbalances in the input and output of literary product, and the rights and obligations of publishers and readers to each other and to the community of scholarship as a whole.

One reason why these issues have remained seemingly quiescent within the American publishing community is that advanced societies have focused on copyright violations and piracy practices within the Third World. The recent statement by Eric H. Smith typifies this legitimate mainstream Western concern.

> In part due to the growth in world trade and the explosion in inexpensive and accessible reproduction technology, book piracy has become a worldwide problem. U.S. publishers and their foreign subsidiaries and licensees are increasingly threatened by worldwide piracy and, in the last few years, the problem has tended to focus on the developing world. Combatting piracy in the developed world has been aided by the inherent interest of these countries in providing protection to their own authors and publishers, resulting in improvements in legal protection and enforcement domestically and a willingness to participate in internationalizing that protection through the international copyright convention process. Unfortunately the same cannot be said of the developing world, where

resort to, and reliance on, piratical activity has significantly increased.[1]

To this position, the Third World response has typically been to emphasize rights to access to information, rather than obligations to copyright holders; a position similar to that taken by librarians with respect to publishers in the United States. Advocates of this view assert the right to access as nothing short of a new "human right." Indeed, one ambitious formulation holds that the right to access to information and ideas "surpasses considerably the known list of human rights, including those in the Universal Declaration of Human Rights." Against such assertions of rights and principles, American concerns for the property rights of publishers and authors seem narrow and self-interested, while their efforts to enact trade legislation to persuade Third World countries to make substantive improvements in their protection of creative and intellectual property appear downright punitive.

Despite the fact that Argentina has the strongest publishing network in the Latin American world, an Argentine jurist Aldo Armando Cocca, has asserted the right to access in such unambiguous terms, that the products of authors and publishers would virtually become a natural resource to be tapped into at will by a user-public. This is how he sees it:

> An access to all possible forms of the exercise of the right to communicate should be guaranteed on a basis of equality. Access is especially important in *tele*communication. Benefit: in contemporary international law, humankind is the beneficiary of all progress. The benefits must include humankind, as a whole, and the human person as its natural components. States should assure that these benefits reach both without hindrance and delay. Resources: this concept should be extended to communication, although it differs in kind from energy and material resources. Technology: creates a new dimension because it holds the potential both to dehumanize as well as to humanize contact across distance.[2]

The division of global political positions can be seen to divide along conventional ideological fault lines. Not uncharacteristically, the European community has become the fulcrum for intense debate and discussion. And well might this be the case. European publishers, like their North American counterparts, still work largely within private enterprises. They represent capitalism at the economic level. However, many also hold to socialist and radical political orientations, which tend to be far more pronounced than those of their counterparts in the United States. For the most part, mainline publishers in France, Italy, Germany, and England, have sponsored major works supportive of no less than analytically concerned with Third World systems. As a result, the political proclivities of European publishers offer a fascinating window on the struggle between First and Third World demands.

Second World, or Soviet-dominated, points of view tend to straddle intellectual fences. On one hand, they too raise the slogan of a right to access; but in practice and law, they recognize and impose severe constraints upon communication. They also are torn between a desire to pirate and a reluctance to have their own materials used without prior permission, and without payment in hard Western currency. Internally, the Soviets are torn between the choice of widening access to information and hence opening their "closed" society, or limiting such access and jeopardizing their status as a leading world power in scientific and technological innovation. As the price of technological change speeds, the problem intensifies. How this issue is resolved will say much about the future direction of Soviet society as a whole.[3]

The Soviet dilemma is that it shares with the West concern for economic development, but it has even greater political isolation than most parts of the Third World. As a result, the computer revolution, as exemplified by the shift from a mainframe system where access is easily controlled to a distributed and easily accessed mini- and microcomputer system tends to sharpen the contradictions. As Loren Graham has noted, the Soviets have a major challenge on their hands. The problem is that the terms of competition are against them. They want to have the ecoonmic efficiency of the computer without losing control of information.[4]

The concern over copyright in Western publishing terms is focused upon the loss of income and profits. This same concern in government circles is focused upon the loss of what is deemed to be vital, sometimes confidential, information and ideas. The widespread efforts of the United States in the 1980s to control access to unclassified no less than classified research, as well as the technical products that result from such ideas, may increase the financial pressures on American adversaries. In essence, however, the issues are national security and rates of economic development. Inevitably, under such polarized global conditions, there is a confusion between the objectives of control and copyright, between denial of access to others and insistence upon payment for legitimate uses. This confusion is shared by both sides; since not a few Third World ideologists explicitly propose the right to access without corresponding recognition of the obligation to pay for such uses. But equating human creativity with natural resources is so transparently a falsity that posing the issue in this way only hardens the position of advanced nations, especially the United States. It also stimulates dangerous equations of control and copyright.

Comparing and contrasting the European Member Associations of the International Publishers' Association with the position of the leadership of the International Association of Scholarly Publishers provides insight into the present mode of relationships and suggests yet wider rifts within the empire of publishing. And there are few signs of a healing process. The umbrella International Publisher's Association weakly reaffirms the publishers' role in the modern world.

> Publishing is primarily a private sector activity, Publishers will retain many of their present functions: the selection within a competitive system, editing and presentation of documents, the endorsement of material through their reputation, the marketing of the publications, stocking and, particularly in a period of deficiencies in public funds, the major responsibility for initial finance. Original publishers will have a legitimate interest in the control and protection of works that they have published when they are disseminated through other channels. Many publishers are likely to continue to use intermediaries for production and distribution as they do at present. This, however, presages considerable changes for the printing industry, the book trade and journal agencies if they are to retain their role for electronically produced materials.

The librarians and publishers also reaffirm the place of copyright in this modern post-industrial world. Like their American counterparts, they tend to cast solutions of technological problems in legal rather than technical terms.

> Librarians will accept, both for themselves and in relation to their users, that copyright will be respected and protected within the new systems. Fees will be paid as required and libraries' use of the systems will depend on ability to pay. Librarians recognize the need for proper control over access to electronic systems. They will not download information without the agreement of copyright owners.[5]

The Asian wing of the International Association of Scholarly Publishers (Asia Pacific Seminar/Workshop) contemptuously dismisses such concerns with a wave of the economic wand. The issue becomes the inadequate flow of books from South to North. It is claimed that this uneven flow has made it difficult for the Third World to maintain viable indigenous book publishing. We are told that "the works of First World scholars have practically inundated the South's centers of higher learning."

Such a position poses the issue exclusively in quantitative terms—it gives absolutely no attention to qualitative factors—the *cause* of the one-direction flow—such as the production of advanced technology in the First World that the Third World needs and must have for its own growth. With unabashed enthusiasm, some members within IASP, uncritically adopt the Leninist doctrine of imperialism nearly a century later:

> The book flow has been and continues to be a one-way traffic—from North to South. This uneven flow has made it difficult for the South to keep its book publication programs viable; it has also deprived both the North and South of the wisdom in the books of local authors that the South publishes. Nowhere is this lopsided situation more apparent than in the world of scholarly book publishing: the world of First World scholars, for instance, have practically inundated the South's centers of higher learning, while Third World scholarship is practically unheard of in these centers. The causes for this unbalanced flow of scholarly books are many and varied. The underlying cause, however, appears to be the wider economic fact that much of Asia continues to be merely a market of the producer North's products, including its scholarly book.[6]

A nod to realism is made, albeit reluctantly, by indicating that language diversity encourages small market outreach, and backward-looking marketing and production techniques further contribute to these limitations. But rather than recognize that English is the universal language of twentieth-century science, the way that Latin and French served international and trans-regional communication in earlier centuries, the IASP report simply urges aping of Western marketing techniques—again without taking into account what works are produced in Urdu vis-à-vis English.

By far, the most sophisticated, and at the same time, peculiar expression of the right-to-access thesis has been developed by Rowland Lorimer, associate director of the Centre for Canadian Studies at Simon Fraser University. Here the argument to violate copyright is based on the alleged fact that information once universally available through the printed page and public library has become a commodity that is privately owned and purchasable. It is his view that the implications for the restraint on access to information through such developments as full-text databases is such as to warrant guerilla warfare of scholars, universities, and nations against publishers—those selfish vestiges of private enterprise.

Lorimer notes two developments: libraries charging for exchange of information, and authors demanding payment for the use of their works in libraries. The instrument of this diabolical turn of events is the computer. It can charge users and allocate and restrict use. But the computer is not to blame—society is. Let us hear from Mr. Lorimer directly on this key point:

> The computer has made it possible to so assess the user with relative ease. Or will a more communal policy prevail? These are questions of policy—of the commitment of public resources by society to deal fairly with increasing amounts and complexity of information. Does the increasing distance between information "haves" and "have-nots" warrant a counteractive public policy, or will we let the inequalities fall where they may? In shortening the time it takes to gather background information, the new technologies have exposed what was previously a hidden cost—the cost of the time of an individual scholar developing a bibliography. In making this phase of research purchasable, information entrepreneurs have transformed a function into a commodity and have exposed the relatively incomplete economic recognition we have traditionally given to information and its manipulation.[7]

Such a view is not above invoking a conspiratorial theory. "Access[7] tends to be curtailed by the market interests of the owner of the database as well as by traditional protections like copyright." The "design of the new technologies facilitates private ownership of information" and worse, "decisions about access to information have shifted from the librarian to the marketer of data." Under such circumstances, a call for "knowledge strategies" to create "cultural survival" has a theoretical flavor, but lacks substance, and may be distinctly parochial in outcome.

The source of such widespread animus is twofold: the denial that those who develop a service, for example, create a useful database or bibliography, have a right to a reward for their efforts, that is, a right to charge for their labors. This in turn derives from an historical myopia all too common in Third World polemics. Library charges for services have been typical over time in the West. British libraries have always charged for usage. The free public library largely subvented through local taxes is an American concept, as is a free public education. Precisely for this reason the Soviet library model derives from the United States and not Western Europe.[8] But whether the source of payment is direct as in Western Europe, or indirect as in the United States and the Soviet Union, advanced industrial societies have few illusions that knowledge acquisition represents a cost as well as a benefit. In short, Third World luminaries notwithstanding, the dissemination of information has always been both a social function and an economic commodity.

II

Before considering the connection between intellectual rights and property rights, it might be well to dispense with a fundamental illusion: namely, that prior to the new technology there was a common book culture. The historical literature makes clear that there has never been a common, popular culture in which all people have participated with equal access. The advent of printing on a mass scale in the mid-fifteenth century increased the number of books, and also decreased the man-hours required to turn them out. But this did not eliminate the class basis of learning—it only exacerbated the differences between those who were literate and those who were illiterate; and among those who could read, those who could purchase books, and those who could not.

The rise of a distinct printing industry served the needs of merchants, bureaucrats, preachers, and the literati. But it did not filter down to the peasantry and certainly not to an expanding urban proletariat, the old "new technology," the print revolution, was a key instrument in the bourgeois revolution in economics and the Protestant revolution in religion. Printers were placed in the same exceptional position as software engineers today: both sought larger markets for their own products, and also contributed to and profited from the expansion of commercial enterprises.[9]

Advocates of the MacBride report on the right to communicate not only deny obligation to those whose imagination leads to creations, but they also deny the material foundations of an advanced culture.[10] Classical Marxism is distinguished from utopian radicalism precisely because the latter, in order to insinuate a new "right" must falsify the historical and social contexts of the printing industries in the first information revolution and of the computer industries of the second information revolution. The great lesson of the printing revolution of the past and the computer revolution of the present is that the people so involved were instruments for disseminating the creative output of a vital and functioning segment of society. The counter-attack on the economic rights of publishers and proprietary claims of authors is nothing other than the assault on the intellect as such—a denial that intellectual labor, the work of the head, has a status equal to that of manual labor, or the work of the hand, and must be equally protected by the legal system and normative codes.

This is not to deny that there are serious problems of imbalance between advanced societies and less developed societies. Because the revolution in information technology is still in its early stages, the need for accurate assessment and appropriate strategies is vital. Several trends are already apparent: information interdependence, capital-rather than labor-intensive activities, and a general rise in service-sector rather than industrial-sector growth.[11] Most Third World nations are simply not prepared to confront such challenges: and they seek recourse to pirating inventions, avoiding payment for research and development, and second-hand absorption of often inappropriate technologies as dangerous short-term alternatives to indigenous autonomous development.

The new information environment threatens to become more rather than less competitive. Those who expect special favors by claiming a less-favored-nation status are in all likelihood doomed to under-development. But for those nations who seize the opportunity provided by cheap labor markets, internationalize their services, and compete in culture and in kind on a global scale, the situation is becoming increasingly attractive. The alternative is a protectionist cultural environment matching a closed economic environment, which leads to a sealed, totalitarian environment, impervious to a larger world. In short, not information welfare but special efforts to help Third World efforts to participate in gaining its fair share of benefit from the information revolution is the order of the day.

Stripped of elegant pleas on behalf of the Third World, and sledgehammer assaults against the rights of intellectual property in the name of a vague commitment to a mythic socialism, opposition to copyright protection or legislation against piracy sows the seeds of a massive anti-intellectualism, denigration of the rights of authorship or the protection of print. This inevitably spreads to all forms of information.

The new information and communications technologies are changing the public's expectations about its rights to use them. For just
as the public became readily accustomed to photocopying books,
journals, and other printed materials, so too it is now learning to
routinely copy films, disks, and tapes and to make unauthorized
copies of electronic data. Software creators, producers and providers call this "stealing"; some software users call it "sharing."
Thus there is a growing gap between the theory of intellectual
property law and its practice. This gap is likely to widen in the next
several years, potentially challenging the legitimacy of the law and
creating significant problems of enforcement.[12]

What starts as an assertion of freedom of access to information
too often ends in the denial of any claim of a proprietary rights in
intellectual products. The MacBride Commission report represents
a frank effort, legal actions notwithstanding, to circumvent fair-use
legislation. The loophole rather than the law becomes central. In the
United States there are unusual publishing efforts such as Kinko copying centers, in which those who compile collections are referred to
as authors, and in which the usual processes of review and referee
are forsaken in the effort "to professionally publish and copyright
their work independent of the complicated politics and stringent policies of traditional publishing."[13] In other words, the presumed allies
of Third World free communication are none other than the most
marginal, least principled segments of First World high technology.
No amount of vague rhetoric can disguise a confluence of evils
paraded about as a higher right. The corollary of there being no free
lunch is that there are no rights without obligations. It would be
wise for advocates of free information to learn this lesson well.

What is being played out on a small scale is a global information
mosaic: a First World community of publishers, printers, and authors
who see a new technology increasingly used to circumvent rules and
regulations which have governed, however imperfectly, the transfer of
information and ideas throughout the century, confronting a Third
World ideology based on the politics of resentment expressed as the
economics of exploitation. Once the natural history of publishing is
conceptualized as the exploitation of poor people by wealthy information entrepreneurs, with "Northern" exporters and profiters versus
"Southern" importers and peasants, then it becomes a short moral
step to encourage the violation of already barely enforceable laws
against piracy and copyright infringement.

What has been largely overlooked by Third World professional spokesmen and their advocates in advanced nations are the consequences of equating requirements of payment for work performed, or valued added, with exploitation of under-developed nations and peoples. Precisely such an approach, in which the end products of modernization are insisted upon without the research and development to achieve such products, is an essential source of backwardness itself. In a world of uninhibited copyright infringement and legitimized piracy of intellectual product, there is little incentive to develop an indigenous publishing industry. In consequence, there is little encouragement for scholars to publish nationally or perhaps even to remain in the nation. This misguided notion of information as a higher right undermines the very objectives of indigenous and autonomous publishing which Third World advocates strive to achieve.

What adds a note of pathos to this situation is the support, within the West, of such infringements in the name of "higher laws" of free communication. What is overlooked is the damage such a position does to the Third World: it permanently enshrines dependence on foreign culture and science; encourages contempt and ignorance for the processes involved in achieving sound intellectual craftsmanship; and not incidentally, leads to a collapse of any sense of the universality of learning as it is displaced by a welter of nationalisms. Not the free flow of information but a new information order based on the *restriction* of this "higher right" is a consequence of the imposition of ideological tests of allegiance on the struggle to control knowledge. Nothing could be more dangerous than the emphasis on the need to control the product rather than on the hard work and skill necessary to create knowledge and wealth.

I should like to conclude this section, not with soothing predictions about a brave new world in which rich and industrial nations will cooperate with poor and backward nations to create a new international economic order, but rather, I would like to present a bona fide exchange of correspondence between one Nigerian scholar and two publishers, one British and the other American. I shall forgo naming names, since the tale of woe described here is doubtless oft-repeated among many publishers.

First, we will hear from the British publisher, who suspended work on a book by a Nigerian scholar, trained in the United States, who was under contract.

You must be wondering why I have not replied to your letters before now. This is because I have been waiting for the economic situation in Nigeria to improve. The fact of the matter is that we have not received any money in the UK for books we have sold to Nigeria for over a year now. This has forced the Board to take the short-term decision to suspend investment on any projects for the Nigerian market until we receive that payment. Tragically, your book has been caught up in this dreadful situation. This means that I cannot put your book into production until we receive some money from Nigeria. I do ask you to understand the extreme pressure that there is on a number of British publishers as well as ourselves in these present difficult times.

Next we hear from the beleaguered author, whose chances for promotion and professional recognition depend upon publication of his major work. He is not bitter or angry. He is frustrated and anxious. He is also shopping about for an alternate publisher, with the enthusiastic collusion of the original British publisher.

I am enclosing a manuscript completed, delivered and accepted by a publisher in 1982—after the usual rigour of assessment, rewriting and resubmission. Unfortunately, just before the book was to go to press, the publisher suspended work on everything pertaining to Nigeria. This is due to foreign exchange problems. Past due bills have not been paid. You are well aware of wrangling between IMF and Nigeria. Book publishers were particularly hard hit, and most of them suspended activities in Nigeria until their past bills are settled. This is an unfortunate thing for academics in Nigeria. Although some of the work we do is attractive for an international audience, the major target of the companies is the local market.

Finally, we hear from the American publisher, one for whom the Nigerian debt is not indicated as being central, but who nonetheless, reacts to this global reality with scarce hope for utopian outcomes.

The problem we have with respect to your work is less fiscal output than order input. For a book on Nigerian Cities to be even marginally successful, a publisher requires substantial orders from a host nation. Clearly, if invoices are not paid, and that situation is not confined to British publishers, orders cannot be rendered in good faith. Under the circumstances, I can only advise you to retain your present agreement. There are serious penalties on both sides for defaulting on payments. It is tragic that an innocent scholar should be trapped in the middle by such an ever reoccurring situation.

One detects in these three letters none of the ballast of international publishing associations and their pontifical resolutions and recommendations. Nor is there great delight or even hope at the prospect of publication within the confines of Nigeria. If payments for books imported cannot be rendered, how can the entire process of printing, publishing, and maintaining of inventory be supported? Further, and beyond nuts and bolts, are larger considerations of organization and legitimation.

Achieving the hopes of authors and publishers alike requires fiscal solvency and a viable market. Only a healthy short term will permit a long-term situation to come about in which a national publishing effort can be established, one that can compete on a world scale while satisfying the needs of scholars on an individual basis. This simple set of truths, rather than the steamy prose of ideologists is only now being understood by much of the Third World; there is still, however, the bittersweet awareness of what advanced nations can produce while they themselves postpone achieving modernization for an indefinite period.

III

My discussion has been restricted to what might be viewed as the private-sector aspects of the publishing environment. But there is a public-sector element that is critical to mediating the claims of publishers from the First World and ideologists of the Third World. And here we must make some effort at resolution and recommendation.

Having spoken frankly about the need for Third World nations to deal with greater market integrity in this world of publishing and communication, it is also nonetheless the case that such long-term ambitions cannot easily be met without weighing non-market or directly political considerations. It is one thing to argue a free market position in advanced industrial conditions, but quite another to do so in relation to pre-industrial, agrarian-based Third World countries. It is this confusion between the ideals of the marketplace and realities of subsistence economies that has led to a dramatic fall-off in support for indigenous publishing in the Third World by industrialized nations.

The data are grim. To give but a few examples: USIA (United States Information Agency) translation book publishing production has gone from approximately 35 million copies between 1960 and 1965 to 25 million copies between 1966 and 1970, to 8 million copies between 1971 and 1975, to 4 million copies between 1976 and 1980, to 2 million copies between 1981 and 1984 (a four-year period). Text purchasing has shown an even more dramatic erosion—with no support over the past five years in contrast to millions of copies of English language reprints between 1964 and 1975. In the same category are low-priced books published in the United States for Third World consumption. For the twenty-year period covering 1956 to 1976, nearly 19 million such books were produced. For the ten-year period covering 1976–85 absolutely no books were provided under this program.[14]

If one simply examines a microcosm of this data we see that between 1965 and 1975, roughly 7 million copies were produced in the joint Indo-American Textbook program (P.L. 480). Between 1976 and 1985, less than 10 percent of that amount, or 700,000 copies were produced, with less than 100,000 between 1977 and 1981. While private-sector publishing penetration did increase during this period, through the activities of the Export-Import Bank, the Overseas Private Investment Corporation, the Small Business Administration, and Foreign Sales Corporations, even the most intrepid defender of current policies must admit that the publishing industry has not been a significant enough factor to even warrant the maintenance of separate statistics.[15]

What does exist is a matrix of tax incentives, special anti-trust waivers, insurance, loans, and loan guarantees intended to promote export activity, but with no special provisos for publishers. Indeed, government assistance programs have been in a state of remission reaching near-zero proportions. W. Gordon Graham has put the matter quite bluntly: "The United States government's economic aid and information agencies have lost interest in the book."[16] And this takes place at a time of fiscal and organizational crisis for the Association of American Publishers to such a degree that individual major publishers are compelled to address government officials directly and individually, rather than organizationally and cooperatively.

Curtis Benjamin has spoken of "unilateral disarmament" in the publishing field.[17] And when one contrasts American policy toward the book with that of Soviet policy, such a characterization can be seen as no exaggeration. In 1982 alone (the last year for which such data are available), the Soviets published 75 million books in languages not native to the USSR.[18] There is no comparable program in any Western country. One revealing piece of data is that despite the presence of 20 million Hispanics in the United States there is *no* Spanish publishing program in this country; whereas with *no* Hispanics living in the Soviet Union there were 11.6 million books in that language published in 1982. In macro-economic terms, the Soviet Union has increased exports of their books by 250 percent over the 1975–84 period, while U.S. exports rose by only 25 percent during the same period.

These trend lines indicate a belief that publishing is to be viewed as strictly a private-sector activity, and one that requires no support levels from the public sector. In other words, the idea of the free market has been universalized to include nations that simply have no excess capital and few resources to acquire books or journals in a competitive way. The relative flooding of literature in the Third World by the Soviet Union also means that there is an absence of competitive pressure even to purchase from Western sources—since books are available—often in English—for much less, if not gratis, from Soviet sources. This then is the empirical situation of Western publishing in the Third World.

From a policy perspective, a clear-cut distinction is involved between public sector and private sector tasks. The publishing community and the communications industry in general can urge a greater public funding, or at least a restoration of former tax supports to support inexpensive texts, translation of significant works into native languages, and even hardware and software products to aid indigenous publication efforts. But it cannot do so at the expense of permitting or encouraging piracy of copyright products, violations of copyright conventions, or sheer profligacy in the name of the politics of information.

The actual fault lines in such a policy posture are more quantitative than qualitative; that is to say, the debate is over how much public-sector funding should go to support and underwrite efforts to penetrate Third World, and no less, Second World markets. At this level, the dramatic weakening of such supports over the 1975–85 period indicates the relative inability of the publishing community to make its position clear and its will known in the halls of governmental power. Why should this be the case? What are the causes of this precipitous decline? Or put differently, is it the relative increase in power of other industries? Answering this question is beyond the ken of this chapter; but the facts of the decline are plainly visible.

To some limited extent, each publishing firm like each nation might be said to have a "foreign policy" dictated by the larger parameters of global struggles between democratic and totalitarian forces. It would be gratuitous and even dangerous, however, to think that even the most powerful publishing firms can set in motion the sort of efforts reserved for governments. The pressures on the private sector to produce profits in a competitive, market-driven environment itself delimit its range of foreign policy options. Thus, only as an industry, through its organizational arms and limbs, can policy be urged, if not set.

The communications industry has multiple "bottom lines." From a strictly economic vantage point it could be argued that there are parts of the world that are neither ready to accept nor capable of participating in what advanced technologies and cultures have to offer. Further, it is probably the case that continued participation in these parts of the world by publishers from developed countries weakens profit margins, exacerbates tensions, and involves executives in quasi-political decisions that are downright murky if not outright treacherous. One cannot disregard such sentiments, but it is also important to realize that the political process, broadly speaking, entails a bottom line of its own: the creation or the maintenance of an overseas environment that either is or has the potential for becoming hospitable to democratic culture.

It might well be that investment in China or India has foreseeable economic consequences that can only be deemed to be negative. Yet, serious publishing organizations continue to make decisions in favor of maintaining, even expanding such overseas operations, because of a clear recognition that the political bottom line has a transcendent value unto itself. We can hold in abeyance the Benthamite-utilitarian argument that in some unforeseeable long run the political bottom line may issue into an economic bottom line. Whether it does or not is less important than the maintenance of the open society where it exists and its establishment where it has not hitherto existed but is now possible.

Involved in this process is a thin line along which publishers and information specialists must insist on the commercial and proprietary claims that keep their business solvent, as well as the public policy and political claims that keep a nation democratic. In this latter sphere the governments of advanced industrial powers, Western powers, must provide a healthy environment that enhances future prospects without damaging present realities. Admittedly, this is easier said than done. The pitfalls are many, starting with the imbalance of interests and concerns between nations and businesses, between public interests and private ambitions. Yet, when the issues are fashioned in a dynamic, interactionist way, we can at least begin to address the major problems that already haunt the end of our century.

The politics of international publishing are probably the most difficult area for the publishing community to absorb easily. For all the stable, steady rules of the bottom line must be put aside in favor of ubiquitous and even dubious claims of public service and ideological advantage—areas not easily appreciated by either business people or investors. Yet, with a steadily increasing share of publishing, especially scientific and technical publishing, dedicated to a global environment, the need for such expertise and wisdom is greater than ever.

Several cautionary notes on policy are in order: first, that the errors of previous generations not be repeated, especially the idea that foreign governments know best what the people need. Hence, the key for publishers is not only to demand restoration of government support, but to make sure that it is funneled through publishers not bureaucrats. In this way, improved publisher to publisher relationships can be developed. Second, the needs of the most industrialized nations must not be superimposed upon the conditions of the least developed areas. Specifically, high technology and outer-space exports are not appropriate in a Third World environment where the book and the journal remain the essential modes of scientific and technical communication. Third, future policy programs must become more conscious of mass requirements and less elite oriented. Specifically, this means to emphasize large-scale translation programs in native languages rather than small-scale programs aimed at a narrow band of educated people who can read or speak English.

These remarks are intended as sensitizing devices and not specific policy recommendations. Those will be made by advanced industrial nations in a variety of ways to meet a set of specific objectives. The increased attendance at international book fairs, the participation of OECD firms in helping establish publishing programs in Third World nations, education exchange programs, and training courses in international publishing, all are significant but still marginal activities. The keys remain publisher-to-publisher connections, adjusting the information explosion to specific national conditions, and concern for mass education and large supplies of key texts.

There was a time in American life, in the late 1950s, when it was felt that such a set of policies required a covert framework. The discovery of such covert supports seriously damaged confidence by eroding respect for learning itself, and for the justifiable struggle of democratic principles and scientific premises. The need for such "covert operations" in the past was, to put matters mildly, dubious. The restoration of such covertness thirty years later would be malevolent. The struggle for democratic culture needs no hiding place. This is a fact, however, which both the publishing community and the government administration must acknowledge and take pride in. Global publishing is a world without heroes and villains; but it is a world replete with competent and at times courageous private firms and public agencies in search of joint survival and mutual sustenance.

10

Scientific Access and Political Constraint to Knowledge

It is clearly much easier to set priorities on who shall have access than to determine limits to access. In a democracy, the very notion of constraint raises citizen hackles, since constraint involves behavioral restraints. Disaggregating the problem of access is the first order of business, in order to deal with specifics rather than abstractions. Similarly, reviewing the actual state of affairs with regard to access is in order, rather than attempting a broad survey of moral postures toward the rights to access and disseminate information. Doing both of these chores simultaneously will help us understand what exists now as a prelude to what ought to exist.

The right to unfettered access to information and the right to privacy are embedded in the American Constitution and as well as detailed in the Bill of Rights. As a consequence, issues of publicity and privacy are part and parcel of a variety of mundane, or at least, everyday activities: from issues of copyright control in the entertainment industry to piracy in the publishing industry (indeed, they often turn out to be the same problems in allied industries). The question of access to information, in other words, is part of the cultural form no less than the legal norm of American society. The magnitude of present-day problems of government secrecy or university science is part of the general fabric of who owns, who creates, and who disseminates information and data. Magnitudes of risk and loss change greatly under the pressure of advanced technology, whereas morals change little under these same pressures.

In the area of science policy, polarizations have occurred around the issue of who shall gain access and who shall be prevented from accessing data. The issue becomes intensified because in our environment, the research and development costs for generating new products are very high, and the ability to "rip off"—or for those more genteel in nature, to replicate such hard-won data—is exceedingly cheap. In software programming it may cost tens or hundreds of thousands of dollars to develop programs for specialized use; yet it may cost pennies to replicate or simply steal that program by illegally running out a duplicate copy. The thin line between legal and illegal usage becomes ever more ambiguous as the line between basic and applied research itself becomes narrower in a world of advanced computers and thinking robots.

What further complicates matters is that access is a geographical as well as a technological issue. The United States receives from the Soviet Union massive data through scholarly channels, i.e., through scientific papers, journals, and conferences. And of course, with even greater laxity, information manufactured and created in the United States flows to the Soviet Union in full force. In part, the issue is not scientific, since at the level of pure science, there are few, if any "secrets." What is under wraps therefore is in applied areas of technology, engineering, and even administration. All of these are more nearly proprietary to the discoverer. But even here, research increasingly takes place in a "team" context, and in a multinational context. What this signifies is the increasing difficulty which a nation or a corporation experiences in maintaining product control (civilian or military) through denial of access. Restrictions exercised through the mechanisms of copyright registration and patent rights are the usual ways of maintaining secrecy. But in areas such as military technology, where governments dominate and the marketplace barely whispers much less speaks, control through such normal, i.e., marketplace restrictions to access are hardly effective.

There are liberal thinkers for whom science itself is endangered by arbitrary political restraint. They believe such restraint may dry up the wellsprings of creativity, thereby denying the fruits of research to broad masses of people who need information to grow and survive, and creating a climate of fear and suspicion that leads to narrow parochialism and ultimately negates science as an honorable research activity. Arguments about national sovereignty barely dent such liberal imaginations. Instead, the universality of science is itself a major factor in establishing a peaceful global political environment, one in which sharing rather than hoarding of practical wisdom becomes the norm. Underneath this point of view is disbelief that denial of access is anything more than a short-term advantage, one best traded for high access and mutual respect.

For conservative thinkers, such a position represents a naïve or, worse, utopian vision of global competitors at the moral level. The conservatives prefer to think that the gulf between East and West can be bridged by science, and attempts to do so only make things easier for totalitarians at the expense of the democracies. Dictatorships have built-in advantages over democracies; they are societies already sealed at the perimeters in contrast to societies that are wide open at the seams as well as at the center. For the conservative spirit, strict reciprocity between sovereign states rather than open access among scientists must dominate government thinking as well as private sector decision-making.

Seen in this light, the problem of access is itself but a specialized rhetoric for expressing general cultural norms and values. If one believes that the Soviet and American systems are roughly at parity (for better or worse) then the tendency to see open access as a good is quite high; but when one believes that such parity between powers does not exist, then "we" and "they" modes of discourse tend to prevail. The control of access to secret or difficult to develop data becomes a critical focus of national science policy.

Treating the issue of scientific access as leading inevitably either to renewed détente and universal peace, or to the collapse of sovereignty and universal destruction, makes it essential to treat the issue of access in a rather more low-key manner. To begin with, denial of access affects only a very small portion of knowledge, information, and data. Literally thousands of professional and scientific publications travel freely between free-market and planned economies. Information travels well across borders when there is shared need for advanced development. Information travels less well on a North and South axis then an East and West axis, despite economic and social similitudes in systems. For example, many Russian-speaking scholars and scientists have a reading knowledge of English, access at the linguistic level is not much of a problem. In the other direction, major Soviet scientific periodicals are translated and made available to scholars in the West. To be sure, translation of Soviet source documents and key scientific articles has been a veritable fixture in the American publishing industry since the *Sputnik* era.

At the macro-level of information exchange, there clearly exists a two-way street: basic scientific research and findings are communicated with relative ease. This is not to deny the existence of pre-screening mechanisms in the Soviet Union that are much more restrictive than in the United States. All research is censored by the State, and a larger portion of scientific research in potentially sensitive areas is not made available in the scholarly literature. But it should also be noted that organizations like the Central Intelligency Agency at times also place restrictions on publication of research funded under classified auspices. Obviously, in areas of peripheral concern to security issues, the amount of censorship in the Soviet Union is minimal—with the exception of local political concerns such as anti-Semitism, which seriously affects publication practices in Soviet mathematics journals. But this is less an issue in access than in totalitarian politics. Similarly, in the social sciences and humanities, there is virtually no censorship of documents and little problem of access. Again, it is true enough that the social science published in East and West is premised on different philosophic or valuational concepts. But even here, as methodological if not ideological universalism becomes apparent, gaps in the structure of social knowledge are being reduced. Historically, the "soft" social sciences such as psychology or sociology have been linked with "bourgeois" modalities of thought. Systematic research in areas such as demography and gerontology will be found in the literature of geography or child welfare rather than sociology or political science. However, the information was and remains universally available; the question of quality of research notwithstanding. The Soviet Union has abandoned earlier opposition to social research done in its own name. Communist authorities have come to see the importance, politically no less than scientifically, in open research procedures in these supposedly soft, bourgeois areas.

The issue of access is complex—pitting civil libertarian concerns again military security interest. As a general rule, areas of no or little strategic military concern do not arouse concerns about restraint or denial of access. In some areas, cooperative endeavors exist, as in medical and cancer research. But when we turn to issues of toxic gases for chemical warfare or laser technology for defensive (or offensive) anti-nuclear launches, then the issue of access becomes lively. But even here a caveat is in order: there is no serious argument favoring restraint on access as a universal principle. Arguments rage over the place of sensitive research in a national security complex and the cost of such research in an international development complex. The United States competition for global supremacy is many-sided: with the Soviets it is a military struggle, with the Japanese it is an industrial struggle. But expressed in such a manner, the issue of access is contextually located and properly focused.

The essential task is to define the problem. Otherwise, the goal of agenda-setting becomes sterile, if not entirely gratuitous. We already know that the problem is not access writ large. Huge chunks of information are entirely available. We know too that the problem is not random access. For example, the issue is not access to a wide range of non-strategic materials. We also know that the issue is not one of physical access. The ability to travel remains largely unimpaired for scholars—with the exception of dangerous geographical areas subject to terrorist assaults in general. And here the issues are not scientific access, so much as political tranquility. The matter of access is thus quickly reduced to what might be referred to as blueprints of strategic materials, information which is programmable, and thus readily transferable or transmitted, and yet a third area is that of dual use technology, that is, hardware which has commercial origins but readily has military applications.

Access seems to boil down to proprietary considerations, strategic-military concerns of primacy, and a general premise that knowledge is a commodity that can be bought and sold and not just a natural resource to be captured in raw form. Seen in these terms, one hopes to get beyond ideological aspects of the Cold War into serious concerns of the importance of privacy or better, the value of invention. One can argue that in a purely Keynesian state the price of knowledge is absorbed into the system of taxation and hence knowledge should be universally granted. But neither the United States nor the Soviet Union is a pure economy. Hence, the costs of acquiring access. Even if we had a harmonious global condition, restraint on access would remain constant. Issues of access are not strictly speaking a function of East-West tensions, but of the structure of the knowledge system as such.

Thus far, we have examined larger issues such as considerations of sovereignty and economic cost in restricting access to advanced knowledge. To this must be added micro-concerns, specifically mechanisms of control that are involved in peer-review processes. Access is further limited by gate-keeping functions to publishing outlets. The peer-review system limits access by filtering out what constitutes poor or worthless information from good or useful information. The more exacting the scientific discipline, the wider is the range of gate-keeping constraints. This is another way of saying that access is neither unlimited nor is it an unmitigated blessing. We do not regard every scrap of paper as sacrosanct, nor do we demand access without a costly system of peer review.

The cutting edge of East-West differentials at the level of scientific information is peer review. For the guiding metaphor behind peer review is the universality of scientific judgment as dictated by the relevant core professionals in any given discipline. It is what defines the notion of Western culture. By the same token, within the Soviet network of science, while peer review operates, it does so precisely within the context of the nation. For the most part, an article or book is not considered published unless and until it has the official sanction of an official national association. This is quite apart from whether a particular research article is considered militarily or politically sensitive. National boundaries limiting publication, rather than the capacity to access information, represents a distinguishing hallmark of Soviet science. In this crucial regard, we can see how the very notion of "Western democratic" and "Eastern authoritarian" styles of research are fleshed out.

Thus, the Soviet system of science, while sharing many characteristics with its American counterpart, reveals noteworthy exceptions. The Soviet system is parallel to the American system, with two noteworthy exceptions: all materials published in potentially sensitive areas are subject to pre-publication review by military experts, and materials in the social and behavioral sciences (not to mention humanities and literature) are similarly serviced by political commissioners who make sure that fundamental orthodoxies are not violated. In both instances a considerable amount of porosity exists. And in areas where closure is total, a *samizdat,* or underground network, operates for disbursement of dangerous intellectual or informational materials.

It might be added that a problem in the reverse also exists: because the United States is a market-driven economy and the USSR is a planned economy, certain liberties with prices, supplies, and demands are feasible. For example, books from Soviet sources, scientific texts no less than Marxist-Leninist classics, are far more accessible to the people of developing nations than to Western counterparts. And in places where both sets of material are available, price often determines what is purchased. In other words, we are dealing with a problem of information overload and not just limits to accessing scarce data. If the advantages of an open system regulated exclusively by peer review are transparent at the advanced end of the knowledge spectrum, the advantages of the closed system are no less manifest in the mass distribution of basic literature without sensitive components.

When we look at physical access, that is of researchers to each other as well as to a field of investigation, then a curious fact compels recognition: East-West problems tend to diminish, and in their place North-South problems tend to expand. One might formulate this in terms of a paradigmatic: the "harder" the science involved the more likely it is that East-West relations are at stake; whereas the "softer" the science the more likely it is that North-South relations are involved. When issues of United States–Third World relations occur, the rhetoric often turns upon phrases like "arrogance of power," "conceit of staff"–"lack of reciprocity"–the sorts of issues that are of particular concern to anthropologists and sociologists who work overseas. But when the issues addressed are East-West relationships, one can, with equal assuredness, be confronted with denial of access in the name of national sovereignty, military advantage, or strategic capability. In short, two quite disparate considerations are disguised by the common issue of access to data.

We must also take into account new forms of constraint on knowledge that are a result of the rising tide of Third World terrorism, namely, denial of access to the field of research, and the denial of admission to the so-called poorer or weaker nation. This is often done in the name of anti-imperialism or anti-colonialism. Thus, terrorism has become a factor in the capacity of field researchers in many disciplines to access their environment. Curiously, and at the same time, it is increasingly the case that these same Third World nation-states which demand open access to advanced technology of the West, in particular the United States, while arguing vehemently for closure in terms of American field researchers or teams of investigators of human rights violations, argue with equal passion against any restraints on communication imposed by the United States government. The problem which internationalism confronts, that of isolationism, is nowhere more apparent–contradictory sets of demands notwithstanding than in this particular Third World context. This imbalance between self-indulgence and demands upon others, while a less than *politesse* subject-area must be dealt with if international science as such is to survive and inform a desperate world of its manifold benefits. In other words, access is a many-sided problem, alive on all sides of the contemporary political and economic spectrum–more so now than in the simpler times of Democritus or Alcibiades.

From my personal vantage point, the best answer to isolationism is the internationalism of science, and of the educated communities. Science provides the ability of people to develop a common language of discourse, not based on the particular biases within the nation, but rather on methodology, core research, style of work, and the capacity to place rationality itself as a goal over and above the claims of nations. This is a difficult goal to attain, since parochial and pedestrian claims have their charms as well as their forces. Scientists, in the West, are able to travel all over the world; speak common languages, and read books and journals deemed universally important. Further, the scientific community has what few other communities have, namely: an institutional base from which to operate in each nation. This base is widespread enough to permit physical movement from one end of the earth to the other. Thus, the informational base and institutional superstructure permit a sense of camaraderie, belonging, and commonality to develop. This is in itself the key to forms of access. Whether the claims of the scientific community are justified or just depends in part on the claims made by other social segments, but for such claims to have practical merit an infrastructure of institutions as well as a network of ideas must be in place.

The struggle to maximize scientific autonomy is the task of scientific organizations. This is a specific mission of a scientific interest group in an environment that is terribly problematic. The administrative response to the global environment, one which witnesses overwhelming Soviet military strength to the point of dominance, has to be addressed by political actors and the political system. A statement of policy on access to information cannot simply take the position that the needs of the American scientific community are the only needs that must be served within this total informational environment. The source of the threat does not uniquely reside in those who administer programs of heavily sponsored research; but in the struggle between world empires that perform and play by different, and at times unconventional, rules.

If a scientific community does not have unreservedly shared values and norms, it cannot hope to achieve its research or theoretical objectives. But if a national commonwealth lacks the capacity for self-defense, and yes, security, then scientific life may run the risk of failing to achieve a common humanity. The issue of access is a small part of this larger, serious problem of surviving in peace and freedom. It would be fatuous to reduce a conference on access to scientific data to a demand to eliminate all varieties of secrecy. No society has survived with such unlimited access; neither diplomatic nor defense capacities would be served by such a posture. On the other hand, no society can maintain an advanced, developmental position without a free scientific environment.

We are involved in a practical dilemma: one person's scientific research is another person's military security. The legitimacy of claims is made hard because the society offers little in the way of adjudicating instruments to distinguish what is absolutely essential from what is quixotic in the way of security requirements *or* scientific requirements. In a society such as ours, both public and private sector organizations, from the American Association for the Advancement of Science on one end to the National Security Council on the other compete not just in the manufacture of knowledge, but in the uses of knowledge. Knowledge more than ever is power. But to achieve such power requires money, investment, and decisions about the needs of a citizenry. Once this broader picture is included into the study of scientific access, a modest agenda might be established, one that will still have to be fought for by the scientific community, but at least one that holds out the possibility of authentic victory.

11

From Means of Production to Modes of Communication

The revolution in communication represents a profound shift from the notion of production as "things" to production as "ideas." As a result, this revolution has forever transformed relationships between people in the work life, no less than the formal relations people have to the sources of "material" and "spiritual" production.[1] Indeed, the quotation marks around such key words is indicative of the archaic nature of such inherited dualisms. Philosophical idealism was nourished in a medieval environment in which rewards for people were viewed as heavenly, i.e., divinely bestowed. Whereas philosophical materialism was likewise nourished in an eighteenth- and early nineteenth-century environment in which rewards were naturalized, brought down to earth by labor and capital.

It is hardly far-fetched in a work on the revolution in communication, albeit with an emphasis on select aspects of that revolution, to raise in the sharpest way the current and likely future status of work. For ideas are not merely communicated, they are struggled for, worked for. One must be careful in the choice of language. For what is at stake is not any notion of labor unions or management associations, or struggles for survival and subsistence, but the very essence of the work process as a major source of human identity and creativity. Thus, the work environment is itself an environment increasingly dominated by generating ideas and the specialized hardware which feeds and nourishes valuable information.

Many of the pessimistic prognoses made at the onset of the post-industrial era, which coincides with the post-World War Two era, have simply not materialized. There has been no noticeable "degradation of work"; there has been no permanent economic crisis within capitalism; nor has there been any appreciable increase in worker

141

speed-up or piece-work expansion.[2] Those who prefer the prophetic mode have mistaken the decline in unionized activity with the decline in the work force itself. To be sure, periods of economic restructuring result not only in the emergence of new industries but also involve related shifts in techniques of production in many older industries.[3]

It is neither a social research secret nor a conspiracy of rightist ideology to take note of the extraordinary decline of "organized labor" in the West. Indeed, the most cogently argued acknowledgment of this fact has been put forth by Robert Wrenn, writing in *The Socialist Review:*

> Organized labor in the United States has declined in strength. It is weaker today than at any time since the 1930s. [There are] four aspects of labor's current weakness: (1) the decline in power at the bargaining table; (2) the decline in union and rank-and-file militancy and in strike activity; (3) the decline in union membership and in the volume and success of union organizing activities; (4) the erosion of the social wage and the increasing "cost of jobs."[4]

Where ideological differences begin to emerge are in the causal assignments for this new phenomenon of inclining work force and declining trade union membership. It is interesting, for example, that the aforementioned article mentions high unemployment rates, non-union competition, the corporate counterattack, changes in government policy, and organized labor's internal dilemmas, but artfully avoids a discussion of such items as protection for workers by appeals to law, union corruption and abuse of pension funds, and above all, the character of the new technology that encourages a dissolution of the very distinctions inherited between management and labor which characterized an earlier epoch.

The essential characteristic of the information society as it now stands is the growth of knowledge industries that produce and distribute information rather than goods and services; and in so doing help dissolve the distinctions between management and labor, while sharpening those between ownership and utilization of information resources. A recent report on Silicon Valley indicates the marked contrast of the new entrepreneurialism with the old forms of labor organization:

> Silicon Valley companies are constantly starting up, growing, merging, being acquired, or fading away, making it difficult to know exactly how many firms exist at any one time. A careful count in

1982 identified 3,100 electronics manufacturing firms in Silicon Valley (Schmieder, 1983). In addition, companies supporting the electronics manufacturers, such as firms engaged in marketing, advertising, research and development, consulting, training, venture capital, legal, and other support services bring the total number of firms in the Silicon Valley electronics industry to about 6,000. Another 2,000 companies are in nonelectronics high-technology fields such as chemicals, pharmaceuticals, and genetic engineering. So the total number of high-tech firms in Silicon Valley is about 8,000, and growing fast.[5]

The burden of my position is carried by the report's subtitle: The Transformation of a Social Class into an Interest Group. This historic development can be seen as the opposite side of the economic alterations in advanced societies as a whole, namely, the changing linkages of human associations in the marketplace—from the area of production of material goods to the production of information services. Admittedly, these are broad categories. The emphasis on material production in the nineteenth century centered on machine tools, mining raw materials, and manufacturing equipment. Increasingly and throughout the twentieth century, material production, aided by new means of mass production, was centered upon consumer goods and artifacts intended to satisfy expanded human wants no less than essential human needs. The production of information services has followed a similar pattern: the earlier phases of computers, for instance, were aimed at satisfying industrial and commercial needs; whereas increasingly the current phase emphasizes computers for home and personal use. The only difference is that massification of goods and services is much more rapidly diffused than it was fifty or one hundred years earlier.

It serves little or no purpose to rehash the issue of "technological determinism" versus "social control" arguments about this new environment in which advanced societies operate. Rather, we are better advised to take a close look at the work force directly: a work force in which 40 percent of the American population is now located in new technology spinoffs; one in which the trade union portion of the work force has not grown in years, and has declined, in the United States at least, in relative size to become less than 20 percent of that force; and one in which service occupations have grown in numbers far greater than the decline of blue-collar work.

In such an environment, to speak of working people as a unified working class is to mock ordinary observation. For the notion of work has far outstripped in significance any notion of class in advanced industrial life. Solidarity takes many forms among working people—from professional identifications ranging from societies to bureaucrats to lawyers' guilds. Further, and of still greater consequence, work may provide the economic sustenance, but not necessarily the ideological commitment, of the work force. Ascriptive associations based on religion, race, and sex, far from dissolving, have expanded in the mid-1980s, to extraordinary degrees. In such a context, those for whom work is more than a task, but also a mission, gradually and imperceptibly shrink to interest group proportions. This is not to demean or disparage such a development. It is, however, to recognize the historic importance of this erosion of class in the social transformation of work as a key instrument in the production of identity as well as information.

Even if we restrict ourselves to developments within the trade union movement it becomes clear that they must operate in conditions of flexible technologies very differently than they formerly did in conditions of mass production:

> General principles, as opposed to specific rules, come to govern labor-management relations; wage determination and work allocation tend to center on concepts such as skill or craft as opposed to a set of particular jobs. The line between worker and managerial responsibility and between union and employer roles becomes a good deal more ambiguous. When general principles as opposed to specific rules govern work relations, the line between contract negotiations and contract administration is also more difficult to draw because there is much wider room for interpretation, and hence for negotiation, in the application of a previously accepted principle to a specific situation. The contrast between industrial relations in the work situation emerges most clearly in industries like construction, where pay is based on craft, the contract is reinterpreted on every major project by the business agent, work assignments are fluid and constantly changing, supervisors are members of the union and sometimes the contractor is a member as well, and where the worker can often lay out a job better than his boss can. But even in industrial unions, shop practice tends to drift in the direction of construction as one moves out of the mass-production parts of the industry toward areas of more specialized production.[6]

The literature on work is so incredibly large and extensive that covering the topic is a strategic problem unto itself. Should one emphasize comparative approaches, case study materials, field ethnography, or in-depth statistical reports of trends and forecasts—or a combination of the above? In short, there are nearly as many ways to examine the issue of work as there are phenomena to be examined. To consider the future of work is above all to review the past and present conditions of labor. The literature on the subject is riddled with an overwhelming contradiction, of sufficient import to be called a primary contradiction. That contradiction is the relationship between meaning and money, that is to say, whether work is primarily to be viewed in psychological terms as the degree to which it provides contentment or discontentment, or as an economic issue of salaries, wages, hours, and benefit packages. This distinction sharply divides social researchers. It is at the core of disputes between socialist and free-market ideologists, and between labor negotiators and management consultants.

Distinctions between capital and labor remain in force in this post-industrial environment. However, explicit doctrines about the inevitable warfare between the two have largely dissolved—in planning as well as free-market societies. Like all momentous contradictions, this one too is not being resolved by policy mechanisms, so much as by changing technological circumstances largely unforeseen by past generations. Whatever we call it: the post-industrial revolution, the new technology, the computerized society, it is now plain that older distinctions between capital and labor are increasingly ambiguous—the ideological proclivities of party spokesmen notwithstanding. Indeed, the extent to which such distinctions retain their sharp focus, to that degree can we designate such societies as belonging to the less-developed nation-states.

Indeed, one recent analyst has shrewdly noted that work can be viewed as either a commodity or a vocation. The former context implies a conflictual model in which laborers search to maximize wages whereas owners seek to minimize wages and maximize profits. The vocational context of work implies a professional interest and commitment; it also implies a consensual model in which the struggle for resources is replaced by a shared struggle to discover. Charles Handy uses the felicitous phrase—"a structure for mattering"—in describing work:

> Work, in some form, is critical to individuals. It is, apart from anything else, a principal structure for mattering. We all need to feel that we matter, that we can contribute, that we are missed in our

absence, that we are respected and liked. If jobs are scarce, or not much good when we get them, we must and will find other forms of work. In the past we were perhaps obsessively preoccupied with the job. Those who didn't have jobs, like housewives or the elderly, were seen in some ways as extras in the play of life, the chorus rather than the principals. No wonder that women have been eager to get in on the act. We badly needed, therefore, to recognize that work did not only happen in jobs. That sort of recognition is beginning to come through, partly because more and more men are finding that work has many faces, a truth that women knew long ago.[7]

A basic way to measure distinctions between industrial and post-industrial societies is to look at the differences between Eastern Europe and Western Europe. Even if we take the most economically vigorous of the Eastern nations, in this case Hungary, sharp dichotomies become readily apparent. Wages are either low or delivered in currencies that are non-transferable and have a limited purchasing power. Technological progress is poorly integrated, with automation below the 5 percent levels. Work organization remains anchored to old-fashioned notions of piece work and mechanized production norms with scarcely any new technologies generated from within or exported from abroad. Socialism, which in theory is pledged to a reduction in working hours, in practice has resulted in a dramatic increase in work time; to the point where the very category of leisure time in contrast to work time is obliterated in even advanced communist states.

As Lajos Hethy, director of the Labour Research Institute in Budapest, recently noted, while the formal hours dedicated to work have declined under socialism, the legal working hours only disguise the substantial *increase* in working time under planned economies:

> If hours spent by all work activities (involving physical and mental efforts) are added—that is activities also in the household, in the so called "natural" and "secondary" economy, as well as commution to and back from work—we will get much higher data. We will even find that actual working hours including the above work activities probably have not decreased, while free time actually have increased, as still too much time is taken by household work (despite an obvious improvement) and by the growing activities of the "natural" and "secondary" economy. For certain groups of workers in Eastern Europe—we can quote some groups of Soviet working class housewives but also Hungarian worker families having an industrial and agricultural background at the same time—working hours "informally" have crept as high as those around the turn of the century—and free time has ceased to exist.[8]

Without resorting to caricature, or ignoring actual developments in health, welfare and full-employment practices in such socialist nations, it is evident that from present data that the difference between a nation entering the industrial revolution late in the present century and one entering the post-industrial, or information revolution, is considerable. One problem is that the post-industrial rhetoric remains sufficiently cloudy as to permit considerable misunderstanding and taxonomic abuse. That is why an emphasis on the *process* of transition from ownership of production to ownership of communication provides a better means of establishing the new conditions for work than an emphasis on the *structure* of these new societies; which indeed remain difficult to characterize or label. But let us turn to just such a structural analysis.

The key elements in the present epoch are as follows: the enormous rise in so-called intermediate sectors—that is, the administrative apparatus of local, regional, and national governments—to the point where they can no longer be accurately thought of as intermediate, but, rather, are central to the survival of advanced macro-economic systems. This phenomenon, ongoing since the turn of the century and accelerating until the very recent past, defines the legal and often the moral character of the work environment. The appeals made by and on behalf of the underprivileged, the downtrodden, or the discontented are no longer focused on direct confrontation with management or indirect remedial activities undertaken by trade unions or other types of work associations, but at the administrative-bureaucratic levels to which ordinary people in advanced societies look for desired readjustments or reorganizations of equity considerations.[9] This key element in the new work environment is itself crucial in setting forth the norms and laws for the work process as a whole.

A more recent phenomenon are the new technologists who as a class of individuals do everything from manufacture to program to service computers and its various hardware and software components. They are in effect engaged in "scholarly communication" at its most elemental levels. This is not restricted to the Silicon Valleys of the world. Since the automotive and aircraft industries have been invaded by robotics, even these older industries have joined the post-industrial information revolution. Industry as a whole has now entered a phase in which labor intensivity has become a capital intensive. This latest development has also tended to erode older programs and sentiments formerly governing labor-management relations. Newer entrants into the work force, whatever their formal training, increasingly view themselves as professionals, not as employees. Data indicate that they worry less about holding a special class position than about issues related to workplace satisfaction—and that includes rewards as wide-ranging as stock options, bonus incentives; and shared participation in decision-making. In such a work environment, older notions of conflict and warfare give way to newer patterns of consensual operation, or at the minimum, conflict within a framework of shared ultimate goals.

A crisis in decision-making occurs in this shift. It is no longer possible to describe the work world in reductionist terms of an exploiting ruling class versus an oppressed proletariat (especially in those societies in which the work force sees itself as privileged vis-à-vis a welfare sector). The very notion of social class undergoes a profound change. Classes and class struggles do remain factors in advanced societies and will continue to be such. But the *primacy* of such forms of struggle over others has been profoundly eroded. Instead, a multivariate environment, with new forms of interest-group competitions emerge, ascriptive features of race, sex, religion, and age resurface; whilst newer forms of distinction and discrimination arise, *i.e.,* differences based on everything from smoking habits to mating preferences. Once this occurs, there takes place a refeudalization of work. The workforce is broken out into new groups with shared research orientations displacing commonalities of particularistic class loyalties. In sum, conflict does not decline in absolute terms, but its sources shift from industrial-achievement to post-industrial ascriptive factors.

Older distinctions between work and leisure, which preoccupied the mass-culture literature after the Second World War, have also dissolved. They too have not been resolved by policy mandates from heaven or planning exercise. Rather, they have been changed by new circumstances in which the work life is invested with ultimate responsibility for personal reward and even private identity. It is hardly an exaggeration to say that, given the decline in communalism and familialism; the purpose of one's life in post-industrial societies is increasingly wrapped up with personal statement of worth. The résumé, and all it says about background and training and previous employment becomes a unique source of independent verification of worth, in short, of identity itself. As a result, pride in work is linked to pride in the organization for which one works. This trend is not only characteristic of Japanese industry, but is a growing factor in advanced industrial societies as a whole.[10] Again, this is not to deny that there are continuing frictions between management and labor. It is rather to assert that such claims are resolved in terms of differences among members of a corporate family rather than demands for total systemic overhaul because of a unique corporate dilemma or struggle. The appeal to information displaces older appeals to emotion.

What takes place is the politicization of corporate life, not in terms of global or even national party loyalties (although these may sometimes be invoked) so much as the politics of the office, and of newer styles of workplace environments. Politics becomes integrated into the psychological processes of moving ahead, and also into the economic process of making more money or improving conditions. For too long politics has been conceptualized as decision-making activities detached from workplace units or its administrative-management functions. We have neglected to appreciate the extent to which the new political environment is itself a workplace and workforce. The emergence of such a new information-rich class thus connects political processes with the economic system and its psychic rewards.

In a larger sense yet, the new work situation herein outlined is directly linked to an ongoing spirit of the century. Egalitarianism is a universally shared valuational code in advanced industrial societies. This statement may appear quioxotic in a century uniquely described as totalitarian, authoritarian, and even genocidal. But aside from the obvious caveat that such contradictory modalities as egalitarianism and totalitarianism can and do exist side by side, there is the question of what constitutes an advanced, post-industrial nation after all. Work advances imply much more than high technology; they imply, and even entail forms of human behavior and interaction in which the methods of custom, tradition, and authority yield to the methods of experience, experiment, and evidence. This is not to imply that scientism is the same as humanism. The experience of Nazi Germany belies that approach. Nonetheless, it is in the nature of advanced science and technology, wherever these post-industrial modes operate, they encourage a kind of egalitarianism that seems to be irrepressible and inexorable.

The pattern of post-industrial attitudes and values toward work show remarkable similarities in cross-national comparisons over time. In a current study under way, George W. England reports only marginal differences among the United States, Germany, and Japan over time. The importance of work is exceeded only by familial values, and outstrips leisure, community, and religious values. Perhaps most surprising is that the new technology has not led to any particular rush to valuational changes, so much as it has kept traditional patterns of industrial life very much intact.[11]

The new technology thus holds the potential for both achievement and abuse. As one analysis recently noted, the new technology restores the potential for the old cottage industries. And this means precisely problems which betoken a new industrial order thought to have long since passed:

> At a conceptual level the electronic cottage holds the potential for both achievement and abuse. To the homebound—the disabled, or those with children to look after—it may represent their only access to a meaningful job. To other workers it offers the entrepreneurial ideal of independence, a liberating style of work that eliminates the routine of set hours and settled pay. To a corporation the benefits can include greater productivity, lower costs in overhead and administration, and access to an untapped labour pool. On the other hand, organized labour fears a return to the piecework sweatshops of the late nineteenth century, with the computer terminal standing in for the sewing machine. The unions imagine companies cutting back office staff and parcelling work out to low-paid clerical workers at home. Essentially unable to organize and to bargain for higher wages, these pieceworkers might try to supplement their earnings by putting other family members—including children—to work. This version of a domestic electronic sweatshop, however, has yet to appear in fact.[12]

Thus, not only are there continuities in value between the pre- and post-industrial orders, but also continuities even in work style, i.e., the return of the cottage industry in the word-processing industries.

Continuities in work values indicate the force of inherited valuational distinctions between good and evil, right and wrong, beauty and ugliness. These still continue much in force. What changes are the criteria for measuring such ethical categories, what might be termed tastes. But what remains is the concern over such issues, augmented by newer considerations of control and autonomy in human existence. Struggle will continue: between the educated and the ignorant, between the rational and the fanatical, between entrepreneurs and managers, between those who are in the work force and those who are in the welfare lines. The future is not utopian, it is only the future. That is to say, optimistic or pessimistic readings are equally problematic. One can hope for as well as anticipate the emergence of sufficient intelligence to employ the forces of modernity to prevent the forces of a new barbarism from seizing control or domination.

This has been the shared hope of humanists and scientists alike. But does this hope warrant expectations for resolving the "two cultures" of technological determinism and social voluntarism?

At the most general level, a cultural phenomenon can be observed: the search for work meanings, or the meaning of work in advanced industrial societies might better be conceptualized as the very essence of an advanced industrial society. The investment of psychic energy and individual worth is precisely that measure beyond Ricardian subsistence that nearly all advanced industrial nations have traversed. As a parallel synergism, work in less-developed countries is linked to collective survival. For most people in Third World nations, work, however harsh, nasty, and brutish is an everyday performance to keep body and soul together. Subsistence, like life itself, is linked to survival mechanisms. That in the late twentieth century, people can and do properly speak of the linkage between work and love, is a measure of displaced psychic energy and recharged individual worth. To be sure, the extent to which the older Freudian paradigm on the antinomic relationship between work and sexuality has given way to a Reichian paradigm of the integrity of work and sexuality is an important, if sorely neglected, element in examining worker attitudes and behavior in a post-industrial context.

Structural data on industrial outputs, plant utilization, inflationary patterns, unemployment levels, etc., show gradations across national boundaries, but just as clearly, in long-run secular terms; show strong commonalities amongst the most advanced nations, and that includes the United States and Japan. This is not to deride the influence of cultural factors; it is however, not to exaggerate such factors gratuitously. Different measures will indeed reveal differences in preferences, attitudes, and aspirations of workers across national boundaries. But as I noted some years ago in a methodological essay on developmental measurement and testing: there is a Heisenberg-effect in social research, such that attitudinal "waves" and structural "particles" can be examined but not as coefficients, only as paired independent variables. The undulating movement between attitudinal "waves" and structural "particles" does not advance the cause of social analysis. Advanced industrial societies, wherever they may be located geographically, are bound by a vast array of commonalities of an economic, political, military, and social sort that will not easily be overtaken in the near future by admitted cultural and area differences.

Too often, in fact, most often, comparative research is basically a cross-compilation of essentially discrete reports on national conditions. Even with efforts to control variances through shared data sets, the temptation to yield to exceptionalism—i.e., the idea that every nation really is different—yields to econometric reductionism, to a condition in which the sociology of everyday work is reduced to monetary equivalences for other varieties of satisfactions.[13] Piecing together a series of national puzzles does not, unfortunately, add up to comparabilities in any rigorous sense of data analysis. There is a need to view comparative research in systemic terms, i.e., planned economies vis-à-vis free-market systems, or more precisely, work under consensual systems vis-à-vis work under command systems. Gorbachev's problems are not unlike those of Mitterand and Craxi; however, Gorbachev's solutions are framed by differences between NATO and WARSAW pact nations—similitudes in the underground economy between Italy and Hungary notwithstanding.

I continue to be impressed by the degree to which work issues illustrate the two cultures within the social sciences no less than between world ideologies. One is empirical, statistical, data-driven, and based on certain assumptions about work as linked to job aspirations and satisfactions; and not simply position in the workplace. The other tendency is a phenomenological or dialectical explanation, a position driven by different assumptions based upon contextual or quotidian events. Survey research and its by-products are replaced by everything from the ethology of the workplace, the economy of exploitation, to the ideology of the special vanguard role of labor in class warfare. This is a serious dichotomization, one that influences not just the character of work; but the way in which the social sciences approach the problem of whole societies.

One curious aspect of this polarization of positivist and phenomenological perspectives is that it cuts across free-market and planned-market societies. Since most communist societies are highly constructivist, they tend to be highly positivist as well. Thus, a kind of optimistic mood impacts social research East and West, encouraging cooperation, but discouraging criticism. The critical perspectives tend to derive from marginal sectors of social researchers in open societies.[14] The anomaly is created that "Left socialist" opposition functions as an embarrassment to its presumed political allies, while being met with a vast sea of indifference from its presumed antagonists in the West. In a larger context, the two cultures of social science are little else than the breaking apart of constructive and critical analytical functions. And the work efforts under way at multinational levels does more to lay bare the issues than—thus far at least—to resolve them.

In conclusion, it is worth reiterating that the rapidity of social change, as reflected in work attitudes and worker behaviors, which profoundly impacts the relative valuational and aspirational measures, does not, and perhaps cannot, translate into the ethical dimensions of behavior. In that particular realm, change remains very slow. Moral change is not only imperceptible in human affairs but, when observed, is not nearly illustrative of higher values. The global designations of our age, to which we are all privy—Raymond Aron's century of war, Elie Weisel's century of genocide, Jean-François Revel's century of totalitarianism—compete for taxonomical honors with Henry Wallace's century of the common man and Daniel Bell's post-industrial century. In short, good and evil do not dissolve in the new work environment, rather they are globalized. Questions of work as such are rather internationalized under the influence of the informational rationalization of the world system as a whole. The hope of the poor is to join the ranks of those privy to the agonies and anguishes of higher moral dilemmas through the acquisition of basic informational skills. To have such a participatory right to the means of information matters, for it enlarges the number of players in the decision-making processes, and in so doing permits more individuals to make the same mistakes. More important, it also introduces fresh possibilities for the achievement of collective goods. And that is what both egalitarian politics and new technologies are very much about.

12

Advertising Ideas and Marketing Products

The essential factor in promotion and advertising is their relation to the marketing environment as a whole. A product which is advertised for sale is inextricably linked to *where* such announcements are placed, whether the media are newspapers, journals, radio/television, or others. Promotion and advertising are necessarily connected with the buying and selling of merchandise. Deciding where to advertise and market immediately raises essential issues not only about the intrinsic advantages of a particular product over and against other products, but the relative advantages derived from the marketing of that product in one medium as opposed to another.[1]

A potential conflict in the marketing decision is that the attention generated only partially centers upon the merits of the product. At least an equal measure of attention is given to the style or form of presentation of that product. It is not simply the worth of the commodity but the impact of the presentation of that commodity that becomes crucial. At this level, most ethical problems of product integrity enter the picture, because selling books or journals involves techniques only remotely (if at all) linked to the intrinsic or heuristic values of the goods sold, or what is often termed "informative advertising." Far more potent techniques are used consistently by advertisers in an effort to *create* demand for their literary products. These include demand manipulation, product differentiation, and the creation of product utility. Demand manipulation involves the technique of creating demand for a product based on extrinsic factors. The mere repetition of advertisements to implant the brand name of a product in the consumer's mind is such a technique. The association of various products with increased sexuality or greater power—as in how to manage or manipulate people—are obvious examples which come to mind.

Product differentiation concerns drawing a distinction between one form or brand name of a product and all others. Where such distinctions are real, such advertising is informative. However, with such products as Bayer aspirin, Pillsbury flour, or Johnson's baby powder, the distinctions made are strictly commercial, not intellectual. Creation of product utility is literally the stimulation of demand (where none existed previously) for a type of product through advertising. Every product presumably promises benefits or satisfactions derived from its use or consumption. To the extent that advertising creates the need that the advertised product satisfies, this special technique is employed in all industries.

The English word *advertising* disguises what the French and Spanish languages make quite clear: namely, the *propaganda* values of selling. This term can be used either as an expression of the promotion of a commodity or an idea or the ideological representation of that idea with a variable amount of fiction thrown in for good measure. For the most part, advertising techniques can ill afford to engage in the complete truth. Advertising addresses an amorphous market, much as an attorney addresses a judge in legal procedure. The adversarial technique is not simply the presentation of the best foot forward of the commodity (or person), but above all, of a general persuasion that the commodity (or person) is above reproach.

Ford Motor Company advertises its product, the automobile, as basically interchangeable with, if not superior to, the Mercedes Benz in physical appearance and even operational functions. But this fails to make clear that this similitude only occurs on day one. No claims are made for parity of the two autos after three or five years in operation. Still, neither Ford nor Mercedes would dare challenge the value of the automobile as the fundamental transportation requisite of modern society. Hence, a sort of noblesse oblige exists between firms, with challenges to product authenticity among firms being rare, even newsworthy events.

There are layers of propaganda, just as there are levels of deception, in the world of advertising. Perhaps the ultimate level is self-deception, the sort of belief in one's own product that transcends any sense of deception, and yet hardly represents the entire range of truths.[2]

The fundamental characteristics of ideology in general can be reduced, for our purposes, to the following seven propositions: (1) Unconscious adherence to patriotic symbols, norms, and values. A singular set of beliefs eliciting strong loyalties. (2) Collectively established values supported by the group over an extended period of time. Its purpose is defined by its content of message. (3) Technique of persuasion in which persuaders are not intellectually distinguishable from persuaded. The ideology is shared by masses and elites, irrespective of whom it serves. (4) The ideology emerges from existing social conditions and relations in which the community finds itself. (5) Shaping of "knowledge" and general theories of science and religion by ideological proclivities. Theories tend to be wide-ranging and universalistic. (6) Ideology is concerned with justification and rationalization of already accepted behavioral patterns. (7) Established systematic connections between theories; that is, laws of historical change, a demand for "rational" motives of action.

In contrast, the fundamental characteristics of advertising as a form of marketing products can be conceptualized along the following lines: (1) Conscious manipulation of symbols, norms, and values. Multiple sets of beliefs, subject to rapid and radical alteration. (2) Individually or corporately, establishes a product over a short period of time. The purpose of advertising is to satisfy basic needs external to itself. (3) Advertising entails a technique of persuasion in which persuaders are intellectually distinguished from persuaded—as myth creator is disinguished from myth follower. (4) Advertising arises out of a need to stimulate and/or revise standards of social cohesion and conflict, for the purposes of selling a product. (5) Advertising entails shaping "opinion" and mass culture; and is generally confined to the "profane" levels of social interaction. (6) Advertising is concerned with multiplying stimuli best calculated to evoke desired behavioral responses in a market context. (7) Finally, advertising establishes fixation of belief in relation to specific products; willingness to defend or attack social structures in terms of "irrational" motives.

A serious issue generated by marketing and advertising in advanced society is whether public media should present only factual information in advertising. The world of television, which is subject to precise regulatory mechanisms in which the exact number of minutes—even seconds—allocated to the advertising and non-advertising portions of an hour are spelled out, is most subject to such controls, presumably because there is finite access to television. There is a crucial recognition within the media that there are differences between what is true and what is advertised. What often obscures the relationship between news and advertising is that both rely heavily upon entertainment. Delivering the news for maximum visual impact itself implies a special emphasis on mass "acts," often at the expense of more complex structural analysis. Hence, even the distinction between newsworthy "truths" and promotional "half truths" is subject to the specific properties of the medium employed. The broader the appeal, the easier it is to make the distinctions; the more scholarly the media, the more difficult such distinctions become.

There is a need to make a further distinction between advertising (that product or idea which is introduced into a market by direct cash investment) and promotion (that product or idea which is introduced into a market by non-monetary mechanisms). A good many questions are now being raised which concern this nebulous area between advertising and promotion. The use of famous celebrities for cover and feature stories that coincide with the release of a new book or film by them or statements of underwriting of public interest broadcasting may in fact constitute cover forms of advertising presented as offering news. For example, the excerpting of a new book by the wife of Francis Ford Coppola to coincide with the public release of his film, *Apocalypse Now,* constitutes one of many such "gray areas" in which promotion and information become hopelessly entangled.

The purpose of scholarly communication is to distinguish between forms of presentation of information as unambiguously as possible, and in this way avoid painting problems with such a broad brush as to obscure rather than clarify the exact contents of ethical dilemmas in advertising. One hesitates to invoke claims of moral superiority; it is rather the claim of empirical clarification that a variety of professional associations aim to incorporate into the public decision-making process.

In a world of publications, there exists a crucial dichotomy between publications that survive primarily because of their advertising revenues and those that survive primarily through their subscribers. In the latter type of publication, advertising revenues are ancillary, and for the most part insignificant. Here we must distinguish not simply between types of advertisements but forms of the medium as well. The larger the size of the journal, for example, the more possible it is to confuse information with promotion. The smaller the size of the journal, the less necessary it is for the advertising media to be responsive. It is not so much a matter of "small is beautiful" as it is that small is less likely to be dependent on advertising considerations; that is, by considerations of "big is powerful."

There are serious empirical as well as ethical issues in the relationship of advertising to society. The exact distinction between advertising and editorial content and just where the tipping point occurs is a matter of constant re-examination and redefinition. The extent to which each medium is committed to the general good or to the particular needs of advertisers and marketers becomes the dynamic relationship which the media must navigate if they are to fulfill their commitments to the public and at the same time survive and compete in a business civilization. In part, the "truth content" is determined by the level of sophistication of the market itself. Hence, claims of one beer or soft drink vis-à-vis another are couched in broad cultural terms having little or nothing to do with the product as such, whereas the information contents on scholarly books must be very exact because of the special nature of the scholarly community of book buyers; and the fine-line distinctions that exist between scholarly journals.

What makes the presentation of propaganda at least tolerable is that the advertising world finds the appropriate media in which to present its images. This permits a relative balance to exist between the means of communication and the instrument of propaganda. The marketing environment presents its own set of requirements, either encouraging or discouraging certain advertising practices responses. This is probably subject to the vernacular of creative tension, but is livable by virtue of the fact of the relative isomorphism between media and advertisers. Scientific books are advertised in scientific journals reaching hundreds, whereas automobiles are advertised during football intermissions, reaching millions. This is reasonable enough. The problem at this level becomes the point at which the public interest must be guarded against this operation of the laws of the ubiquitous market. The banning of cigarette and alcohol advertisements on radio and television is a case in point. The very lack of differentiation in an audience may dictate legislative and legal interventions where none is forthcoming (or need be) in products which cater to specialized audiences.

Dilemmas are also encountered by specialized media; for example, automobile or petroleum firms advertise in technical journals and periodicals, and by so doing, may overwhelm these fragile instruments of information with the very size of their marketing budgets. Clearly, the reverse is unlikely to happen: scientific information or consumer service periodicals are extremely hard to place before large publics. It is not impossible, as the spate of commodity-oriented programming stimulated by government regulatory consumer agencies makes plain. Nonetheless, such public-interest programming is still exceedingly rare and statistically insignificant. For that reason, because the battle between information and propaganda is so weighted, the problem lies much more on the shoulders of advertisers than in the palms of the scholarly communities. For this reason, the need for public-interest pressure groups remains constant; even if they sometimes take on the appearance of a hectoring interest-group in their own rights.

The ultimate dilemma is the point at which advertising and media become thoroughly fused, where there is no clear distinction between the propagandistic functions of marketing information and the knowledge functions of generating such information. We have many instances of this, both large-scale and small-scale. For example, as the Church Committee noted, the CIA sponsorship of certain book or magazine publishing activities led to a laundering of the affiliation and a blurring of the relationship between propaganda and knowledge. Another example is the distribution of a spate of catalogues and promotionals, ostensibly in the public interest, that do not reveal problems of waste, monopoly, cartels, and so on. The programming by network television specifically and exclusively in terms of numbers of viewers, and hence numbers of potential buyers of commodities, also introduces serious problems related to catering to prejudices without regard to "truth in advertising." At such a level, again, the line between advertising making and truth telling becomes subordinate to numbers of viewers or buyers. When the line between truth and propaganda becomes indistinguishable, the potential for a totalitarian regime increases dramatically. An Orwellian world could easily come about in which the means of communication are even more monopolized than the means of production.

Present arrangements which permit a division of labor in the media field, while far from perfect or idyllic, at least provide the basis of tension and opposition and make possible the distinction between knowledge and advertising. Still, the market is a long way from offering a perfectly sound relationship between sellers and buyers, special interest and public needs. The answer is more, not less, competition; more, not less, mass participation.

Democratic societies are characterized by legislative and political remedies to advertising abuses. Quite properly, we have a strong resistance to moralizing about knowledge dilemmas. In this sense, advertising techniques can best be viewed as composing a continuum, with informative advertising at one end and deceptive advertising at the other end. There are few serious ethical dilemmas created by honest, informative advertising. The ethical responsibility for deceptive or false advertising must emphatically rest with the advertiser. And it is in this area that we have witnessed substantive, protective legislation, although those practicing deception also learn techniques for evading legal constraints. However, it is at the center of this continuum that the respective responsibilities of advertiser, consumer, and media become vague.

The line between marketing and advertising is itself in need of explanation. Essentially, marketing is what takes place in relation to the self-promotion of a product line; i.e., one "markets" a list of books to buyers of an "in-house" list; whereas one "advertises" the same list to buyers in an "out-house" list, or publication. Obviously, the purpose of both marketing and advertising are increased sales and profitability. But again, the quest for profits in scholarly communication is severely tempered by issues of image-building, corporate legitimation, and author sensibilities. Thus, what appears initially as a straightforward quest for the "bottom-line" often ends in a variety of competing demands for status no less than profit.

For the most part, the book world recognizes the distinction between information (or entertainment pure and simple) and advertising (or propaganda) by rarely carrying such material in its physical product. The absence of such extraneous material is built into the price structure of the book; on the presumption that without advertisers to defray costs the price of a book is going to be higher than the equivalencies in journal or magazine formats. Every once in a while, a book will carry special messages, but these are jarring, and by their very presence tend to cast doubt on the objectivity of the product. Indeed, even promotions for books in allied areas are restricted to dust jackets, on the presupposition that these jackets can be discarded; they are not a part of the essential fabric of the intellectual contents of a book.

This contrasts sharply with journals and magazines, even scholarly materials, in such serial formats. The presence of advertisement is just about as commonplace in scholarly or popular periodicals as they are absent in books and monographs. Thus, the universe of scholarly and popular information and entertainment contains sharp variances which help define the form, or format. While advertisements in scholarly materials tend to be restricted to information related to the purpose of the journal items, in contrast to advertisements in popular media that tend to be general in character, this does not necessarily assure the truth contents of either. Journals will carry advertisements for books emphasizing only positive comments and extracts that are as often skewed as promotional literature of a more generic sort. Therefore, the distinctions among advertising, ideology, and information, while more complex in scholarly communication than elsewhere, remain very much intact. Subtlety of presentation is, after all, not the same as truth in packaging.

These caveats rendered, it must also be said that an advertisement, even if less than the whole truth, contains important elements of information that make journals (in hard copy form at least) quite special. They sensitize the audience to new currents, provide basic ordering and price information, and provide a sense of currents and cross-currents that are often as important, albeit ephemeral, as the scholarly article as such. The more stratified the advertising environment, the more capable are the individuals who read such publications of making fine distinctions between minor embellishments and major gaffes. There are also cross-over factors: journals are places where selective teaching audiences are reached—hence the need to announce texts. Such stratified audiences are opinion-leaders in their own right, hence the need to reach and to announce select trade-oriented groups. The world of scholarly communication is hardly a vacuum-packed environment. The line between advertisement and information and knowledge also forms a continuum, much to the chagrin of those who prefer purity in all things and ideas.

As the aforementioned indicates, there is still much groundwork to be done, much detailed effort to flush out the connection between directly underwitten information aiming to influence, and knowledge purchased by presumably unencumbered individuals to instruct or educate. Any claims toward fashioning a general theory would strike the sophisticated researcher as pretentious at best and preposterous at worst. The one area where much is known, motivational research, is most directly linked to the area of behavioral psychology. The one area where little is known, the structure and varieties of knowledge, is most directly linked to the area of philosophical sociology. Establishing linkages between fields may provide a first step to resolve the cloudy relationships which exist between advertising products and generating ideas.

13

Gatekeeping Functions and Publishing Truths

When a forgery is uncovered, or a plagiarized volume appears, or a fake letter adduced to support a mediocre manuscript, cries are sent forth that there is a need for tighter security by publishers. This is often coupled with a complaint that authors should scrutinize themselves more carefully. The burden of my remarks is quite the reverse: that the review process works surprisingly well and that authors have enough mechanisms of censorship at work to inhibit all but the most brazen few not to "cross the lines" of sound judgment and good taste alike. It may be the case that on rare occasions serious transgressions are not captured until after publication, but it should be remembered that one of the chief functions of making a work public is exactly to separate sense from nonsense.

Maintaining standards of truth in scholarly communication is an important goal, but it is necessarily a shared obligation. In the main, the amount of intentional deception that goes undiscovered is small. For example, four relatively famous, popular books have received careful scholarly attention: Alex Haley's *Roots,*[1] H. R. Haldeman's *The Ends of Power,*[2] David Rorvik's *In His Image: The Cloning of a Man,*[3] and Timothy J. Cooney's *Telling Right from Wrong.*[4] Each has received different sorts of criticism regarding standards of truth. Apart from the introductory essay, *Roots* was not billed as nonfiction but as a piece of imaginative reconstruction which provided a collective vision of the slave roots of American blacks. It was criticized as inaccurate by those who took it as a literal tracing of a single family tree, but the transgression was quite properly seen as minor and modest. H. R. Haldeman's *The Ends of Power* may be a more revealing statement than many of the fiction and nonfiction pot-boilers that followed Watergate. In part, the book aroused curiosity since Haldeman, although former President Nixon's closest aide, had previously revealed little self-interest by refusing to discuss Watergate in public. One can accuse Haldeman of a stubborn inability, even now, to grasp the magnitude of the Watergate affair, but not even his most severe critics have labeled him a liar on the presentation of larger issues. Certainly his version is as credible as a host of others which came before and after.

The Rorvik volume is more problematic and more interesting, not so much because the author claimed to have evidence that a man has been cloned, but because the promotional copy asserts that the publisher is an adequate judge of the veracity of these scientific claims. Since Lippincott is a major publisher of medical texts, its trade division is clearly suggesting that they consulted in-house expertise on the scholarly side. This may account for the disturbance felt by the scientific community, which was not, apparently, consulted at all. Even the Clifford Irving biography on the late Howard Hughes[5] might have passed muster as imaginative biography—the problem here was fraud in labeling. The author sought a large advance, and the publisher sought big profits by claiming in its advance publicity that the book was autobiographical rather than biographical. But as the Rorvik case indicates, this seems to have been more an example of advertising exaggeration than publisher negligence.

The case of Cooney's *Telling Right from Wrong* provides another sort of wrinkle in the truth-telling paradox. Involved is an author who believed, incorrectly as it turned out, that his book had no chance of being published by a major publisher without a supporting letter from a major academic figure. When the faked letter was discovered, the original publisher declined publication; but another enterprising press picked up the option, and in this case, the plates. Since the quality of the book is not under consideration, but only the authenticity of a supporting document, the issue came down to whether an author-as-faker is any worse than an author-as-murderer. According to Random House, the book would have been materially affected by the author's pre-publication actions. According to the author and his new publisher, Prometheus, the book remained to be judged on its merits or demerits, and not on admittedly shaky ethical behavior in search of publication. In this instance, the question of the "truth" of the manuscript was not in question, rather the "morality" of publishing strategies by a young author was central.

In each case, these are books with a "serious" purpose or message; but published as "trade" rather than "scholarly" works. This is in itself an indication that the problem of truth in publishing, with rare exceptions, is most frequently found in big publishing houses that have comprehensive lists. Books published as fiction are prima facie exempt from "truth-telling" (except when such titles get too close to empirical reality), and books published as pure scholarship are subject to a severe or vigorous review process that screens out works of serious deficiency.

Scholarly publishing has traveled a long way from serving as a printer to scholars in Renaissance culture to functioning as gate-keeper of truth in science and humanities. Indeed, at this point in time, there is scarcely a tenure decision undertaken at a major university that fails to take into account the publishing history of the individual under consideration. In not a few instances, the scholarly press provides the essential bona fide in the form of referee reports that may not determine the truth and falsity of a scholar's work, but certainly determines whether the scholar shall survive or perish in a given university or academy. Given this considerable shift in obligation from academic department to editorial department, the world of scholarly communication has tended to err on the side of severity and caution.

Linkages between universities and their presses has come full cycle. What started out as university support for scholarly publications has reached a point at which the quality of the university press attachment comes to seriously define the worth of the university as such. Charges of slipshod refereeing, ideological bias, or poor managment now reflect on the status of the university as a whole. In such a context, the issue of maintaining standards of truth is akin to beating a straw man to death. These concerns for accuracy are built into the socialization process of scholarly communication. As a result, the real wonder is less the occasional fraudulent work that slips through the net, than the rarity of such an event. Controversies concerning authenticity of historical documentation or laboratory experimentation are so rare that they cause newspaper headlines and stirrings among university managements. In such a climate of opinion, the emphasis on an occasional mistaken publishing judgment in releasing an unsound work must be seen as a minor issue in the world of scholarly communication.

Aiming for the goal of truth in what is published is certainly no less compelling in commercial or trade publishing than in scholarly communication. The problem is that possibilities for deceit are simply greater in trade publishing, not so much because of the greed of one kind of publisher and the altruism of the other, or because one employs lower editorial standards and does not have its books professionally reviewed. Scholarly communication is simply different, more intimate, in its nature. Individuals doing research are well-known to each other, publishing parameters clearly established, and professional constraints or claims are far easier to maintain than is allowed for in trade publishing.

The use of outside readers or referees can serve as a check on questionable material and author reliability, but any argument that commercial houses should adopt university or scholarly standards in this respect betrays ignorance of how scholarly communication actually functions. The outside reviewer of scholarly material does not work simply for financial compensation. It is primarily a professional obligation. Academic reviewers read manuscripts because they are interested in learning more about a subject in which they are already knowledgeable, no less than because they want to avoid publication of poor material. Experts also want to see a good book strengthened insofar as possible, and in directions they deem valid. Implicit in the reviewing process as used by scholarly presses is an understanding that publishing resources for scholarly books are finite, and that a bad book could well take the place of a good book. Furthermore, a bad book could have a negative influence on the development of a discipline. In short, the academic reviewer's purpose is not solely to assess accuracy in a journalistic sense, but to assess merit, which may be quite different. It is the case that some university presses have moved dangerously close to pure profit-motive publishing in its cross-over to trade publishing. But this is less an issue of truth-gathering than boundary maintenance between publishers.

The difference between trade publishing and scholarly publishing boils down to some fine lines and thin hairs: people read scholarship because they feel they must keep up with their field and maintain their professional reputation and personal skills. In trade publishing, people read because marketing has made them want to read a book outside or beyond their professional or work fields. Demand is created; thus the marketing of a trade book is in part the stimulation of interest, rather than, as in scholarly publishing, the tapping of an already existing interest.

When trade houses employ pre-publication reviewers, they do so for very different reasons than scholarly publishers. Trade houses generally are concerned with protecting the author and the publisher alike against outright error that could lead to legal liability. Such reviewers, often editors in-house, perform their work primarily for the money. The fact that his or her book had been professionally reviewed might well make an author more comfortable, and it might result in fewer suits or reduce the loss factor if a suit was brought. But there might also be a risk, for there are far fewer existing norms of advance reviewing of trade books as there is in scholarly publishing. Moreover, the public may not want to read what the experts would have them read and vice versa. Mass taste is not elite taste. The art in trade publishing is balancing the demands of the former against the standards of the latter. For this reason, trade publishing is more closely defined by the marketplace rather than by specific canons of professional responsibility in work output.

The post-publication reviewing process should not be overlooked. It plays an important role in scholarly publishing, but an even more important role in trade publishing. This is due to the fact that reviews are usually published closer to the actual publication date of the book. The vigorous exchanges that characterize post-publication analyses in trade publication are the finest safeguard against shoddy intellectual merchandise. Doubtless there is logrolling and back scratching; the trade publisher's promotion machine is geared up precisely for this purpose. That said, the number of media outlets both great and small and the relative autonomy of journals and periodicals from book manufacturers still provide a meaningful series of forums in which the adequacy of works can be tested.

Gatekeeping issues about truth, as opposed to merit, must be tempered by concerns about censorship. In the case of presumably serious works published in a commercial manner, the question of accuracy has often been more problematic, even as it becomes less important. James Watson's *The Double Helix*[7] may not be an absolutely accurate description of the priorities in the discovery of the structure of DNA. Immanual Veliksvsky's *Worlds of Collision*[8] may be nonsense or an apt, albeit speculative recounting of how our planetary system was formed. Resolving these questions is not the publisher's responsibility. In the case of the commercial publication of books by individuals whose reputation rests on their scholarly achievements, the concerns and the responsibility still belong primarily to the scientific community. That community has ample access to publishers, commercial and scholarly, to make known its objections after publication. Martin Gardner in *Fads and Fallacies in the Name of Science*[9] has made a decent living exposing fraud and chicanery in scientific writing. In the world of politics, where the content of truth is filtered through a series of ideological propensities, it may be dangerous to insist on canons of pure truth. It is both simpler and more efficient that the public is made aware of possible biases and sentiments through the post-publication reviewing process than a denial to channels of communications in the name of truths—often little more ideological biases or dictatorial wills.

There are a variety of techniques employed by publishers in both trade and scholarly activities to reduce the probability of issuing fraudulent or plagiarized materials. They include a heavy reliance upon established authors, firmly drawn parameters of fields of interest, the much mentioned multiple referee processing of manuscripts, down to more mundane matters of insistence upon a ribbon copy and verifiable author questionnaires. While no one mechanism is foolproof, as a collection of safeguards these work relatively well. The problem is that they may work too well. The tendency of publishers to operate within well-defined limits often leads to an overconservatized view of the marketplace and a corresponding suspicion, if not breakdown, in innovation. Thus, extreme caution may have the effect of drying up the well-springs of creativity, and moreover rejecting manuscripts that may be useful to publish, albeit risk on the surface.

The present condition of scholarly journal publishing indicates how serious the problem of the overconservative approach to truth-making can become. In the social sciences at least, most journals have such finely tuned methodological criteria for publication, that the method rather than the findings, or even the theory, become central. The wide gap in style and substance between book and journal publishing in the social sciences is indicative of this gap between information and knowledge. For book publishers to adopt the same standards of rigor is to guarantee an even smaller audience base for their products than presently exists, and a choking off of an area of creative communication currently not available in the journal publications area. Tightening the screws on the truth-error continuum may have the opposite impact of drying up the innovation-convention continuum. In such an environment, to err once in a while in the publication of a manuscript may be far easier than tightening yet further the criteria of publication altogether.

Karl Marx, in an early essay "Remarks on the New Instructions to the Prussian Censors" neatly expresses the rationale behind most publishers' reluctance to censor: "Are we to understand quite simply that *truth* is what the *government ordains*? . . . Freely shall you write, but let every word be a genuflection toward the liberal censor who approves your modest, serious good judgment. Be sure that you do not lose a consciousness of humility."[10] With these mocking words, Marx made plain that the problem for democratic society is less the occasional charlatan or liar who carries off a literary swindle than the much more frequent demands by the state and, in our age, the State Publishing House, to protect the public by preventing access to controversial materials. The best safeguard against fraud is a free and untrammeled publishing network. Fail-safe systems urged by those who would make the publisher a Guardian of Truth represent a cure far worse than the disease. Truth can be guaranteed when the exclusive publisher is the Government Printing Office. But a democratic culture must be protected from that kind of perfection.

14

The Social Structure of Scholarly Communication

Perhaps the best definition to date of scholarly publishing in general, and of the university press in particular, is that recently given by Arthur Rosenthal: "A primary purpose of the university press is to function as a natural outlet for information, theory, speculation, and methodology that will influence human endeavour and enrich understanding in generations to come."[1] The problem begins with the disaggregation of these words, for increasingly, the dissemination of information and the publication of theory and speculation are performed by different structures. Further, what Rosenthal describes as university press functions are often performed by organizations and publications that are not located at universities. To say this is to recognize diversity, not to disparage attempts at definition. My purpose here is to delineate some of these gray areas, and in so doing, come to terms with the reality no less than the rhetoric of the world of scholarly communication.

The essential character of scholarly publishing harkens back to the distinction between information and knowledge made earlier in this volume. Scholarly publishing emphasizes the goals of learning rather than the mechanism of transmitting data. No one has more forcefully articulated this distinction than Morris Philipson, director of the University of Chicago Press:

> All these words which are being spread—bandied about—are concerned with the means of communication rather than the ends to be served. I submit that all of us engaged in the operations of publishing would be much better served if we concentrated more concern on our purposes or the ends and the goals of what it is we are doing than on the means, let alone the new "challenges" to those means. I submit further that the quality of what is communicated

for the purpose of advancing scholarly learning is infinitely more significant than the means by which it is "archived or retrieved." No proposition of the twentieth century is more false or self-destroying than McLuhan's silly idea that the medium is the message. The intellectual "challenge" of Plato's dialogues is the same whether preserved, and therefore available to be studied, on a scroll, in a codex, in a printed book, or on a video terminal.[2]

Such a vision is not oblivious to the variety of communication possibilities; rather, it appreciates the distinction between information and knowledge, between organization of information and filtering of ideas. This distinction must ultimately stand as the touchstone of scholarly communication, a standard that can be evaded only at the gravest peril to the concept of scholarship as such.

Scholarly publishing confronts marketplace considerations indirectly no less than directly. That is to say, the rising costs of production and the declining amounts of subvention compel scholarly publishers to seek direct support from the scholars producing the work or indirect support from agencies or institutions supporting the research to begin with. The current crunch is nicely stated by Edward H. Berman:

> The rising costs of scholarly publishing, coupled with the financial difficulties of so many universities, could require a reconceptualization of the role of publishing in tenure and promotion decisions. This could perhaps be avoided if universities were to show more cognizance of the problem than has generally been the case, and be more willing to appropriate funds to support the publication of solid academic work. Institutions that fail to provide this support will have to fend off challenges by faculty members, beset by the pressures to publish, who must divert a proportion of already inadequate incomes to professional activities from which rewards are by no means assured. Those institutions which do not succeed will face disgruntled scholars challenging the legitimacy of publication as a criterion for advancement in the academy.[3]

The problem, of course, is that such arrangements come perilously close to vanity publishing. Even if one assumes a pure division of labor between scholarly decision-making and commercial dissemination, the possibility that only those who can pay will be published means that considerations of wealth and social class may become an increasing part of the fabric of scholarly publishing. A theory of predestination is at work: if a piece of scholarly research is deemed worthy it can be published, but only if funds are available; whereas if good works cannot be paid for, then such researches will not be published. Thus it is that the Schumpeterian model, one that asserts the needs of the advanced industrial society for hard information, must come into play precisely to avoid publication based on class distinctions, or more bluntly, on the ability of some to generate funds rather than the ability of others to produce meritorious works.

The channels of scholarly publishing are varied and ubiquitous: ranging from the traditional university-based and controlled publishing arm to the entirely independent and off-campus organization that publishes scholarly works without university press committees or university subventions. Between these poles are a variety of identifiable forms that make clear the hydra-headed nature of the entity of which we talk. Some publishing companies carry prestigious university names, but operate off-campus and are responsible for making profits, and as a corollary, some privately owned publishers operate at universities and are fearful of making profits. Purity in scholarly publishing is in the eye of the beholder, but if it is to be found, it will be located in the products produced rather than the nature of the organization doing the production.

Scholarly communication involves multiple, or at least dual, "bottom lines." There is the need to sell no less than manufacture books and journals, but there is also the need to serve an elite minority of scholars and intellectual toilers who need to learn about specialized or even outrageous viewpoints that cannot readily be gleaned from purely commerical publishing publication. Scholarly communication concerns less the *type* of book produced than the *substance* of what is produced. At both "bottom lines" there are causes for embarrassment and pride. The fact that university presses contribute little to the profits and sometimes add much to the loss of the host institution is sometimes viewed as an indicator of virtue and frequently as mismanagement. Likewise, scholarly publishers are proud of the quality of the materials published, but also somewhat embarrassed over the "elitism" of such activities.

A keen insight into the tensions, the parallel bottom-lines, of university-based scholarly publishing has recently been given by Jack Miles; executive editor at the University of California Press.

> The faculty committee forces the eye of the publishing professionals away from the bottom line, not because the professors are incapable of being canny about money—far from it!—but simply because, by prior design, this bottom line is not their bottom. By this division of powers the university and ultimately the state make their

support of the university press amount to something more than a
safe berth for a sleepy crew of editors. The faculty-run editorial
committee is the mind of the academic minority mobilized on behalf of a particular class of books, and as such it presents an enormous counter-force to de Tocqueville's "tyranny of the majority,"
our distinctive, democratic form of intellectual oppression. Inevitably, however, the same division of powers introduces into the publishing decision not just the unique strengths of the professors but
also their institutional vulnerabilities and the full range of their
personal and professional biases, notable among these a reluctance
to engage in politics.[4]

Far from seeing such elitism as a negative feature, this view holds
scholarly publication to be "a desperately needed corrective to an
all-pervasive system of political censorship." University press publishing is "one among several real, if far less desperately needed, correc-
tives to a less pervasive system of economic censorship. As *samizdat*
escapes the tyranny of the people so the university press escapes the
tyranny of the market."

However, these escape hatches have quite real limits: scholarly
presses, whether based at universities or otherwise, can lose money
only within the limits of the subvention, and only for a certain length
of time. The character of scholarly publication compels more specialized efforts to reach the market rather than indifference to market
forces. These forces are circuitous, and in an expanding economy or
economy with high profit and productivity, they are rarely felt. But
those publishers who have failed, both on and off campus, can attest
that market forces remain quite real. An alternate model to the conventional "us" and "them" is Schumpeterian: to wit, both society
and economy need scholarship, need scientific publication, precisely
because such "truths" cannot readily derive from other sectors of
mass society. Thus, it is the marketplace as such that creates the economic basis of scholarly communication. It is to this economic ground
that we now turn.

How does one distinguish scholarly communication from commercial publishing? Clearly, there have always been similarities:
commercial firms have published serious books on subjects of scholarly interest, and both have sometimes published the same authors.
But increasingly, many university-press titles—cookbooks, novels,
books of poetry—might have been published by commercial houses.
Indeed, some university presses enter into joint publication with

commercial publishers in marketing and distributing books and journals. The answer in part is found elsewhere. University presses differ from the commercial in their organizational structure. As part of a university they are responsible to people for whom economic factors are not necessarily the most important. The board to which they are accountable is likely to be a group of scholars rather than stockholders. In any case, at some level, university presses are part of a world of learning that is in some respects remote from financial concerns.

Non-economic factors account for a large part of the challenge of university-press life. Making money may be a shared objective, but in scholarly communication trouble brews when poor books are published. Such trouble may result in the removal or reduction of subsidies. Trouble can also come from a failure to meet sales objectives needed to offset the cost of producing books that are qualitatively superior—or that are thought by academics to be qualitatively superior—to their commercial rivals. In short, the market operates, albeit ubiquitously, in scholarly communication.

There is no automatic correlation between the size of the university and its security or power. One can have a large university and a relatively small press, or a small university with a powerful press. Indeed, some outstanding universities have no local press to speak of. Some university presses fail, much as presses do in commercial life. What then gives special character to scholarly publishing? Horizontally, the world of scholarly publishing can be effectively divided into three areas that operate simultaneously to help create the character, the tension, and the strain within university and academic life.

First, there is what might be termed the medieval element: the prestigious or the status factor in publishing. These university press books are often attractive, often expensive to print and bind. They represent a best-foot-forward for the university in its public relations. These prestigious books are produced with the full knowledge that they may never recoup their investment directly, but they must be published in order for a university press to exist—not in commercial terms, but as an ideological or theological entity.

The imagery with which this goal is sometimes posed, service to God rather than Mammon, is indicative of the medieval characteristics, or at least pre-capitalist characteristics of the scholarly publishing enterprise. Marsh Jeanneret, former director of the University of Toronto Press, places this issue in frank terms:

University presses were invented to meet the needs of academic authors who wanted a better mechanism than commercial publishing to present new information to other researchers regardless of its saleability. In North America, at least, firms that were earnings-oriented could not be expected to treat academic writers and profitable authors evenhandedly. Nor was it practicable to modify the goal of profit-seeking enterprises simply by supplying grants-in-aid. It was unreasonable to expect any business firm to publish without the prospect of financial gain; on the other hand, why should a foundation, for example, support needed publishing if its subsidies would create private profits— Yet this happened whenever a grant-in-aid exceeded the difference between costs and revenues . . . But it would be unjust to say that commercialization led university presses to abandon their original mission; instead, most did their best to serve God and Mammon both.[5]

The difficulty with this feudal model is that books are a commodity, and as such must compete for the same readership and in the same marketplace as all other commodities, not the least commercially produced books. Thus, the scholarly book environment has had to take on the coloration of that which it presumably is not, a commercial venture. The rise of sophisticated advertising and promotional campaigns, the search for academic "stars," the forging of sound business organizations, led to both competition and simulation of the commercial publishing environment. Traditional self-imposed constraints as to what could be published by a scholarly publisher were eroded, sometimes to a point where the themes no less than contents of a work resembled the more overtly commercial product. In this way, the commercial elements became very much ingrained alongside the feudal element as a cornerstone of scholarly communication. That this became an uneasy alliance is unquestionable. Universities began seeking profits from their presses, foundations withdrew support, and scholars wanted to be treated like novelists. But the alliance persists, becoming even stronger in the current era than in earlier decades.

The capital element introduces a notion of profits not just markets. Such books, however medieval in character, must be sold by people using advanced entrepreneurial methods who are keenly aware of the fact that there are other publishers and other books. This aspect of scholarly publishing calls into play intense feelings about the kinds of books that are being published these days. As financial considerations penetrate, permeate, and percolate through the university system, the issue of whether the press should publish cookbooks, self-help books, and the like becomes very important. A university press can justify publishing a cookbook from, let us say, the People's Republic of China; but the twentieth cookbook on the list becomes significant, since it will undoubtedly push out some of the status books. Negotiations between the medieval and the capital sector help define the character of a university press list.

The emergence of the capital sector in scholarly communication does not, however, signify the demise of the feudal element. We are not describing the displacement of old regimes by new revolutionaries. First, there is the tradition of scholarly publication which is a factor unto itself. Second, there is the academic committee which reviews and judges which books should be published. These people, directly responsible (or at times responsible simply as paid referees), have a considerable predilection to publish only the best of outstanding scholarship. Their mission is defined in feudal terms, and their cogitations are carried out in cloistered settings which reinforce tradition and resist innovation for its own sake. Third, there are the consequences to the university or institutional affiliation of moving too perilously close to commercial criteria. If a series of fiscal failures can be damaging, a series of status assaults in the form of poor reviews can prove fatal. Thus, an uneasy alliance persists.

The third structural component in this social structure of scholarly communication might be called the socialist element, but in order to avoid any hint of the pejorative, or the celebratory as the case may be, we shall call this the social sector. This structural component has to do with the social psychology of people in the business of publishing. One of the attractions of publishing for many people lies in the hope it offers of escape from entrepreneurialism in its raw competitive form. And that anti-capitalistic impulse is a particularly important element in the collective character of university-press personnel and in the character of university-press publishing. University presses have many employees who, while sharing the traditional values of the university, are also in the vanguard of the population as a whole in terms of civil rights—of women, of homosexuals, of blacks and other minorities. The social component, when added to the medieval and capital components, provides another key variable in the character of university-press publishing. How these components are balanced defines the nature of the press, and often, what is published.

It is not without meaning or consequence that the publishing community, like the university environment it often serves, is considerably to the political left of the society as a whole. One might well argue that this is a fitting posture for a "vanguard" agency of intellectual life. This of course presupposes a pure isomorphism between serious ideas and left politics. In a variety of forms—from publishers' biographies to manifest statements from organizations such as the Society of Scholarly Publishing and even more, the Association of American Publishers—the dominant mode of ideology is best characized as main-line Democratic rather than main-line Republican. That this is a far cry from the nineteen-century inheritance, when publishing was a far more elitist activity, should certainly come as little surprise or shock to the *cognoscenti*. But it does raise elements of ideology and bias no less disquieting, if colored differently, than those of the distant past.

Publishing is therefore an industry in which the linkages between "economic infrastructure" and "ideological superstructure" are anything but direct. The idea that publishing is an environment in which the profit margin is the central concern misses not only the non-economic factors endemic to academic and scholarly publishing but also the deepest proclivities of the actors involved in this part of the publishing process. The "reform" of language, the widespread "purging" of sexist language could only occur in an environment where the political disposition had crystallized into an overwhelming consensus. In brief, scholarly publishing is unique not only in its organizational structure but even more substantially in its ideological proclivities. And whether one applauds or bemoans this condition, it at least deserves frank recognition as the very essence of scholarly communication in the United States.

In part, the "vanguard" position of scholarly publishing is not as eccentric as it may appear. For while the scholarly publishing world is hardly synchronous with the political persuasions of Americans as a whole, it is quite in tune with that highly select audience to which the works of scholarly publishers are addressed: academics, librarians, researchers, advanced students—in short, people whose lives are in certain respects marginal by choice from the main-line of economic alignments no less than political persuasions. The social world of scholarly publishing is a sub-culture, an environment with its own guiding universals, in which change is more impressive than order; innovation more critical than stability, and in which the revolutionary holds a fascination that can scarcely be equalled by tradition.

It is not that political conservative forces lack for publishing outlets; they have an entire panoply of periodicals, journals, and book outlets. But they are viewed, like the extreme left, as just that—extreme. The dominant culture of publishing is so automatically tied to left and liberal sentiments, that the capacity of the left to formulate its own organizational expressions in publishing, ironically enough, has been for some time quite difficult. The lists of major publishers are dotted, inundated might be better, with works on women's liberation, Marxian and socialist theory and doctrine, the condition of minorities and small nation groups, revolutionary doctrine, etc. One is less likely to find materials on business history, or heroes of commerce and industry, the social role of the police, or the values of law and order. Thus, whether looked at from the point of view of the internal organization of the scholarly community or the product output, the ideology of American publishing is clearly distinct from that of American society as a whole. Elitism becomes a left-property in publishing, whereas it is part of rightist ideology in the general rhetoric of American society.

In addition to these social structural elements, however, there are cultural components that loom quite large in scholarly communication, often larger than the structural components. First, there are regional elements. University-based presses in New Mexico and Oklahoma exhibit a strong emphasis in their lists on books on Indians and native culture generally. Indeed, nearly every university press caters to such regional concerns, and curiously enough, many have carved out a cultural market of people interested in everything from local family history to regional artifacts. Some of the smaller presses have a near-exclusive cultural emphasis, leaving to larger publishers cosmopolitan considerations or global pretensions.

Another division is areas of specialization. Scholarly publishers become known for their fields of concentration. Scholars know through the folklore of publishing itself that Oxford University Press emphasizes studies in social and intellectual history, the University of Massachusetts Press emphasizes literary criticism, M.I.T. Press is known for its varied series in urban affairs and architecture. And, because of its linkages to the Bollingen Foundation, Princeton University Press has developed an outstanding list in psychoanalysis, art history, and the foundations of religious belief. One can extend this sort of cultural specialization to nearly every publisher: Greenwood, Sage, Westview, Lexington are known as places for the publication of younger scholars and dissertations they produce in social and political science and in international relations. In such cases, ideological proclivities tend to be submerged to area of concentration considerations.

Some major houses, with relatively large resources and the support of big foundations and universities (sometimes working in conjunction) do tend to publish across-the-board, that is in all areas of a university's strength. Thus, houses like Chicago, Harvard, and California publish in biological and psychological sciences, Oxford (England) publishes widely in everything from mathematics to theology. These major presses clearly dominate the field of scholarly communication. But their very omnibus characteristics, i.e., their range, permit small publishers to fit into the interstices. Large networks also tend to have large budgets and large obligations, sometimes making the more dangerous or esoteric book the risky book to publish. In short, the larger these houses are, the closer they come to simulating the problems of large commercial establishments.

Thus, we have a horizontal (social structural) and vertical (cultural) pair of axes to contend with when disaggregating the character and decision-making capacities of scholarly communication. Clearly, the tilt in commercial publication is sales; just as clearly, the tilt in scholarly publishing is status. It is not that such concerns are diametrically opposed. All publications, book and journal, scholarly and commercial strive to achieve a synergy and symmetry. But the fine tuning of distinctions is precisely what this subject is about. Even if we confine ourselves to the question of reviews, certain differences become apparent.

The commercial publisher will look for big reviews in *Time, Newsweek,* or *Fortune,* or, as is more likely, in the pages of the *New York Times Book Review.* The academic publisher derives its payoff from positive comments in the leading journals and review media of each particular technical or scientific specialization. The commercial house will seek to place its authors on television and radio talk shows, while the scholarly house will try to synchronize its efforts with the appearance of its authors on major plenary addresses at professional meetings. It is not that either cluster of publishers would spurn acceptance in the bailiwick of the other. Rather it is a clear-cut recognition that there are bailiwicks to begin with. And that these constitute macro and micro markets and audiences that are served and serviced in distinct ways by different publishers.

Scholarly communication has been subject to a set of contradictory pressures to create organizational forms that will give shape to its professional substance. But thus far, this has retulted more in balkanization than unification. There is the American Association of University Publishers, embracing the 80-odd members considered to be university based. There is the Society of Scholarly Publishing, embracing a plethora of organization and professional groups from the American Geophysical Union to the National Parks Association, each of whom has a publication arm, sometimes equal in size and outreach to the university press group. And there is the Professional and Scientific Publications division of the Association of American Publishers. Add to that a variety of smaller international groups organized around firms doing business in the multinational arena, and one witnesses a networking of scholarly communication that is at once sizeable and uneasy with respect to boundaries.

Scholarly communication, in its own way, replicates the demands for specialization that characterize professional life at the end of the twentieth century, and a contrasting set of demands for some sort of integrated framework that can permit unified action on basic concerns such as postal rates, copyright clearing-house functions, and piracy questions.[6] That the two sets of desires do not always mesh is hardly news. More newsworthy is the emergence of professional commonalities and intellectually unifying threads that have been virtually absent until this point. With the emergence of journals such as *Scholarly Publishing* and *Book Research Quarterly,* not to mention the growing number of books on books, what was once an accidental profession entered into by gentlemen and gentleladies is rapidly becoming a professional entity with a sense of core and periphery to match the publications per se. The professionalization of scholarly communication constitutes a revolutionary development unto itself; with what consequence we have yet to see.

But we are at least far enough along the way to detect some new trends: a higher standard of competence at all levels of management; a realization on the part of universities and institutions of learning generally that scholarly publishing is a major criteria for advancement and promotion, and finally, the heightened awareness that scholarly publishing is the quintessential mechanism for the maintenance and promotion of democratic culture—not as a formal expression of democratic beliefs so much as a plural existence of institutional outlets. So it has come to pass that what started one hundred years ago as an accoutrement of university life has now become the essence of professional association and definition.

What constitutes the strength of scholarly communication is the plurality of interests and themes among scholarly people. Because the publishing world in the West does not have ideological unanimity, and the political system does not determine every phase of the publishing programs, scholarly publications have become a crucial ingredient of democracy. Clearly, the university press must be realistic about economic factors in order to survive. But scholarly communicators must also be aware of the dangers that result from an overemphasis on commercial factors. There are roles that scholarship and its publishing vehicles can accomplish in free societies that are simply not feasible in totalitarian societies. Precisely because scholarly communication is largely beyond national policy debates it is a foundation of cultural democracy. The ultimate value of the medieval, capital, and social factors, and of cultural and organizational vectors, what makes them work, is their coexistence. In their cacophonous diversity the scholarly presses represent an essential element for the survival and expansion of democracy.

15

Social Science as Scholarly Communication

One difficulty in measuring the social science component in scholarly publishing is the way in which statistics are gathered and maintained. For example, social science sometimes falls within the rubric of technical, scientific, and medical publishing—a category of activity which can be viewed as the creation of books to satisfy the continuing educational needs of the practicing professional after he or she has completed the use of textbooks. Within this category are to be found physical, biological, geological sciences, as well as technology, engineering, and the omnipresent social sciences.[1] Books like *Human Sexual Response* by Masters and Johnson are published as medical works but could just as easily be issued by a social science publisher. Likewise, a popularization of the Masters and Johnson technique for sexual fufillment, *Surrogate Wife,* published under a pseudonym, is released as a mass paperback. Thus, along with the rise of narrow specialization, there is also the emergence of extraordinary ambiguity within the publishing community as to which categories or rubrics such specialized works belong—in marketing no less than production terms. The need for record-keeping rather than real-world concepts often dictates the categories to which books are consigned.

Raw numbers tell strange tales. On one hand, the total number of books listed in the "sociology and economics" category for the years 1982–84 indicates that out of an average total of 51,000 titles published in the United States, approximately 8,000 fall into this broad, omnibus category. It is more than twice that of juveniles and medicine and science—the three runner-up categories. And yet when one turns from gross figures of titles to mass-market paperbacks, the same category dwindles to 45 out of 3,800, or 1.18 percent.[2] Social science publishing, other than the text market, is aimed at the professional librarian and scholar. It produces many titles in small press runs, and operates in a narrow intellectual environment where sales of more than 1,000 copies are good, and sales of 5,000 are considered extraordinary.

It is further necessary to place social science books and journals in a larger context of sales statistics for the book industry as a whole. Data compel modesty. The social sciences scarcely figure in trade, religious, mail order, book club, mass-market paperbacks, and other dominant industry-wide categories. Social science books do figure prominently in university and scholarly presses, college texts, and somewhat less in professional books. This already signifies a social science publishing universe of approximately 20 percent of the total range of bookselling activities. Now within this smaller pie, the combined totals of sociology, anthropology, political science, psychology, and economics—the five basic fields—constitute roughly 17 percent of domestic net sales in the textbook area and 15.5 percent in the area of professional books.[3] Again, a further subdivision is in order, since the sociology portion of these sales is 3.4 percent in the college-text field, while in the area of professional book sales, the numbers and percentages are so minuscule that they are lumped together with "other social sciences" to form 8.3 percent of the relatively modest dollar amount in professional titles.

Upon close inspection, what has been observed and recorded for the 1975–85 period is a pattern of broad stability with some moderately downward tendencies in the last years, reflecting declining enrollments in graduate centers of an area called social science that represents optimally 1 percent of the total book sales in the United States. This is not intended to minimize the importance of the subject matter at hand, but rather to indicate the strict market segmentation involved. Qualitative as well as quantitative measures indicate that such books are purchased for research and policy guidelines in contrast to those purchased for sheer entertainment. This confirms a broad pattern of a restricted market share.

Even if we are talking of a 1 percent sales factor, we are still dealing with a one-hundred-million-dollar area of activity in the United States alone. This constitutes a remarkable form of growth from a starting point at the turn of the century, when such a field of publication as "sociology and economics" did not even exist, at least not in statistically significant sales terms. Finally, the thousands of books and hundreds of journals appearing annually in sociology, economics, psychology, political science, and anthropology warrant serious scrutiny as a measurement of the changing cultural impact of professional and scientific disciplines. It is important to maintain a careful balance between the big picture of publishing as a multimillion-dollar communications industry and the intimate but infinitely smaller picture of professional social-science publishing.

At the same time, and to prevent a constant oscillation between these opposite magnitudes, one must retain a clear appreciation of the mediating role of a significant portion of social science publications. They provide an interface between what might be called the "pluralistic culture" of the academic community and the "class culture" of a broader community based upon market segmentation and segregation.[4] The level and degree of calibration is of exceptional importance. The role of major social scientific books, monographs, and reports cannot be reduced to a narrow, purely commercial vision of sales and profits. Many of the final research products of social scientists land on the office desks of political and administrative elites—of national, state, and local policy and decision-makers, bureaucrats involved in testing, evaluation, and measurement as a way of life. To such a specialized network of critical communities, to the "new class" of bureaucratic intellectuals (or, if one prefers, intellectual bureaucrats), social science publishing is a critical pivot in the performance of their central tasks. Add to this the normal, that is, traditional, purposes of social science publishing, its role in achieving academic positions and securing tenure, and one can readily perceive that interrelations between social science and scholarly communication are a critical, if sadly neglected, area of social research. Publishing remains a central measure of professional achievement in American social science, and in turn, social science remains a central source of scholarly publishing.

The dissemination of social science information comes in two essential forms: books and journals. Indeed, there are a number of intermediary forms extending from popular format magazines to video cassettes to internally prepared monographs. But still, it remains the case that one-time book publication and a serial journal publication represent the principal modes for delivering most social-science efforts. The differences between media forms and how they impact the world of social science dissemination of ideas would itself provide a major research activity. But the main thrust of these remarks, while remaining fully sensitive to differences between forms of presentation of materials, aims at understanding the overall pattern and framework of social science publication. There are enough commonalities within the social sciences to permit a tactical waiver on the finer nuances amongst them.

Still, one should take note of several new trends that deserve at least cursory examination, since they form part of future research tasks: the growth of annuals or serial publications which often serve to bridge journal article and book-length investigations. These annual reviews often retain a sense of big issues while remaining alert to the methodological emphasis of the periodical literature. The annuals are a response to the rapid expansion of subfields of specialization. The second area of significant trend is the extraordinary multiplication of journals in areas that formerly merited an article in an organizational journal or an occasional book. Third, there is the growth of regional publications that serve as filtering agents for tenure and permanent appointments as much as sources of scientific innovation. Fourth, there is the emergence of publishing research reports, which operate quite beyond the traditional book or journal markets.[5]

Differences between social science publishing in book form and journal form do exist. Quite simply, book publishing in social science has reached a plateau and has even shown downward tendencies; some major firms have either discontinued or severely cut back their sociology programs, for example. On the other hand, journal publishing has continued to expand. From a purely economic standpoint, both books and journals have shown what Fritz Machlup has referred to as a "sick" pattern: increase in cash flow derived almost exclusively from higher prices, and an excessive increase in numbers of titles and journals published.[6] At the same time, the units sold of books and journals have decreased markedly. This is partially a result of the sheer specialization of social research and, in addition, new computerized services that provide copies of articles on demand speedily and at modest expense.[7] These by now well-known and frequently documented economic conditions do not, however, have the expected deterrent effect on growth, since more than market conditions are at stake.

These non-market conditions are critical in establishing variations between book and journal sales. Books are often underwritten by market conditions, for whether commercial or scholarly presses are involved, a strong entrepreneurial incentive is clearly in evidence. But the journal area is often under the control of professional associations, regional societies, research agencies, and so on, that serve to offset marketing considerations. Journals come to serve interest group or regional functions. Many social science journals reflect pressure groups, such as Latin American or Middle Eastern associations. Not that these are poor quality journals; indeed, because of access to powerful resources and top-flight academic talent, they are often superior to so-called strictly academic periodicals. Other journals reflect ideological standpoints: from socialist to conservative impulses, again such journals may carry first-rate social research, but their sponsorship, from the American Enterprise Institute to the Union of Radical Political Economists, signifies a pattern of evolution more linked to organizational imperatives than individual purchasing habits.

Most recently, journals have begun to mushroom on a regional or sectional basis. These have traditionally existed, for example, *Social Forces, Social Science Quarterly,* and *The Journal of Politics,* but they have expanded considerably under the impact of the tenure system which, far from crumbling, has expanded in recent years. To service criteria of "scholarly publication," regional associations have begun sponsoring regional journals, which become a touchstone for hiring practices in the academic community. Publication in a regional journal, or an organizationally sponsored agency, may not "count" for much in an Ivy League situation, but in the 2000 + universities and colleges who have come to accept hiring and tenure-track practices of the higher learning at face value, such sectional journals serve as an acceptable *bona fide*—certainly superior to vanity press book options that existed in an earlier period, since some sort of referee system in these regional journals is in evidence. What this again indicates is that social science publications are not constrained by general market conditions; they have clearly demarcated guidelines that emerge out of the inner requisites of the discipline of social science and the vagaries of academic employment.

Another indication of this differential response is that books strongly reveal classical concerns for good writing, broad themes, and a macroscopic and cross-disciplinary relevance. Whereas journal publication tends to be increasingly specialized, emphasizing methodological niceties, sharply delineated theses, and a strong sense of a narrow, cross-sectional reading of a particular problem. In part, this distinction reflects the difference, mentioned above, between books published by independent agencies and journals published by trade or professional associations. To be sure, some journals are dedicated to broad issues and qualitative analysis, while some books appear in specialized formats and under series imprints dedicated to quantitative studies. However, it is fair to say that, in the 1980s, the form of publication has been subject to increasingly stylized responses by professional social researchers.

If social science publishing, whether in the book, monograph, or journal areas, were exclusively a function of the economic marketplace—that is to say, uniquely tied to individual tastes and preferences—there would be far fewer such products available. Whether by direction or indirection, by membership in an organization, agency subvention, or university support, monographs on the social sciences are underwritten and produced on the basis of a presumed transeconomic necessity. That necessity may be related to specific areas of knowledge decision-making. Social indicators may be representative of an area of information deemed vital to national security, such as terrorism or conflict resolution; or simply related to a need to measure potentials for tenuring younger people in areas of the country or institutions below Ivy League standards. In short, the reasons why books or journals expand in social science, even as professional memberships decline or become stagnant, are as varied as the vocabulary of motives itself. There is hardly a simply one-to-one ratio between scientific input and economic outlay.

Once this distinction between an economic market and an academic milieu is properly digested, it adds a major component left out of much discussion of commercial or strictly profit-making publications. The free force of market supply and demand may ultimately operate to curb or delimit social science publishing. However, it is an ultimate equilibrium which is a long way from effecting present realities. Public planning economies recognize quite frankly the need for public support of scientific endeavors—including applied social science. But private sector economies have a more difficult time to both conceptualize and implement a "social good" beyond the economic calling itself. In part, commercial viability remains the vague hope of many working and writing social scientists; in equal part, the fact of subventions that underwrite many publishing programs strongly smacks of vanity publishing. And within the academy "vanity" is a word which ranks on a draconian scale second only to plagiarism. Yet, unless the existence of non-market forces involved in social science publishing is acknowledged, the range and extent of this area of publishing will be profoundly misunderstood and undervalued.

What begins as an innocent adventure in search of the relation of social science research to social science publication quickly becomes entangled in a web of commercial, political, and technical considerations that takes us far beyond our simplified starting point. Perhaps this is what makes the subject at hand so fascinating: social scientific publishing immediately raises fundamental issues about the organization of the academy, the processes of communicating ideas, and the constraints of the marketplace. The sheer attempt to disaggregate and distinguish these different parts of the puzzle moves us also into areas as wide-ranging as class stratification and personal stress. Scholarly publishing is not only a specific industry; no less it is a microcosm of social aspirations. Scholarly publishing in social science reveals a strange mixture of different types, people drawn from capitalist bastions of sales force to anti-capitalist centers of learning, from flinty accountants who deal in units of sales to professors who deal far more readily in bruised egos. The book and/or periodical is often the most central encounter between the higher academics and the middle echelons of business. Little wonder that the academic publishing of social science is a subject which until recently was hardly considered fit for public consumption.

Many editors and most authors come either from academic or editorial backgrounds. As a consequence, directing a publication is, at first glance at least, a shocking experience. Such chores have little to do with anything such scholarly types have previously experienced. There exist few training procedures, or formal categories that correspond with university or editorial situations. A publication recently released by the Association of American Publishers, has described the publishing industry as "the accidental profession." One could scarcely find a more apt description of what social scientists in the publishing world are all about. The truth of this situation is vouchsafed by the fact that nearly every journal or book also represents an editorial idea or an organizational imperative, or some combination of the two. Few social scientists have had backgrounds in the concrete tasks of publishing. For the most part, scholars are at universities that rarely even offer courses on the kind of activities that occupy social scientists centrally on a daily basis. This gap between an editorial ideal and a technical chore is an anomaly that is at the basis of the continuing tensions between a marketplace imagery of most publishers and an intellectual faith characteristic of most social scientists.

A complex dilemma for social science scholars functioning as journal editors or book authors is their strong proclivity toward anti-establishment values and belief systems. In some measures at least, the latent purpose of many journals and scholarly books is a belief that much is wrong with the present society, and that technical, exact research can, in some small way, right inherited wrongs. Yet, when these books and journals enter the marketplace, the problems confronting them become acute. The "bourgeois" system represented by the commercial market rears its hydra-head, and compels an embarrassing realization: at a technical level, putting out a publication is not qualitatively different from marketing any other product. The same considerations of audience size, product enhancement, design and layout, soft sells, customer servicing, and so on, exist in publishing as in the manufacture of steel—to distinguish the product from all others, service a clientele on time and with precision, and—lo and behold—pay invoices and meet all sorts of omnipresent commercial obligations.

What starts as a rebellion of revolutionary innocence against a guilty society ends as an understanding that innocence and guilt are accoutrements that live in uneasy partnership in scholarly publication. However, moral language does not necessarily describe the processes by which books and magazines are put together and promoted. Those who fail to understand the delicate thread between critiquing a system and living through one soon fall by the wayside; or they are left without copyright ownership and editorial control of their own creations—wondering in fear and trembling at their own weakness and society's draconian strength.

As a result of books and journals, social scientists are accidendentally involved in the education, training, and recruiting of an industry called publishing. Social analysts and researchers are very much a part of this industry: not only as authors, but as editors, reviewers, and even owners of publishing programs. Indeed, a primary justification of elevating these discussions to a central consideration resides precisely in righting this inherited wrong; that is, in converting accident into necessity, and providing a balanced view of what social science as a quasi-commercial product is really about. Even if most social scientists do not necessarily make a living from publishing, it is important to understand how and at what levels social scientists connect up with a printed world of scholars, partisans, and interested users.

The easiest tasks are those connected with pre-publication: gathering and preparing manuscripts for publication. The toughest tasks are connected with post-publication: the proper printing, binding, shipping, followed by careful marketing, advertising, and promotion, which in turn, require accurate subscription fulfillment, file maintenance, and billing to avoid complaints. Even in farming out these technical tasks each publisher must make serious choices about the costs for such services and the benefits yielded. Each publication comes with particular strengths and weaknesses: of personnel, organizational linkages, professional competence. That is why the services required to manufacture books and periodicals must be disaggregated and treated in a distinctive, non-mechanistic way.

The hope for conglomerates and consortia in social science publishing derives from the fact that very few publications could survive as an isolated entity, and fewer still could achieve sustained growth. Costs and services are too high, and revenues are too low. For most journals or book programs, amalgamation is not an abstract idea, but the basis of survival. Social scientists had to innovate or run the serious possibility of failing to reach their potential or actual audience. Personnel costs are too high; editorial costs are too high; printing bills are too high. Some were suddenly informed by a home university or professional association that the honor of housing a specialized publication was no longer sufficiently worthwhile to merit the expenditure of general university funds. At the other end of the spectrum, a granting agency gave the charge of starting a publication without either funds for marketing or talent for editing such mandated publication. What brings social scientists together in the publishing arena is therefore a common need to survive and an uncommon disposition to learn new skills that make survival possible.

A seemingly paradoxical situation obtains when one contrasts the problem of publication in book and journal forms. Simply put: the book area in general is undergoing a profound case of monopolization, whereas the journal area is undergoing an equally exaggerated movement toward pluralization and multiplication. The book area, for example, shows strong linkages not only toward monopolization within the field through mergers between publishers, for example, the absorption of Prentice-Hall by Simon & Schuster; but also vertical monopolization between paperback houses (such as Avon, Dell, Fawcett, New American Library), hardcover affiliates (such as Random House, Holt, Rinehart & Winston, Harcourt Brace Jovanovich), and conglomerate parent firms (such as RSA, IFI International, MCA, Gulf & Western, and CBS).[8] The situation in the scholarly magazine field is considerably different, with new journals springing up to meet quite detailed scholarly interests. What were formerly considered topics for occasional articles are now seen as fit subjects for journals, for example, *Agribusiness, Computers and the Social Sciences, International Journal of Terrorism; Teaching Sociology; Youth and Society;* and *Public Budgeting and Finance,* among others.

However, in certain crucial respects, the general condition of publishing is in marked contrast to the specific character of social science publishing. To fill the void of monopolizing tendencies and soaring costs to major publishing firms, a host of new and aggressive publishing programs has come into being, specifically aimed at servicing an exacting social-science market. In addition, university presses and scholarly presses are increasingly finding social science volumes entirely suitable for their programs. At the same time, the very multiplication of journals has led to the rise of consortia, often attached to university presses and sometimes to privately owned scholarly concerns; these provide either ownership or management services to new and/or struggling periodicals. Meanwhile, professional organizations of social scientists and social researchers themselves have spawned a series of new journals for members. Hence, sociologists or political scientists in the United States received as a benefit of membership a plethora of periodicals, everything from newspapers and newsletters to trade monthlies and scholarly quarterlies. The emergence of pluralization in professional products has given rise to a new industry: the consortium or press affiliate designed to handle issues and problems in small book and journal publications.

Even representatives of the Authors' Guild are aware of the inevitable trend toward amalgamation, consortia, and cooperation. As Alan U. Schwartz recently observed: "Given the cost and interdependence of our society, it is naïve to think that publishing can survive without a certain amount of economic unification. Combined printing, production, distribution and even selling operations will have to be encouraged if the publishing community as such is to survive."[9] If one examines the *Literary Market Place* and notes that among Chicago, Sage, Transaction, and Pergamon, more than 100 scholarly periodicals are represented in the social sciences, some idea of how far and deep this trend toward interdependence has evolved becomes evident. The real threat facing publishers and authors alike may not be internal monopolization but rather the increasing domination of the publishing industry by richer and more powerful communications media with an insatiable appetite for that multimedia creation called product. Thus it is the specific character of the arrangements and agreements entered into rather than any general concern over monopoly that increasingly has come center stage in social science publishing interests.

Earlier in this chapter, emphasis has been placed on critical discontinuities between the publishing industry in general and social science publishing in particular. It is also important to take proper note of basic continuities between the general and specific. Social science publishing is still part of the publishing industry in general; and however special the nuances may be, long-run secular trends do reveal strong linkages that also deserve to be placed in a larger context.

There has been a general decline in the average per capita dollars spent on books and periodicals of all kinds. The proportion of family expenditures that went for reading materials declined from a not very munificent sum of 0.9 percent in 1967 to 0.6 percent in 1977. According to a special report on family spending habits, conducted by the Bureau of Labor Statistics, the average household expenditure on books and periodicals is between $55 and $75 per annum.[10] This provides some idea of the limited amount of money being spent in this area of publishing. This decline is partially disguised by rising living standards and inflated dollar values. Yet the steep 33 percent decline reflects itself all down the line. Inflation and the great expenditure of the household on necessities rather than peripheral wants ramify throughout the publishing industry. Magazines can be borrowed, read in libraries, or simply deferred for another occasion—a far cry from food and shelter requirements. Yet, it remains the case that scholarly publishing, because it is often insulated from swift changes in economic fortunes, tends to be countercyclical, i.e., may do well even as the overall economy does poorly.

There can be no question that marketing to individuals of social science works in cloth has virtually dissolved. The same tendencies in purchasing books generally can be observed in social science monographs. Clothbound editions are small, anywhere from 500 to 2,000 copies, and library and institutional purchasers rather than individual scholars are those serviced. Paperback sales have shown some increases in volume, but also sharp decreases in profitability. Without classroom adoption and educational bulk orders, paperback costs and prices would soon soar and again serve to freeze out a buying population of any great size. The limited nature of social science publications, in sharp contrast to mass paperbacks, means that costs of production remain high. This is reflected in the rapidly inflated nature of paperback prices. Within two decades, the average retail price has gone from $1.95 to $4.95 to $7.95 on most items. Further, since many readers of social science books and journals are academics, with easy access to good core libraries and even better reproduction equipment, specific chapters or articles can be photocopied (not infrequently by defraying costs to the universities or colleges) rather than volumes purchased or subscriptions renewed. General market trends, far from being uniformly reversed, can be exaggerated in the world of social science publication.

Another area of sharp decline is in certain ancillary-subsidiary rights and sales. There are fall-offs in classroom orders, bulk sales, and income from secondary republication rights for readers and/or anthologies. This is in part due to the new copyright technology.[11] "Instant" books and readers, on-demand publishing, and information retrieval services are easily available to the academic and professional communities. There exists a plethora of reproducing equipment that makes it just as convenient to go to the local photocopying office as it is to prepare a reader or make purchases that require an expenditure of money. These ancillary-subsidiary sales have resulted in a huge new industry called "on-demand publishing." This activity (pioneered by University Microfilms International), in bypassing orignial publication sources, or providing insignificant royalty fees to authors and publishers of record, takes away classroom and subsidiary and ancillary sales. For example, an area of substantial subsidiary revenue in the past, classroom copy adoptions, has just about vanished for most journals and periodicals in the social sciences. This means a fall-off in revenues at the same time that there has been an increase in usage of articles from social science sources. New copyright legislation and technological screening devices may alleviate this state of affairs, but not in the foreseeable future, and certainly not as long as librarians and publishers are cajoling each other rather than making joint representation to the manufacturers of reproducing equipment.

The decline of library subscriptions to technical periodicals of all sorts has also led to serious problems: a decline in unit sales of books and, if past evidence is any indication, subscriptions to journals, which are even harder hit. As a result of budget restraints, overall library sales dropped 28 percent between 1974 and 1981.[12] The most obvious way to reduce costs is to eliminate book sales, or avoid new journal orders. There is a direct linkage here with the new technology. There exist library networks, online computer services, for entire city-wide and now state-wide systems. For the entire state of Ohio, only one copy of a periodical is needed. Within twenty-four hours, any article can be rotated to 258 participating libraries.[13] This means that of 258 potential subscriber units 257 do not require a subscription. This is the challenge brought about by the new reproducing equipment. Couple this decline in institutional and library budgets with a huge increase in available publications, and the magnitude of the problem can be gleaned. For example, if a comparison is made between Ulrich's *International Periodicals Directory* 1969–70 edition with the edition a decade later of 1977–78, one finds more than a doubling in scientific literature published in one decade, and a trebling in social science literature within the same time period. Illustrative of this situation is that a majority of periodicals in sociology and political science are less than fifteen years old. The number of new magazines started in 1975–77 alone was up 30 percent over the previous totals. A total of 334 publications were started in 1976 as against 254 in 1975. And the majority of these new periodical starts were in the broad area of consumer and social interest.[14] Each publication is therefore itself part of a syndrome of an expanding informational base taking place at a time which is witnessing a precipitous decline in the marketability of social-scientific and public-interest periodicals; and for that matter, in the membership rolls of some main line social science organizations.

It might well be the case that the new technology provides new access for social science information. Certainly, the growing acceptability of intermediary forms of delivering information—such as typescript manuscripts bound in spiral looseleaf form, on-demand anthology programs, and facsimile editions of dissertations—provides several such indicators. But the effects of this new technology on the structure of publishing have powerful short-run effects. We are only now beginning to realize that the structure of social science itself is involved. For example, the extreme specialization of newly emerging journals may be a function of declining professional reading markets, no less than an ideological or intellectual strategy within social science. If the purpose of publication is to vouchsafe scholarly merit, a work which is referred by peers, then the print run or salability of a given title becomes virtually irrelevant. These are at least some areas worthy of further exploration.

There is little purpose in ignoring general tendencies in communication, or fabricating beliefs that social scientific publications are unaffected by events. I have cited only a few of the more pertinent indicators that affect the life of professional publications and, indirectly, professional standing. While decreased circulation figures become an industry-wide norm in certain "basic" areas, other "applied" areas (such as health and environment) show patterns of growth. But whatever fluctuations exist in the types of social research being produced and published, the increases occurring in the costs of book and journal production are seemingly as constant as inflation itself. Over the past several years, and despite the most imaginative kind of management innovations, publishing has witnessed an increase in basic, non-reducible costs. These increases are taking place at a point of increased competition from other publications, higher postal services which affect every part of our collective effort, and declining university enrollments in the social sciences. Beyond these more obvious forms of accelerated increases are those new methods of research and design that also increase editorial and production costs. Articles with a simple and straightforward text have become the exception rather than the rule. Every publication now has charts, tables, graphs, special notation systems, photographs, line drawings, and so on—in other words, a plethora of items that increase cost. These hidden costs of doing business are increasing at the same time that basic costs continue on an upward spiral.

In carefully monitoring continuities between publication in social science and publishing in general, I have singled out areas of recurring problems. Many social scientists and publishers have understood the practical problems of survival. But there are deeper strains, more difficult to isolate, and hence to overcome. I should now like to address these.

Above all, we share a common need to appreciate more urgently the product-nature and sales-nature of journals and books. There should be a greater emphasis on marketing and advertising social science publications before rather than after materials are placed on sale. There is a strong tendency to give away the product manufactured as a public relations device; and failing that, the product, that is, the book or journal, is itself considered to be the marketing device or promotional piece. In place of generating and developing an overall conceptual program, copies of the publication are simply given away randomly. Unless there is a specific target population in mind for a specific periodical or monograph, it is, in my opinion, a colossal mistake to give away to some the same product intended for sale to others. General Motors does not give away a Cadillac to convince consumers that such a vehicle is a car that one should buy.

What corporations do, and quite properly, is create an undertow of marketing interest that makes consumers want to go out and make the necessary purchase. In publishing, because of the relatively low initial unit cost, social scientists in particular have developed a peculiar habit of self-destructive celebration by giving away their creative products, often forgetting how negatively we as consumers react to items received without charge and unsolicited.

As a consequence of high initial unit costs, publishers are not interested in developing a counter-tendency and a counter-flow: specifically of not giving away the book or journal, unless by so doing, a definite marketing advantage can be ascertained. To continue giving away mechanically that which so many people work so hard to produce, and at such high costs, is clearly poor business and probably poor scholarship. Beyond purely commercial concerns, the give-away raises the specter that what social scientists produce is ideology or propaganda rather than the best information and ideas available. The moral of this tale has now begun to dawn on even the most obtuse, cash-rich publishers: do not lightly give away that unique product which is being offered for sale.

Survival and growth is the alpha and omega of the information industry: the marketing of ideas is not the same as packaging a product. Free periodicals should be viewed with the same suspicion as free lunches: the burden of the costs is simply shifted from scholar to student, schnorer to buyer. If the purpose of social science information is simply to convince the uninitiated, or lobby for a cause, the rationale for giving away is self-evident. But if the purpose is distributing vital information or specialized ideas, then evaluating (and recovering) the costs of manufacture becomes a reasonable goal. The play of market forces, while not necessarily the only item for consideration, is at least one central element in assessing a book or a journal.

There is seemingly lack of awareness and sensitivity on the part of the social sciences, to what other publications in allied fields are accomplishing in terms of editorial content, technical innovation, and printing processes. Editorial myopia is natural enough given the limited time of each person and the anarchy of production. Social scientists are led to think almost exclusively of their own publication; and editors and publishers show similar limitations of focus. As a consequence, neither social scientists nor scholarly publishers are properly geared up to recognize the multiple journals or books in related or cognate fields.

Books and journals in the social sciences face keen competition. The plethora of publications which characterizes a pluralistic society, indicating who is buying, printing, and editorializing about what, is fully in evidence in the United States and Europe. Competitive journals inform us about the qualities periodicals possess or lack, not only in technical matters of layout, format, and design, but editorial leadership and changing readership needs and composition. Competing books on the same subject are not anathema or necessarily redundant, but alternative visions of a particular field. To be sure, distinguishing pluralism from multiplied waste itself becomes a contentious issue dividing social scientists from scholarly publishers.

The need to appraise properly social science ranking in publishing terms is central to scholarly publishing. Criteria for such rankings are clear enough: for journals, they are subscriber base, advertising revenues, renewals, levels, and article submissions. For books, they are volume of sales, citations, reviews, number of editions and translations, and continuity of demand over time. The problem is how to convert a decent editorial product into a readable volume, or at least one that is read. Social science and public interest books and journals are partly a business. At the risk of inviting scorn, publishing (at times) is even a modest growth industry. Rank ordering is not only desirable but necessary. Too often, the medieval backdrop of the academic environment disguises the intensity of extant competition. In political science and sociology alone there are now close to one hundred periodicals published in the United States and Canada. This is a remarkably big market for the buyers. Suppliers, i.e., writers of articles, are abundant, whereas data users and idea buyers are quite limited.

Technical publications operate in a highly competitive market and, despite handicaps, competition is likely to increase for the balance of the century. In terms of start-up costs for the physical product, book and magazine publishing are the least expensive. The possibilities of beginning a new automobile corporation are virtually nil, but in a new research field an issue of a social science publication can be marketed for less than the cost of one new automobile (or even less than the funds required for a basic marketing brochure), so the possibilities of accelerated competition are just about infinite.

It is the relative scarcity, or at least finite limits, of scholarly and literary talent rather than cost factors in production that keeps some sort of lid on book and journal publication multipliers. This is not to suggest that competition is intrinsically evil. The emergence of new journals or the flow of new book titles indicates the existence of hitherto untapped markets. Such growth may also indicate an audience size and potential not properly thought through by any single publisher. New publications are excellent sources of cross-fertilization, at the level of marketing as well as of scientific ideas. In an admittedly finite market situation, to ignore competition, to dismiss rival viewpoints, or to disregard new periodicals is to ensure a dangerous and perilous course. This is a problem which only individual publishers and journal editors can properly evaluate. And they can do so by paying strict attention to the new intellectual currents within the social research environment.

There is a powerful tendency among social scientists to emphasize editorial leadership at the risk of dismissing reader wants—put more bluntly, to assume the existence of a perfect isomorphism between contributors and readers is to guarantee a very small audience. Too often, editors are motivated by a guiding idea or ideology that they believe is not being met by other publishing programs. Rarely, however, do technical periodicals or scholarly publishers in social science seriously inquire whether an actual audience exists, or is currently being satisfied. Scarcely any journal can boast of having an updated readership survey, or using survey tools often advocated for others. What features of any particular periodical are most appreciated, most widely read, easily remembered, or quickly forgotten? What articles are often cited, or rarely referred to, or quickly passed over? Which book titles are translated? Which merit reprinting or new edition? Library surveys reveal that some journals and books produced are not so much read as being received as part of a membership program. If this is the case, the question of the worth of the publication certainly takes on added urgency for all concerned.

The style or form in which books and articles are published is often crucial to the success of a publication. Social science publications are often seen in purely functional terms. In this regard function comes to signify the absence of stylistic or physical accoutrements. As a result, such publications provide a service for those who write the articles rather than for those who read them. In some instances, editors assume a perfect isomorphism between writers and readers, thus condemning from the outset audience size to minuscule figures. Books and journals which exist to provide prima facie evidence for a tenure ruling by a promotion committee have already reversed reality tests: emphasizing the writers' needs at the expense of readers'. Beyond even this dangerous notion is the further assumption that a publication has no worth over and above the constituencies presumably being serviced.

It is a profound mistake to think that, because readers are specialists, their general needs can be perpetually ignored with impunity. The true requirement is to find out what specialized readers want, what they require, and what they are not getting from other publications, without ignoring larger themes and disciplinary cross-overs. This is the best way to preserve the integrity of each social science and strengthen the relative position of a publishing effort. Otherwise, in addition to fiscal shortfalls, books and journals will run the inevitable risk of ideological special pleading, the tendency of editorial management to substitute its own proclivities for the judgment of specialized readers, and its own restricted sense of values for that of the audience for which the book or journal is intended.

There are times when editorial prerequisites demand policy decisions which may risk readership loyalties. But at least, each publisher and editor should know the depth, or lack thereof, of these loyalties. In this regard, communication between authors and editors, and the specific universe serviced by the particular social science, would assist in converting subjective pulse feelings into an objective appreciation of an actual readership profile; something still carried on in a remarkably cavalier fashion.

I should like to conclude from the Association of American Publishers' report cited at the outset on publishing as an "accidental profession": this time, to provide a general philosophic perspective which I believe social scientists and scholarly publishers share concerning what is in its absence a shared enterprise:

> It is important, even urgent, that we look again at the medium in which we work, and at those with whom we work and whom we intend to reach. Because it is important, possibly urgent, that we concern ourselves not only with the education of our audiences but with education of those of us who will publish for them. What they learn—or do not—about publishing; whether they come into publishing, or never think of it, will have a great deal to do with what books are available, authors published, readers reached, houses prosper. Because in a world of underdeveloped, overdeveloped, and underassisted and overreaching peoples, the people of the book—its creators, consumers, and purveyors—matter. Stand for something. Should represent something special. Like the book itself, more is expected of the people of the book.[15]

Much of this chapter has emphasized forebodings and difficulties ahead. But one should be careful not to understate the enormous achievement registered by book and journal publishing in the social sciences as a whole. In addition to growth in volume and sales for most categories of social science books and journals is the vast improvement of format, layout, and design. Beyond that, direct advertising, subscription fulfillment, and customer service have all been dramatically expanded. Most recently, and under the impact of economic exigencies, the idea of sharing technical services and staffs has proven its worth beyond a shadow of a doubt. The contribution of cooperative efforts between social science and book and journal publishing is the best evidence of its value to the world of scholarly communication.

The openness with which the communications network promotes interaction without monopolization is the surest guarantor of the continued integrity of social research. The shared values and mutuality of interests between social scientists and scholarly publishers provide the best climate for the continuing survival and maturation of both a viable publishing program and a democratically rooted social science.

16

Experts, Audiences, and Publics

In this final chapter, I shall take certain liberties denied to me in the rest of the book. A last chapter carries with it a notion of entitlement, of freedom to speak plainly, that might be intrusive elsewhere. Here I shall draw upon experience no less than evidence to defend the notion that communicating ideas is a multi-layered activity technically, and more importantly, a multileveled activity ideologically. Communicating ideas confronts us with a plethora of "bottom lines," some of which relate to product management, others to market orientation, and still others to normative judgments of good and evil.

Social science publishing operates within parameters set by American capitalism. The social system is the context within which social science survives. These conditions are not a curse but a challenge. In a country like the United States there are essential contradictions. However, these are mediated by considerations of the nature of the social system no less than of the social sciences. The nature of that economic entity called the free market is in fact what publishers learn to live with every day, even if they are socialist presses aiming at the overthrow of the very marketplace within which they operate.

Scholarly communication is linked to a mature capitalism, and also to a mass media within that structure. Thus the dissemination no less than the creation of ideas is influenced by an information environment that increasingly insists upon speed, accuracy, and skill in dissemination and retrieval of information and ideas, and shows impatience with words or language that fail to offer gratification or pragmatic results. Thus the market for scholarly publication is aided and abetted by the larger information environment, but frustrated by the limits of such an information environment.

The core social-science market in the United States is approximately 200,000 to 250,000. While this estimate is probably a trifle low, the secondary market for popular social science would number about ten times that amount, or about 2 to 2.5 million. I base that estimate on the readership of magazines such as *Psychology Today, The Atlantic, Harper's, The New Republic,* and *National Review.* This market of 2.5 million is probably the largest potential buying public of social science outside the communist world (even if one considers Marxism as a social science). The likelihood is that the United States has the largest audience potential, or actualized potential, for social science literature in the undiluted, prosaic sense of the term social science.

In the socialist countries, where social scientists of necessity strongly identify with Marxism-Leninism, definitions or statements of the character of social science are wrapped up with economic issues. In the United States there is a powerful identification of social science with psychological issues of a very intense sort. Neo-Freudian, self-help approaches to social science are often viewed as modern ways toward personal salvation. The people who read *Psychology Today,* whatever else they get from the magazine, expect to receive help for their personal problems, even as they are wrapped in public issues.

The therapeutic potential of social science is terribly important to American buyers or users of social science products. This is especially the case for the peripheral market, that group beyond the core group of 250,000. In American life, if one excludes the portion of the market interested primarily in self-help, a potential audience of 2 million to 2.5 million shrinks right back down to that core of 200,000 to 250,000. The ideological challenge for social science communicators is to move beyond information and into learning, knowledge, and values. The conversion of intellectual self-help into a vision of the world, or a view of how the world operates beyond personal therapy, is a major challenge to those involved with communicating social research findings.

Another contradiction confronts social research communicators: on one hand social science is well covered in the media, yet on the other hand, in relation to mass media, the specialized social science media are quite small. That is to say, not only are the social sciences a small part of scholarly publishing, but that they are an even smaller segment of publishing in general. If social science publications compare themselves with mass media publications such as *Time, Newsweek,* or *Fortune,* or any of the monthlies, they are scarcely in competition, much less at the forefront. The minimal participation of social scientists in the delivery of their products to a communications market can be seen as a high order problem in helping set national or international agendas.

In the United Kingdom social science operates within a much smaller total population. But because of the social policy tradition, social research remains a powerful factor in publishing. Social research publications can be purchased along with other weeklies on the newsstands; social research has the active support of political party intellectuals. Although the United Kingdom has the edge in having a reading culture, this in no way minimizes the achievement of social science communication in Great Britain, where, proportionately, it reaches a much larger audience than its counterpart in America. Social science involves a network of beneficiaries and recipients of the data and findings, but turned around and looked at in another more inclusive mirror, social science is a small fish in a substantial communications pond.

Many sectors of the mass media area in the United States have similar kinds of problems, i.e., of dilution of professional influence coupled with popular expansion, and they feel them keenly and acutely. Popular media publish summaries of basic social science, but the social sciences also seek an innovative role in their own right. How do the social sciences currently meet such problems? Or better, how do intermediary publications within social research come to terms with the double bind of being a big fish in a small pond and a small fish in a big pond? Those who are in an intermediary position are also mediating periodicals. Social science calibrates in two directions: toward the mass media and toward scholarly confirmation.

The number of journal subscribers may be uniquely important to its revenue, but not necessarily to its calibrating effect. For example, *Society* ran an article a few years ago on the Philadelphia prison system. It formed the basis of a 20-minute segment on a program on CBS-TV that was watched by approximately 25 million people. On the basis of the original article, the social researchers had an impact of considerable dimension beyond the *Society* subscriber base. The transportation and incarceration of prisoners in Philadelphia were modernized and humanized on the basis of this exposure. This itself led to all kinds of action nationwide on the rights of those picked up and taken into custody by officers of law-enforcement agencies.

This scale of impact is still rare in social research. Where there is a meliorative possibility social research findings tend to calibrate widely; where the possibilities are non-meliorative social science tends not to calibrate widely.[1] An important characteristic of social science is its potential for initiating change despite a relatively small constituency. Here the word *media* should be taken in its exact sense. The task of social science publications is not uniquely to deliver the goods to readers or to publics but rather to deliver messages to other publishing organs and agencies. Social research rarely tries to deliver directly the informational yield to large masses, but instead tries to deliver that yield to other media, to calibrate widely, throwing stones in a pool of water with the hope they will make wider and wider ripples. This is a sound metaphor because it preserves social scientists from arrogance and conceit; it gives this group a realistic estimate of what can really be done, without at the same time being unduly discouraging or self-defeating.

One important function of such mediating publications is rarely talked about, but is of great importance. Mediating publications have an impact both on and for the professional side of social science. Specialized monographs or journals selling in numbers of 500 or 1,000 copies may reach far larger audiences in popular versions, summaries, reprints in larger media, and so on. Thus, scholarly communications are filtering devices by means of which elites transmit important findings and opinions to masses. In turn, the mass media challenge such elite publications to improve formats, modernize typefaces, and simplify language in presenting ideas, thereby providing a constant spur to scholarly publications to look alive, to sharpen up, to have a better kind of presentation of self, and perhaps to reach wider audiences. The aesthetic or physical functions are extremely important too. If one examines the transformation of scholarly products since the end of World War Two, it will be plain just how wide the influence has been. We tend to look at how specialized journals help mediating publications without appreciating how popular organs affect specialized journals. Many technical publications have developed new formats to reflect the more aggressive search for markets and customer satisfaction that have been longstanding in commercial publishing.

This is a healthy development. It is a recognition that people read specialist materials, even if institutions usually buy them. There may be a wider audience for technical journals than we imagine from limited circulation bases. The source of this audience is ubiquitous. *Time,* with its Behavior section, helps stimulate an interest in scholarly work. This mutually reinforcing relationship of interests is exceedingly important in broadening the social science constituency. Without it, scholarly communication would become dangerously circular—locked into a closed network in which readers and researchers are always and only one and the same set of people.

The popular media and mass publication can be seen as training grounds for future social scientists. They pose the moral concerns which feed the sociological imagination, but which may not always be realized in the classroom or in the everyday practice of a social science discipline. Their role is that of missionary, helping people to understand that the social sciences perform a unique role in the area of social analysis; a role important not only for the semi-professional or lay groups but for pre-professional constituencies who are career-oriented but not yet served by professional relationships or technical literature. It is absurd to think that a young person is going to be influenced to enter professional life by reading professional books or journals. Such materials are simply too inhibiting and make imposing assumptions of linguistic familiarity. Thus mass communications periodicals perform a very important function, and they will do so increasingly as the contents of social science research become more specialized and even more removed from everyday accessibility.

Mass communication also serves the scholars by familiarizing them with developments in allied fields. The Science section of the *New York Times* is avidly read by scientists. The proliferation of information is such that a political scientist cannot read every journal of sociology, and a psychologist cannot read every journal of political science. Mediating publications serve a post-professional constituency no less than a pre-professional constituency. This transfer of knowledge is also a mediating function.

Let me turn from general purpose considerations to a more detailed examination of the more pedestrian aspects of communication: promotion, marketing, fulfillment, and reaching an audience in general. Most concerns in this area are prosaic, but complicated, in nature. They have to do with mailing and franking privileges; they have to do with promotion budgets; they have to do with finding new audiences.

Advanced nations have special problems deriving from capital intensivity, and other nations, where labor intensity is still viable, have other kinds of problems. In some countries, mass publications are still hand-bound and shipped by slow-moving surface mail. In the United States and the United Kingdom, it is financially impossible to have people hand-wrap magazines and send them out, or provide manual billing. How does a labor-intensive society work with a capital-intensive society at the level of computer mechanization and rapid information retrieval? How do we generate a uniform source of data that will match information needs with human ability to use the data? These actual and hypothetical concerns are sufficiently complicated within one nation, but in a communications environment still largely limited to hard-copy materials, they appear almost insurmountable. For example, many people do not receive their foreign journal subscriptions regularly. At this prosaic level of marketing, distributing, and computerizing information, we move into an area that cannot be managed by calls for democracy, free speech, or a uniform information order.

The simple case of socialist nations, with their subsidized periodicals, and free market economies that do not have direct subsidization (at least not to the same extent), reveals the organizational and fiscal complexities involved in comparing scholarly communication across social systems. Even within systems, sharp distinctions arise. Profit-making and not-for-profit organizations are subject to different rules and regulations. Even philanthropical agencies concerned with the social sciences have legal constraints and charters which prohibit support not only to minimally private enterprise organizations but also to agencies that fall outside the mission of the granting agency.

Business problems are of extreme importance and cannot be dismissed in a cavalier way simply because one defines a mission in noble, scientific, or value-neutral terms. But scholarly communication is not simply part of a magazine business, media business, or printing business. There is a business entity, a world called the "social sciences," that requires distribution and communication. Its message is delivered in whatever ways are possible: audio or video cassettes for people who are doing classroom assignment; film for those going to movie houses; magazines and books for those who prefer the printed word; cable-television for regional use in remote area. Whether in book, film, or cassette form, one delivers the informational goods that exist, no less than an ideology based on that information. In short, the social science environment is larger than the social sciences. Scholarly communication is at the heart of that environment.

Social research findings are not restricted to any one level of sophistication or any one kind of information system. The rise of specialization means that decisions about the form of delivery, and the amount delivered, must take into consideration the exact nature

of *both* the product and the marketplace. In short, commercial considerations force a re-examination of social science as itself a nego-
tiable commodity at many levels. Social science has its own laws,
dynamics, traditions, and values. But to have meaning it must be
delivered and understood in whatever formats are available. One does
not put square pegs in round holes. Journals, books, magazines, cassettes, and films all have their own inner dynamics, their own inner
requisites. But each has to be harnessed as a means to an end for
social science. Publishers are generally locked into one kind of activity: magazine publishing, a professional association's journals, book
publishing. We have to get to the *idea* of communication itself, if we
are to deliver the social science message to the market in its multiplicity of forms and formats.

This raises an ancillary but important point. If social science
is itself an ideology, it has its own requisites. These involve scientific
norms that are based upon internationalization rather than national-
ization, evidence rather than emotion, an entire series of presuppositions and presumptions that are fundamental to the conduct of
science. The main point here is that historicism, functionalism, or-
ganicism, and so on, may be part of social science, but not the other
way around. Ideologies that presume to study human behavior are
part of a plethora of things known in their collectivity as the social
sciences. The priority of science over obscurantism is the essential
battleground of all modern social science. Social science has to perceive itself as an embattled ideology, or it will perish. In short, reason
itself is embattled—and not just a quiescent add-on to the madness
of everyday life.[2]

Social science does not survive to serve the interests of political
systems, networks, or ideologies. Nor does it expand by disguising
its mission behind other frameworks. Social science has a unique and
sometimes dangerous role to play. There are many political systems
in which social science has perished, sometimes permanently. The
delivery of the social science message, while performed by elites, is
after all a populist message intended to have remedial impact upon
anonymous and ordinary people. Social research fastens on what they
think, what they feel, what they do, why they live, how they die—a
series of messages in fact central to democratic life. The form in
which the message is delivered is only a single component. Whether
a technical monograph or a mediating periodical is involved is not
of primary concern. What does matter is the idea of social science
itself. It must be allowed to live, be permitted to flourish. That can

only be accomplished by the most vigorous collective pursuit of truth across national boundaries as well as within the nation, and by attention to every possible detail of how the *ideals* as well as the *ideas* of social science are transmitted.

The ideology of a political system always deals with ideas in survival terms. Social science must accomplish nothing short of that. Social research must be able to match idea for idea, and inculcate commitment for commitment. The marketplace becomes the place in which the values of social science, in relation to other ideological systems, must be fought out. If the social sciences perish, it should not be for lack of effort. The key aspect of all social science is communication, whilst its own partisanship is science. This unique blend of communication and orientation makes the social sciences a special force in the contemporary world.

Social scientists do not lack the virtues that other people possess. Nor are they more heroic than those in other professions. Rather, they have such a strong urge to separate fact and value at the methodological level, so powerfully dualistic in their distinction between citizen roles and scientific roles, that they often become inhibited and enfeebled as public figures. As a result they have internationalized dualism as the essential fuel to maintain their professional identities.

The notion that social science stands apart from citizen activity or political participation is very strongly held. The problem for social science in the United States extends beyond scholarly communication. It involves bridging the gap between science and politics. It is almost impossible to get the social science community to take responsibility for their recommendations. This is a consequence of philosophic dualism. Current issues of wide importance take a great deal of time to get sifted and filtered into the professional literature. The ideology of social science is not just a notion of rationalizing and humanizing collective behavior, but also a profound sentiment that there is an unbridgable gap between what exists and what should exist. The management of that dualism is serious for those concerned with and involved in the broad dissemination of social science findings and theories. For it is in dissemination that these dualisms tend to dissolve.

The number of individuals who read and the amount of reading done has to be divided and subtracted by other entertainment media and other forms of learning. For example, television is a powerful and time-consuming medium. It is difficult, but not impossible, to look at television and read a technical professional journal at the same time. This is a good reason to maintain a fluid notion of social science delivery systems. What first appears as a magazine article may filter into the network of social science users differentially. For example, the same article may be delivered in preliminary form to a professional society, then published as a scholarly essay, then be transformed into a popular magazine, finally to be made part of an anthology. Admittedly, there are limits to how far and how wide any one article may calibrate. The further away one gets from the printed word, the more difficult it is to capture the theoretical aspects of ideas. But the great chain of being is also a great interlocking network.

Visual images are more concrete. But it is exactly this effort to fuse and link the written word with the oral tradition that makes the multimedia approach so central, and at the same time so exciting, a prospect for the social sciences. The academic tradition still dominates the social sciences, and this tradition places an extremely high premium on the written word. The mass communications tradition, much newer and less secure, places an equally high priority on the spoken word and upon visual images. The creation of new linkages between these two traditions becomes both a task for social science and a problem in social sciences analysis of mass culture.

The notion of multiplicity and media is important. The small technical journal is a place where only specialized kinds of information get sifted and sorted. A magazine is not superior or broader than a technical journal nor is a book somehow inferior or superior; status concerns notwithstanding, they all function in different ways to satisfy different kinds of audiences. What one witnesses is the same cluster of scholars writing at different levels of technical sophistication and different sets of assumptions concerning evidence. Thus, the area of scientific communication witnesses a multiplicity of forms but by the same cluster of scholars.

At what point can notions of fastidiousness, care, exactitude, be employed as a shield against public responsibility? There is no ready answer to the question, every publication has to work it out for itself. People perform multiple roles, which is one reason why one cannot answer certain questions categorically.

To what extent does social science permeate the larger world, the public debate on major issues, and to what extent do social scientists take it upon themselves to comment on those public issues? This extent determines degrees of responsibility and involves the risk of public criticism. Within the American culture the same people who lay claim to fastidiousness, under the cover of social science, and who are no doubt entitled to it, feel quite free once they play their other role, to jettison all sense of fastidiousness. Sometimes such people lose their common sense entirely. When a citizenship role is performed, a certain amount of fastidiousness is also called for.

The general public does not have a critical role toward information, but an accepting one. Consequently if a person identified as a professional economist makes a political statement, he or she is utilizing legitimacy as a scholar to tell the listener or reader in positive terms, "Do thou likewise." Somewhere along the line an illicit jump has been made. Nobody is contesting the obligation to be careful in research or take an extra six months to perform such chores. Rather, those who are fastidious ought to take an equal amount of care in their public, non-professional pronouncements. That is not always the case, certainly within the context of American social science.

Part of the conservative climate of academic life arises from Luddite refusals to adapt to new modes of technology. The University of Chicago and the University of Michigan have microfiche and microfilm programs that can deliver a dissertation instantaneously, unabridged, and perfectly well. The interesting question is whether an academic community will accept this as a legitimate form of publication. Can one write in a curriculum vitae that one's work is on microfiche, and will academics invest a very minimal sum to buy the machinery necessary to retool themselves to read from a different kind of screen, i.e., from a source document? There are very complicated cultural and economic questions here but if one wants to transmit information quickly, this can now be done quite rapidly. At the moment, there is no reward network to pay off for such screen-delivered information. But this is a slightly different question than the potential for dissemination no less than communication.

We still do not have a sociology of the printed word. For example, it is no accident that elite periodicals adopt to mass journal models. We sense, even if we don't know, that the distinction between an aristocratic audience and a mass audience can be overcome only in certain ways. The printed word itself changes. A British publication originally put out by the Fabian Society under the name *Empire* endured for forty years. For another ten years it was known as *Ventura,* then it finally evolved into *Third World.* Interestingly too, under the impact of having to internationalize, this journal had to break its old format, which was a narrow, small one, and had to adapt to an international format, generally changing the character of the printed world itself. One of the things that we must understand is the relationship between the processing of information and the form in which it is delivered. There is still no social science treatise on the nature of composition and printing as it affects this kind of process, and yet it is vital to the notion of the worth of the printed word.

I would like to conclude this chapter and this volume by offering five recommendations for the integration or at least interfacing of experts, audiences, and publics. The first is the establishment of an international commission or committee for diversity of the press, promotion of the social science press, and guardianship of intellectual freedoms in the area of social sciences. We have such a committee in the United States called the Committee on the Diversity of the Press, the purpose of which is to keep alive the flame of liberty in the area of scholarly communication. It is very much within the charter of both the United Nations and the United States to extend the libertarian spirit in the area of the social science press and to act as watchdog or guardian for any abridgment or any impingement upon the right to untrammeled communication and dissemination of ideas and information. This is an alpha and omega of any discussion about the nature of social science.

The second recommendation is to encourage the diversity of languages served by international scientific publications. While English is clearly now the language of science, the foreign language sections of publications should be expanded and there should be a strong commitment to the idea that all scholarly publications, whatever their language of origin, contain summaries in the other major languages so that journals can be made more international in a much simpler way than the process of translation, which is very difficult and often not warranted by low volume outreach. At the same time, nations must understand that translation involves openness in ideas, and correspondingly, a reduction in secrecy and control.

The third point I would make is for greater international exchange at the level of marketing, at the level of advertising, of standardization of computer information on subscribers so that publishers and professionals may begin to build on one another's databases. It would be quite conceivable, for example, without any exchange of currencies, to institute highly useful commercial list exchanges on a barter basis, and in that way develop strong international ties through the promotional activities which each periodical or set of periodicals undertakes in their own self-interest. Likewise, advertising exchanges should be more systematic to draw attention to other publications so that appropriate audiences can be reached in a more effective manner. Some kind of clearinghouse network would be an extremely useful device in advertising as in intellectual materials.

The fourth venture that I personally would like to see and that again one would hope could be sponsored by an international publishing agency is the development of an international bibliographical data bank of specific bibliographic information on specific research areas, so that the information can be input and retrieved very quickly. If one wanted to find what materials are available in all languages about agrarian reform in Algeria, there should be an information retrieval network that would allow us to obtain such data. We already have several services in different languages along such lines, but we need a central clearinghouse for information in the area of social science. What we have now suffers from the anarchy of the marketplace—and the meanness of ideology. For example, little information comes out of China or Eastern Europe except that which is translated by machine technology. A serious imbalance between inflow and outflow occurs. Only about 2 percent of all available material from the Soviet Union gets translated. We therefore need a central clearinghouse; it is theoretically possible; it is currently prohibitively expensive.[4] There is enough hardware but not enough organizational will in OECD or at UNESCO, or any of the central international agencies, to commit the resources needed to create that kind of network of information input and information retrieval. When we talk about exchange across national lines we ought to think more in terms of information retrieval than personal travel. This would be a more modest but at the same time more realizable goal with respect to accessing foreign cultures.

My final and fifth point is probably the most difficult and the most painful one for it concerns the development of mechanisms of financial or fiscal support for scholarly publications perhaps on a pro rata basis, perhaps on a neediest-first basis. Thus, for example, the development in Africa of social science journals which has already begun would be supported by a mechanism or subsidy to the extent that their contents went beyond purely national considerations. Perhaps direct international fiscal support to national ventures is impossible, but one would hope that some mechanism of support for those publications which already exist could be found, especially for new journals, new ideas, and new forms of presentation of media, particularly in the developing areas. But in exchange for such support must come a guarantee of untrammeled research, and assurance of safe passage for the researcher.

Dialogue takes place not only between the North and South, i.e., advanced nations and the less-developed nations, but within the advanced nations themselves. Certainly within the United States, there is a struggle among social scientists on such questions. There really is no U.S. social science posture throughout the world. That might have been conceivable in the 1950s, but not in the 1980s. The mechanism of an international ideology broke down somewhere along with the end of hegemony. What we have now is a plethora of pluralism, very similar to what is going on in the political process of the West as such. There is the Cologne school, the Frankfurt school, and various other schools of thought, representing very different postures and frames and opinion and reference in one science after another.

It is important not to overlook the inner history of the social sciences and how they evolved in relation to more general considerations. One tends to ignore that inner history and identify the course of social science with the course of empire. But this creates an extraordinary and dangerous deformation of reality. Disintegrations occur throughout the entire world. The same process is under way in the Soviet Union, where there are Parsonian factions, for example, survey research of the Lazarsfeld type, phenomenological work at Leningrad, more orthodox and other types of factions at Kiev. Thus even within the context of a totalitarian environment there are tendencies of differentiation that must be taken into account if we are to get a feeling for the realities of social research as well as scholarly communication throughout the world.

Underground (*samizdat*) publications in the social sciences are quite important, and they too must be factored into the scholarly communication network. The point is not to ignore these essential communication structures of the social sciences in relation to the overall history of a given science. We must not get into the habit of thinking that every social scientist necessarily reflects or speaks on behalf of dominant political trends. Very often, in point of fact, dominant social science trends are forged in opposition to the main political currents and tendencies of a nation. In short, it is not always the case that trends and tendencies within the social sciences represent a mirror image of tendencies within the national structure. To think thusly is a form of vulgar Marxism, which is dangerous and also pernicious because it transforms everyone who writes or speaks into a representative of the nation, whether or not that person wants to be, or whether in fact there even are views in their home countries that can be represented in a monolithic way. A mark of democratic culture is precisely the right to appear at a gathering to represent one's own personal views and not a prefabricated national consensus.

The tragedy in the present situation, certainly in the Third World, is that very often just as the inner history of a social science unfolds, political circumstances arise which frustrate the effectiveness of the communication of its results. In some countries, the expulsion of social scientists and the decimation of a social science tradition has taken place, making a shambles of the national tradition and forcing many scholars into exile. This is a problem which social scientists must begin to face with greater candor. What do we do, for example, when there is a coup in a country which deeply affects the social science community and its institutions? How do we develop a sense of international community across national boundaries? These are serious matters for which we need a proper forum.

There are struggles in every nation, problems of exiled social scientists and those under attack. We would better serve our own constituency in our own community if we abandoned the largely desultory assumption that at all stages the external factor or the dependency variable is the only one that really counts. Although I do not believe external factors are insignificant, the good fight has to be fought by social scientists within their home countries, within the cosmopolitan centers, no less than in the peripheral areas. The methodological canons of scholarship as such permit a kind of community; were that not so, there would be no possibility of communication.

For example, the entire Chinese situation can be considered within a social science framework. Whoever handles areas like language reform, urban sprawl, population concentration, is in some sense functioning as a social scientist. Under such conditions that literature created elsewhere in the world will in fact be used by the Chinese to make policy, to bring about reforms that society deems essential in character. The social science done by Walt Rostow on modernization, for example, may be more useful to the Chinese than that done by Paul Baran on colonialism. A majority might think that the Parsonian framework is better than the Marxian framework for studying social systems. There are non-ideological components to the research process. Certain types of social analysis or social research may appear conservative merely by virtue of dominance but may not be conservative in any other sense.

There are two points hidden in this digression: one, that the body of world social science may be used in China, and parenthetically, that the Chinese experience can be viewed as a social science experiment. The very complicated, empirical, and analytical problem of figuring out which social science is better may not be answerable by ideological criteria. It may be answerable by much more prosaic criteria, such as experimental veracity and empirical verification. The problem of evidence always remains. It is much too comforting and much too pleasant to think that because we are morally pure we are also empirically right. The history of social science proves that many immoral people have a lot to say empirically, while nice people may be lacking in intellectual worth. This is not necessarily a correlation that one likes, but it is widespread.

Scholarly communication suffers from different kinds of problems, from those of success as much as those of failure. The appropriate revolution cannot necessarily be found in international agencies or outside traditional publishing networks. Arrangements have to be thought out organizationally in every country. At some point, one is dealing with organizational networks, not with individual preferences, although whoever is head of an organization, whatever their sentiments might be ideologically, becomes a representative person. But networking ideas must begin at a much more fundamental level. That is one reason why a meeting of those who edit periodicals may be very useful but limiting; a meeting of forty or fifty editors may not even begin to cover the field.

There is a need to communicate successful and unsuccessful models of social science intervention. This is in fact an ongoing activity of many people, but models of social science interventions which are successful involve a consensualist social situation to begin with. There can be successful application only when there is fundamental agreement on goals within a society. Otherwise a successful intervention might lead to much less enthusiasm about the success; or even a kind of negative sentiment. Some research projects come under assault, not because they are unsuccessful, but rather quite successful in instituting techniques that serve special interests. Thus the degree of success is not the only determinant in the institutionalization of social science. What may be a more critical variable is the existence within a society of a consensus about what needs to be done. That may be why we have much less success in domestic research than in overseas research.

In the area of foreign affairs, there is substantial agreement about the goals. What is at stake is not the validity of the social science methodology or enterprise, but rather the moral purpose of science. That is why the distinction between the social scientist and the social engineer is blurred. If there were no normative structures, distinctions could be made easily and would have already been institutionalized. Even in the United States, where social engineering is esteemed, it has not institutionalized itself. For example, we do not have a clear discipline of social policy-making as an academic subject. We do not have a policy science in the 1980s even though Lasswell announced it in the 1950s precisely because of the intervention of ethical concepts that prevent the notion of policy science from being carried out unilaterally, in the absence of a shared cluster of interests and values.

Social research is bought and sold by individuals. When one points to the political process, one may as well point to the theological process; the point of reference is always extrapolated from place or time. Revolutionary theorists would maintain it is not a task for social scientists, but for broad masses, for the political process. In our culture, we refer to the political process in modest terms when we make appeals beyond the framework of the social scientists. The very fact that we are driven to that means, that we cannot have a dualism between the social scientist and the social engineer without surrendering the critical faculty or the critical capacity, is presumptively inherent in the training of all social scientists. Because if there is a division or a dualism along that line, the critical capacity of a social scientist will be forfeited, the possibility of asking questions about the limits of policy itself would be forfeited, and that might make the solution more dangerous than the existing problem.

We have admittedly come far afield from a simple discussion of the management of social science information. If the scope outweighs the coping mechanisms, then at least some sense of the magnitude of the issues involved in experts reaching audiences and publics can be gauged. Scholarly communication does not exist in a vacuum, but in the context of larger national goals and international pretensions. Every international book fair, every translation of a journal or book, every trip by a dissident author to a foreign land, reveals as much.

Partisanship is part of the fabric of publishing. Shocking as it may seem, so too is partisanship built into the system of social research. The question is complex because one must address the matter of partisanship to what and to whom, no less than publishing for what ends and what people. In the crucible of this mixture, the politics of scholarship and the economics of publishing meet—not so much in deadly opposition as in the uneasy alliance to maintain and extend the open society.

Notes

1. Valuational Presuppositions of the New Technology

1. Irving Louis Horowitz, "Engineering and Sociological Perspectives on Development: Interdisciplinary Constraints and Social Forecasting," *International Social Science Journal*, vol. 21, no. 4 (1969), pp. 545–556.

2. Joseph Weizenbaum, *Computer Power and Human Reason: From Judgment to Calculation* (London: Penguin Books, 1984) with a new Preface.

3. Norbert Wiener, *Human Use of Human Beings: Cybernetics and Society* (New York: Avon Books, 1967).

4. Robert Jastrow, "The War Against 'Star Wars,' *Commentary*. vol. 78, no. 6 (Dec. 1984), pp. 19–25; and James E. Katz, *People in Space: Policy Perspectives for a 'Star Wars' Century*. (New Brunswick and Oxford: Transaction Publishers, 1985).

5. Sean MacBride, "The Cause of Liberty," in *The Right To Communicate: A New Human Right*, edited by Desmond Fisher and L. S. Harms (Dublin, Ireland: Boole Press, 1983), pp. xv–xxvi.

6. Iuri Kolossov, "The Right To Communicate in International Law," in *The Right To Communicate*, pp. 112–19.

7. *From Gutenberg to Telidon: A White Paper on Copyright*, by Judy Erola and Francis Fox. (Ottawa, Ontario, Canada: Government of Canada, Department of Communications, 1984), 117 pp.

8. Herbert I. Schiller, "Information: A Shrinking Resource," *The Nation*, vol. 241, no. 22 (Dec. 28-Jan. 4, 1985–86), pp. 708–10. For a more technical, but similar, standpoint, see John M. Hoar, "The Politics of Information: Libraries and Online Retrieval Systems," *Library Journal* (Feb. 1, 1986), pp. 40–43.

2. New Technologies, Scientific Information, and Democratic Choice

1. Jay Scholl, "The Videotext Revolution," *Barron's National Business and Financial Weekly*, vol. 62, no. 31 (2 Aug. 1982), pp. 6–8; and Martin Mayer, "Coming Fast: Services Through the TV Set," *Fortune*, vol. 14 (Nov. 1983), pp. 83–92.

2. Tom Forester, "Introduction" to *The Information Technology Revolution* (Cambridge: The MIT Press, 1985), pp. xiii–xiv.

3. Pierre J. Vinken, *Information Economy, Government and Society* (London: European Information Providers Association, 1982).

4. Wilson P. Dizard, *The Coming Information Age* (New York: Longman Publishers, 1982); and Tom Stonier, *The Wealth of Information* (London and New York: Methuen, 1983).

5. Ursula Barry, ed., *Proceedings of EEC Conference on the Information Society* (Dublin: National Board for Science and Technology, 1982). See especially, Nicholas Garnham, "The Information Society Is Also a Class Society."

6. I emphasize *Western* Marxists, since in fact the Soviet Union has moved rapidly into the new technology. Journals such as *Journal of Computer and Systems Sciences* (now in its twenty-third year) and *Automatic Control: Essential Serials in Electronics and Cybernetics* (now in its seventeenth year) have made the transition to the present without much concern for critical Marxian interests. Both journals are available in English through Scripta-Technica, Silver Spring, Maryland—a subsidiary of John Wiley & Sons, Inc.

7. Dan Lacey, "Publishing and the New Technology," *Books, Libraries and Electronics: Essays on the Future of Written Communications*. Foreword by Carol A. Nermeyer (White Plains, N.Y.: Knowledge Industry Publications, 1982), p. 85.

8. Bernard Berelson and Morris Janowitz, eds., *Reader in Public Opinion and Communication*, rev. ed. (New York: The Free Press of Glencoe, 1953), especially pp. 309–16, 469–82.

9. John Senders, "The Electronic Journal of the Future," *The American Sociologist*, vol. 11, no. 2 (1976), pp. 160–64; and Lauren H. Seiler and Joseph Raben, "The Electronic Journal," Transaction/SOCIETY, vol. 18, no. 6 (Sept./Oct. 1981), pp. 76–83.

10. George B. deHuszar, ed., *The Intellectuals: A Controversial Portrait* (New York: The Free Press of Glencoe, 1960), especially pp. 477–532.

11. Bernard Rosenberg and David Manning, eds., *Mass Culture Revisited* (New York: Van Nostrand Reinhold, 1971), especially pp. 3–21.

12. In this connection, the papers by C. Wright Mills on "The Cultural Apparatus" delivered initially as BBC lectures in the 1959–60 period, deserve special commendation. See *Power, Politics and People: The Collected Essays of C. Wright Mills,* edited by Irving Louis Horowitz (New York and London: Oxford University Press, 1963), pp. 405–22.

13. One of the curious byproducts of this information explosion is the growth of "hard copy" books and magazines. *Satellite Orbit,* for example, now has the size and appearance of a Sears Roebuck catalogue. Thus, in this area, as in the field of computer publications, the growth in new areas of information create expansion, not retraction, in older forms of printed communication.

14. F. Wilfrid Lancaster, *Libraries and Librarians in an Age of Electronics* (Arlington: Information Resources Press, 1982), pp. 199–203.

15. Lewis A. Coser, Charles Kadushin, and Walter W. Powell, *Book: The Culture and Commerce of Publishing* (New York: Basic Books, 1982); also Manfred Stanley, "Marketing as a Liberal Art," *Scholarly Publishing,* vol. 13, no. 4 (July 1982), pp. 293–308; and most recently, Walter W. Powell, *Getting into Print: The Decision-Making Process in Scholarly Publishing* (Chicago: The University of Chicago Press, 1985).

16. Juan Rada, *The Impact of Microelectronics.* Geneva: The International Labor Organization, 1980; and Juan Rada, "Information Technology and the Third World", in *The Information Technology Revolution,* edited by Tom Forester (Cambridge: The MIT Press, 1985), pp. 571–89.

17. Victor Rosenberg, "Information Policies of Developing Countries: The Case of Brazil," *Journal of the American Society of Information Science,* vol. 33, no. 4 (July 1982), pp. 203–7.

18. Irving Louis Horowitz, "Corporate Ghosts in the Photocopying Machine," *Scholarly Publishing,* vol. 12, no. 3 (July 1981), pp. 299–304; and Irving Louis Horowitz with Mary E. Curtis, "The Impact of Technology on Scholarly Publishing," *Scholarly Publishing,* vol. 13, no. 3 (April 1982), pp. 211–28.

19. Dorothy Nelkin, "Intellectual Property: The Control of Scientific Information," *Science,* vol. 216 (May 1982), pp. 702–8.

20. See William J. Broad, "Journals: Fearing the Electronic Future," *Science,* vol. 216, whole no. 4549 (28 May 1982), pp. 964–68; and responses by Benjamin Lewin, Joseph Raben, Lauren H. Seiler, and Charles M. Goldstein under the title "Electronic Publication," *Science,* vol. 217, whole no. 4559 (6 Aug. 1982), pp. 482, 484.

21. David L. Altheide, "Keyboarding as a Social Form," *Computers and the Social Sciences,* vol. 1, no. 2 (April-June 1985), pp. 97–106.

22. Brent D. Ruben, Josephine R. Holtz, and Janice K. Hanson, "Communications Systems, Technology, and Culture," in *Communications and the Future* (Bethesda, Md.: World Future Society, 1982), pp. 255–266. Howard F. Didsbury, Jr., ed.

3. Technological Impacts on Scholarly Publishing

1. Such discussions often appear in trade periodicals. For examples, see Frank Romano, "All Together Now: Standarization Helps Publishers Benefit from Photocomposition Technology," *Book and Magazine Production* (Sept. 1981), pp. 43–45 and "Demand Printing Could Provide Economical Reprints, Monographs," Management Update, *Folio,* p. 4.

2. "The extraordinary capabilities of information machines has tended to obscure the impact such machines are having on the very fabric of our economy-society . . ." *The Information Resource: Policies-Background-Issues,* edited by Forest Woody Horton (Washington, D.C.: Information Industry Association, 1979), p. 1.

3. Susan Wagner, "New Copyright Law Primer," *Publishers Weekly* (26 Dec. 1977), pp. 37–42.

4. "The emergence of electronic publication does not resolve the confrontation between the First Amendment and its strong belief in the free use and exercise of information and statutory provisions for fair use under copyright protection. To be sure, such electronic transmission of copyrighted data and images, like the publication of hard copy itself, is coming under the increasing scrutiny of courts seeking not so much to inhibit consumer usage as in assuring proper payments to publishers and authors alike—whatever the forms may be of information transmission." See Harriet L. Oler, "Copyright Law

and the Fair Use of Visual Images," *Fair Use and Free Inquiry: Copyright Law and the New Media,* edited by John Shelton Lawrence and Bernard Trimberg (Norwood, N.J.: Ablex Publishing, 1980), pp. 268–86, and Irving Louis Horowitz, "Corporate Ghosts in the Photocopying Machine," *Scholarly Publishing,* vol. 12, no. 4 (July 1981), pp. 299–304.

5. See Bill Esler, "The Printer Strikes Back," *Book and Magazine Production,* July 1981, pp. 39–42. A Wiley survey conducted in the Spring of 1981 found that over half of Wiley's authors have some kind of word-processing capability available to them, and 30 percent use word-processing technology to prepare manuscripts.

6. One advantage of having manuscripts in electronic form is that given an age of the electronic dissemination of textual materials, publishers with words in machine-readable form will be able to sell their "books" in either or both hard copy or disk form. See Sandra K. Paul, "Roadblocks in Typesetting from the Word Processor," *Scholarly Publishing,* vol. 12, no. 4 (July 1981), pp. 324–27. Also, see Robyn Shotwell, "Getting into Database Publishing: Some Possibilities and Pitfalls," *Publishers Weekly* (11 Sept. 1981), pp. 45–46.

7. One serious source of potential, and actual, litigation among publishers is in the area of unauthorized abstracting services. The *New York Times's* KIT, for example, is embroiled in serious controversy with McGraw-Hill's *Business Week*. The latter charges that such abstracting is based on exclusive copyrighted material which is being recycled and illegally sold; the *Times* claims that there is no copyright on facts. This is an area of litigation that will grow as computer technology of the printed word expands. See John F. Berry, *"Times* in Copyright Controversy," *Washington Post* (8 Nov. 1981).

8. Given an annual worldwide market for information technology now roughly worth $110 billion and expanding at 10 percent annually in real terms, the impact on publications reckons to be substantial. Journals and books, especially those of a data-rich variety with highly refined audiences, are prime candidates for electronic counterparts to conventional journals. The mechanisms for publisher participation in such efforts are still experimental, but quite real. See Allan Singleton, "The Electronic Journal and Its Relatives," *Scholarly Publishing,* vol. 13, no. 1 (Oct. 1981), pp. 3–18; and Lauren H. Seiler and Joseph Raben, "The Electronic Journal," *Transaction/*SOCIETY, vol. 18, no. 6 (Sept./Oct. 1981), pp. 76–83.

9. For a discussion of these issues see Robert D. Stueart, "Great Expectations: Library and Information Science at the Crossroads," *Library Journal,* vol. 15 (Oct. 1981), pp. 1989–92; and Mary C. Berger, "The Endangered Species: Can Information Service Survive?" *ASIS Bulletin* (Oct. 1981), pp. 12–14.

10. Nicholas A. Alter, "Microfilm: The Next Ten Years," UMI International reprint, June 1981; and George H. Harmon, "Micrographics: Return of the 25-Cent Book?" *The Futurist* (18 Oct. 1981), pp. 61–62.

11. See "Making Journals Fit for Readers," New Journals Review, *Nature* (Oct. 1981), p. 341. The point is also forcefully made by Cuadra Associates, a California consulting group, in their formal presentations.

12. See Robert Dahlin, "Consumer as Creator," *Publishing Weekly* (27 March 1981), pp. 11–18.

13. Liz Roman Gallese, "Publishers Try Adapting Print to Video Uses," *Wall Street Journal* (2 Nov. 1981), p. 1.

14. Henry B. Freedmen, "Paper's Role in an Electronic World," *The Futurist* (Oct. 1981), pp. 11–16.

15. "As publishers we are opposed to the regulation of content in any form . . . Democracy cannot exist without unfettered freedom of speech, and both government and private citizens must constantly be on guard against any encroachments and any forms of censorship" (from the American Association of Publishers' invited policy statement, filed on 23 Sept. 1981, in response to legislative efforts to rewrite the Communications Act of 1934, *AAP Newsletter,* 9 Oct. 1981).

4. The Political Economy of Database Technology

1. My chapter should be viewed as part and parcel of an ongoing effort to connect the social structure and scholarly publishing. In this regard, I would suggest the following three pieces in particular which I authored to be read in conjunction with "The Political Economy of Database Technology"; "Fair Use Versus Fair Return: Copyright Legislation and Its Consequences" (with Mary E. Curtis), *Journal of the American Society for Information Science,* (vol. 35, no. 2 (March 1984), pp. 67–75; "New Technology Scientific Information and Democratic Choices," *Information Age,* vol. 5, no. 2 (March 1983), pp. 67–73; and "The Impact of Technology on Scholarly Publishing," *Scholarly Publishing,* vol. 13, no. 3 (April 1982), pp. 211–28.

2. For a useful overview, see Ian Montagnes, "Perspectives on the New Technology," *Scholarly Publishing,* vol. 12, no. 3 (April 1981), pp. 219–23.

3. Stephen P. Herter, "Scientific Inquiry: A Model for Online Searching," *Journal of the American Society for Information Science,* vol. 35, no. 2 (March 1984), pp. 110–17.

4. Alan Singleton, "The Electronic Journal and Its Relatives," *Scholarly Publishing,* vol. 13, no. 1 (Oct. 1981), pp. 3–18.

5. J. Franklin, "Primary Information On-line in Biomedicine: An Appraisal," *Scholarly Publishing,* vol. 13, no. 4 (July 1982), pp. 317–25.

6. Roger Benjamin, *The Limits of Politics: Collective Goods and Political Change in Postindustrial Societies* (Chicago and London: University Chicago Press, 1980), pp. 86–87.

7. Ithiel de Sola Pool, "The Culture of Electronic Print," *Daedalus: Journal of the American Academy of Arts and Sciences,* whole no. 111, no. 4 (Fall 1982), pp. 21–22.

8. Murray A. Straus, "Social Stress in American States and Regions." Conference Paper for International Conference on Databases in the Humanities and Social Sciences, Rutgers University, June 11–12, 1983.

9. Joyce Duncan Falk, "America: History and Life Online: History and Much More," *Database,* vol. 6, no. 2 (June 1983), pp. 114–25; see also Dan Lacy, "Culture and the Media of Communication," *Scholarly Publishing,* vol. 13, no. 3 (April 1982), pp. 195–210.

10. Harry N. Rosenfeld, "The American Constitution: Free Inquiry, and the Law," in *Fair Use and Free Inquiry: Copyright Law and the New Media,* edited by John Shelton Lawrence and Bernard Timberg (Norwood, N.J.: Ablex Publishing Company, 1980), pp. 238–309.

11. J. Michael Brittain, "Internationality of the Social Sciences: Implication for Information Transfer," *Journal of the American Society for Information Science,* vol. 35, no. 1 (Winter 1984), pp. 11–18.

5. *Fair Use versus Fair Return: Copyright Legislation and Its Consequences*

1. R. Gibbon, Curtis Publishing Company. Comments and Views Submitted to the Copyright Office on Fair Use of Copyrighted Works, Oct. 24, 1958, Studies prepared for the Subcommittee on Patents, Trademarks, and Copyrights of the Committee on the Judiciary, U.S. Senate, Eighty-sixth Congress, Second Session. Washington, D.C.: U.S. Government Printing Office, 1960.

2. A. Wittman, Statement before the New York Hearings of the Library of Congress, Register of Copyrights. *Library Reproduction of Copyrighted Works* (17 U.S.C. 108). Appendix VI (Delivered Jan. 28, 1981). Released as *Report of the Register of Copyrights,* Jan. 1981, pp. 95–106.

3. S. E. Palmer, "Copyright Suit: What Effect on Professors." *The Chronicle of Higher Education,* vol. 25, no. 17 (Jan. 5, 1983), pp. 16–27.

4. R. Wedgeworth, Executive Director, American Library Association. Public Hearing on the Report of the Register of Copyrights on the Effect of 17 U.S.C., 108 on the Rights of Creators and the Needs of Users of Works Reproduced by Certain Libraries and Archives, Jan. 28, 1981, New York. *Report of the Register of Copyrights,* Appendix VI, Part 1, p. 61.

5. J. G. Howard, "Electronic Journals: Potential Dangers" (letter), *The Chronicle of Higher Education* (July 27, 1983).

6. N. H. Marshall, "Comments of the American Library Association on the Report of the Register of Copyrights to Congress: Library Reproduction of Coppyrighted Works (17 U.S.C. 108)." Released by the Washington, D.C. office of the American Library Association. June 1983.

7. L. F. Seltzer, *Exemptions and Fair Use in Copyright: The Exclusive Rights Tensions of the 1976 Copyright Act* (Cambridge: Harvard University Press), pp. 116–117.

8. Testimony of the Information Industry Association before the Copyright Office, Jan. 29, 1981. *Report of the Register of Copyrights,* Appendix VI, Part 2, p. 4.

9. K. Nadeski, J. Pontius, "Developments in Micrographics, 'Fair Use,' and Video Technology." *Library Resources and Technical Services,* vol. 27, no. 3 (1983), pp. 278–96.

10. R. Campbell, "Making Sense of Journal Publishing." *Nature,* vol. 299 (Oct. 7, 1982), pp. 491–92.

11. See Summaries of Commission-Sponsored Studies, "An Analysis of Computer and Photocopying Issues from the Point of View of the General Public and the Ultimate Consumer, Public Interest Economics Center, Final Report of the *National Commission on New Technological Uses of Copyrighted Works.* July 31, 1978 (Washington, D.C.: Library of Congress, 1979), p. 129.

12. N. H. Marshall, "Comments of the American Library Association on

the Report of the Register of Copyrights to Congress: Library Reproduction of Copyrighted Works (17 U.S.C. 108)." Released by the Washington, D.C. Office of the American Library Association. June 1983, p. 9.

13. H. S. Bloom, "The Copyright Position in Britain"; and A. A. Keyes, "Copyright and Fair Dealing in Canada," in J. S. Lawrence and B. Timberg, eds., *Fair Use and Free Inquiry: Copyright Law and the New Media* (Norwood, N.J.: Ablex Publishing Company, 1980), pp. 198–221.

14. O. Karp, (ed.), "Authors League Symposium on Copyright-Protection of Non-fiction Works and Literary/Dramatic Characters," *Journal of Copyright Bulletin* (Aug. 1982), pp. 611–16.

15. I. L. Horowitz; M. E. Curtis, "The Impact of Technology on Scholarly Publishing." *Scholarly Publishing,* vol. 13, no. 3 (1982), pp. 211–28. I. L. Horowitz, "New Technology, Scientific Information, and Democratic Choices," *Information Age,* vol. 5, no. 2 (1983), pp. 67–73.

6. Knowledge and Property—Big Issues in Small Machines

1. While most legal decisions have tended to confirm the rights of publishers to claim the protection of copyright, the courts have tended to construe such decisions on narrow grounds. In the 1985 case, Harper & Row won over *The Nation,* the Supreme Court made a point of emphasizing the specifics of the case in order to avoid any "chilling factor" on the dissemination of information.

2. After the legal verbiage of recent Supreme Court decisions are stripped away, it is clear that the courts have resoundingly argued in favor of the maintenance of copyright protection for publics and potentates alike. Even the most vigorous argument in favor of the right to know, when it comes to presidential figures, acknowledge as much. See, Victor Navasky, "Monopolizing the News," *The Nation* (June 1, 1985), p. 657.

3. Christopher Wilson, The Making of a Best Seller, 1906," *New York Times* (Dec. 22, 1985), pp. 1, 25.

4. There are, of course, certain cases, such as University Microfilm, wholly owned (until recently) by the Xerox Corporation, where industries find themselves on both sides of the copyright dilemma. But these exceptions are relatively unusual, growing less so with the recent Xerox and IBM divestitures of their publishing divisions.

5. One such device, manufactured by Manitou Systems in Chicago, is in Levi Strauss, DuPont, Simon & Friedlander, the University of San Francisco, and scores of other industries, banks, law firms, and accounting firms. See *New Product Marketing* (May 1977), pp. 24–25.

6. For an excellent summary of public libraries and private levies, see William B. Goodman, "Readers' Rights and Writers' Property," *The American Scholar,* vol. 54, no. 3 (Summer 1985), pp. 389–96.

7. Zygmut Nagorski, "For Whom Does Jaruzelski Speak?", *New York Times.* (Sept. 23, 1985), p. 19.

8. Douglas C. McGill, "Copyright Dispute Swirls Around Sculptures," *New York Times.* Aug. 29, 1985, p. 15 (section C).

7. *The Rise of Information and the Fall of Knowledge*

1. The literature on this distinction between information and knowledge is more vast than deep. My own favorites, from the contemporary period at least, are Anatol Rapaport's two books, *Fights, Games, and Debates* (Ann Arbor: University of Michigan Press, 1960); and his *Strategy and Conscience* (New York: Harper & Row, 1964). In this same category of excellence are the works of Lewis F. Richardson, *Arms and Insecurity* (Chicago: Quadrangle Books, 1960); and his classic work, *Statistics of Deadly Quarrels* (Chicago: Quadrangle Books, 1960).

2. For a contemporary exploration of this distinction between power and authority as it relates to information and knowledge, I would recommend the two volumes of Hannah Arendt's *The Life of the Mind* (vol. 1, *Thinking;* vol. 2, *Willing*) (New York and London: Harcourt Brace Jovanovich, 1977). Also see her Lectures on Kant's *Political Philosophy,* edited with an interpretive essay by Ronald Beiner (Chicago: The University of Chicago Press, 1982).

3. Irving Louis Horowitz, "Methods and Strategies in Evaluating Equity Research," *Social Indicators Research,* vol. 6, no. 1 (January 1979), pp. 1–22.

4. Andrew H. Neilly, Jr., "Professional and Scientific Books," *The Business of Book Publishing,* edited by E. A. Geiser, Arnold Dolin, with Gladys S. Topkis (Boulder and London: Westview Books, 1985), p. 337.

5. T. W. Collins, "Social Science Research and the Microcomputer," *Sociological Methods and Research,* vol. 9, no. 4 (Autumn 1984), pp. 438–60.

6. John Shelton Laurence, *The Electronic Scholar: A Guide to Academic Microcomputing* (Norwood, N.J.: Ablex Publishing Co., 1984), pp. 135–36.

7. *McGraw-Hill Annual Stockholders' Report,* "Special Report: Focus on the Future" (New York: McGraw-Hill, 1985), pp. 9–22.

8. Frederick A. Praeger, "From the Publisher" *Westview Publishers Catalog* (Spring 1985). Inside front cover.

9. Patricia Battin, "The Electronic Library—A Vision of the Future," *EDUCOM Bulletin* (Summer 1984). Issued as Scholarly Communication Reprint: 2, by the Office of Scholarly Communication and Technology. Washington, D.C. (June 19, 1985). pp. 7.

10. Robert Bogdan and Margret Ksander, "Policy Data as a Social Profess: A Qualitative Approach to Quantitative Data." *Occasional Papers Series of the Center for the Study of Citizenship.* Syracuse: Maxwell School of Citizenship and Public Affairs, 1985. 22 pp.

11. James N. Danziger, "Social Science and the Social Impacts of Computer Technology," *Social Science Quarterly,* vol. 66, no. 1 (March 1985), pp. 3–21.

12. Isaiah Berlin, *Four Essays on Liberty* (New York: Oxford University Press, 1970), pp. 33–34.

13. Steven Sieck, "Information Storage and Retrieval," *Publishers Weekly,* vol. 226, no. 21 (Nov. 23, 1984), pp. 36–42.

8. Scholarly Communication and Academic Publishing

1. Arthur J. Rosenthal, "University Press Publishing," *The Business of Book Publishing,* edited by Elizabeth A. Geiser, et al. (Boulder and London: Westview Press, 1985), pp. 344–49.

2. Marsh Jeanneret, "God and Mammon: The University as Publisher," *Scholarly Publishing,* vol. 15, no. 3 (April 1984), pp. 203–4.

3. Herbert G. Bailey, *The Art and Science of Publishing* (New York: Harper & Row, 1970).

4. Fritz Machlup and Kenneth W. Leeson, *Information Through the Printed Word,* three volumes (New York: Praeger Publishers, 1978).

5. Irving Louis Horowitz and Mary E. Curtis, "On Truth in Publishing," *The Nation,* vol. 226 (1981), pp. 660–61.

6. National Endowment for the Humanities, *Scholarly Communications: The Report of the National Enquiry* (Baltimore: Johns Hopkins University Press, 1978).

7. J. Michael Brittain, et al., "Is Information International?", *Transaction/SOCIETY,* vol. 22, no. 5 (July-Aug. 1985), pp. 3–19.

8. Lewis A. Coser, Charles Kadushin, and Walter W. Powell, *Books: The Culture and Commerce of Publishing* (New York: Basic Books, 1982).

9. Expropriating Ideas—The Global Politics of Publishing

1. Eric H. Smith, *New Strategies to Curb International Book Piracy: A Survey of The New Foreign Trade Legislation* (New York: Paskus, Gordon & Hyman, 1985). 34 pages (mimeographed).

2. Aldo Armando Cocca, "The Domain of the Right To Communicate," in *The Right To Communicate: A New Human Right,* edited by Desmond Fisher and L. S. Harms (Dublin: Boole Press, 1983), pp. 24–37.

3. Iuri Kolossov, "The Right To Communicate in International Law," in *The Right To Communicate,* pp. 112–23.

4. Loren R. Graham, "Science and Computers in Soviet Society," *Proceedings of the Academy of Political Science,* vol. 35, no. 3 (Fall 1984), pp. 124–34.

5. J. Alexis Koutchoumow, et al., *The Impact of Electronic Technology* (A Joint Statement of European Librarians and Publishers). This group included representatives of the International Federation of Library Associations and Institutions, International Publishers' Association, and The International Group of Scientific, Technical and Medical Publishers. 7 pages (mimeographed). Amsterdam, Holland, IPA, 1984.

6. Esther M. Pacheco (seminar director), "Disseminating Asia's Scholarly Books," in *IASP Newsletter,* whole no. 2 (April 1985), pp. 1–2.

7. Rowland Lorimer, "Implications of the New Technologies of Information," *Scholarly Publishing,* vol. 16, no. 3 (April 1985), pp. 197–210.

8. Dee Garrison, *Apostles of Culture: The Public Librarian and American Society, 1876–1920* (New York: The Free Press/Macmillan, 1979), pp. 237–38.

9. See the brilliant work of Elizabeth L. Eisenstein, *The Printing Revolution in Early Modern Europe* (Cambridge: Cambridge University Press, 1983), esp. pp. 29–106.

10. Sean MacBride, et al., *The Right to Communicate: A New Human Right,* edited by Desmond Fisher and L. S. Harms (Dublin: Boole Press, 1982), pp. xv–xviii.

11. A singularly worthwhile overview of Third World options, remarkably free of overheated rhetoric, is Juan Rada, "Information Technology and The Third World," in *The Information Technology Revolution,* edited by Tom Forester (Cambridge: The MIT Press, 1985), pp. 571–89.

12. Office of Technology Assessment, *Intellectual Proprety Rights in an Age of Electronics and Information.* 18 pages (mimeographed). Washington, D.C.: OTA Project proposal sponsored by House and Senate Committees on the Judiciary. 1984.

13. Kinko's Graphics Corporation, "Custom Publishing," *Professor Publishing Newsletter,* vol. 2, no. 1 (Spring 1985), pp. 1–4.

14. William M. Childs, "A Book Publishing Program for USIA," in *American Books Abroad: Toward A National Policy,* edited by William M. Childs and Donald E. McNeil (Washington, D.C.: The Helen Dwight Reid Educational Foundation, 1986), pp. 161–89.

15. Donald E. McNeil, "The Role of Private, Public, and Independent Organizations," in *American Books Abroad,* pp. 147–60.

16. W. Gordon Graham, "The Shrinking World Market," *Publishers Weekly,* May 4, 1984; and his earlier piece, "Publishing in a Major World Market," *Publishers Weekly,* February 6, 1978.

17. Curtis G. Benjamin, *U.S. Books Abroad: Neglected Ambassadors* (Washington, D.C.: Library of Congress, 1984), pp. 71–74.

18. William E. Freeman and Scott Righetti, *Soviet Book Exports 1973–1982* (Washington, D.C.: United States Information Agency, 1984).

10. Scientific Access and Political Constraint to Knowledge

1. Perhaps the first major scholar to recognize and codify this great transformation is Fritz Machlup, in *The Production and Distribution of Knowledge in the United States* (Princeton: Princeton University Press, 1962).

2. Harry Braverman, *Labor and Monopoly Capital: The Degradation of Work in the Twentieth Century* (New York: Monthly Review Press, 1974). For a more recent, and more sophisticated analysis see Phil Blackburn, Rod Coombs, and Kenneth Green, *Technology, Economic Growth and The Labour Process* (New York: St. Martin's Press, 1985), pp. 200–208.

3. Nowhere is this process better observed than in the printing industries which "leap-frogged" the older Merganthaler hot-lead equipment with everything from cold-type processes to word processing that simply bypassed older stages of print technology. See, Daniel Bell, *The Coming of Post-Industrial Society: A Venture in Social Forecasting* (New York: Basic Books, 1974).

4. Robert Wrenn, "The Decline of American Labor," *Socialist Review,* vol. 15, nos. 4–5 (July-Oct. 1985), pp. 89–117.

5. Everett M. Rogers and Judith K. Larsen, "Silicon Valley Fever: The Rise of High Technology Culture," in *The Computer Culture,* edited by Susan H. Evans and Peter Clarke (Indianapolis: White River Press, 1984), p. 17.

6. Michael J. Piore, "Computer Technologies, Market Structure, and

Strategic Union Choices," in *Challenges and Choices Facing American Labor,* edited by Thomas A. Kochan (Cambridge: The MIT Press, 1985), pp. 199–200.

7. Charles Handy, *The Future of Work: A Guide to a Changing Society* (Oxford: Basil Blackwell, 1984), p. 55.

8. Lajos Hethy, "Today's Workers in the Socialist Countries of Eastern Europe." Paper delivered at a Conference on *Workers' Values and Behavior in the Industrially Advanced Societies,* Castelgandolfo, Rome, Italy. June 20–21, 1985 (mimeographed), p. 8.

9. See Irving Louis Horowitz, "Bureaucracy, Administration and State Power," in *Winners and Losers: Social and Political Polarities in America* (Durham, N.C.: Duke University Press, 1984), pp. 115–25.

10. Ezra F. Vogel, *Comeback: Building the Resurgence of American Business* (New York: Simon & Schuster, 1985), esp. 263–77.

11. See George W. England, "Major Work Meanings in the USA Workforce—A Comparative View," Monograph prepared for Conference on "Workers' Values and Behavior in Industrially Advanced Societies." Rome, Italy, June 20–21, 1985. Mimeographed. Also see, R. P. Vecchio, "The Function and Meaning of Work and the Job," *Academy of Management Journal,* vol. 23, no. 4 (Autumn 1980), pp. 361–67.

12. David Clutterbuck, *New Patterns of Work* (New York: St. Martin's Press, 1985), p. 134.

13. One recent effort to address this problem is Edmond A. Lisle, "Validation in the Social Sciences by International Comparison," in *International Social Science Journal,* vol. 37, no. 1 (1985), whole no. 103, pp. 19–30.

14. See, for example, George Gerbner, "The Importance of Being Critical," in *Ferment in the Field: An International Symposium.* Published as *Journal of Communication,* vol. 33, no. 3 (Summer 1983), pp. 355–62.

11. From Means of Production to Modes of Communication

1. This chapter is not intended to provide a practical, "how to" approach to marketing and advertising. Indeed, this task has been splendidly pre-empted, for some time to come I should think by Nat G. Bodian, in his *Book Marketing Handbook: Tips and Techniques,* Vol. One (New York: R. R. Bowker, 1980); and *Book Marketing Handbook: Over 1000 More Tips and Techniques,* Vol. Two (New York: R. R. Bowker, 1983).

2. For a further elaboration on these distinctions in the forms of information, see my earlier work *Philosophy, Science and the Sociology of Knowledge* (Springfield, Ill.: Charles C Thomas-Publisher, 1961), esp. pp. 79–91.

12. Advertising Ideas and Marketing Products

1. Alex Haley, *Roots* (Garden City, N.Y.: Doubleday, 1976).

2. H. R. Haldeman, with Joseph DiMona, *The Ends of Power* (New York: Times Books, 1978).

3. David M. Rorvik, *In His Image: The Cloning of a Man* (Philadelphia: Lippincott, 1978).

4. Timothy J. Cooney, *Telling Right from Wrong* (Buffalo, N.Y.: Prometheus Books, 1985).

5. Clifford Irving, with Richard Suskind. *Clifford Irving: What Really Happened* (New York: Grove Press, 1972). The "original" title to the unreleased "autobiography" is called *The Autobiography of Howard Hughes* (New York: McGraw-Hill, 1972).

6. Elizabeth L. Eisenstein, *The Printing Revolution in Early Modern Europe* (Cambridge: Cambridge University Press, 1983), pp. 97–106.

7. James D. Watson, *The Double Helix: A Personal Account of the Discovery of the Structure of DNA* (New York: Atheneum, 1968).

8. Immanuel Velikovsky, *Worlds in Collision* (New York: Doubleday, 1950).

9. Martin Gardner, *Fads and Fallacies in the Name of Science* (New York: Dover Publications, 1957).

10. Karl Marx, "On the Freedom of the Press" (1842), in *Karl Marx: Selected Writings,* edited by David McLellan (New York and London: Oxford University Press, 1977), pp. 17–25.

13. Gatekeeping Functions and Publishing Truths

1. Arthur J. Rosenthal, "University Press Publishing," *The Business of Book Publishing,* edited by Elizabeth A. Geiser, Arnold Dolin, and Gladys S. Topkis (Boulder and London: Westview Press, 1985), pp. 344–49.

2. Morris Philipson, "Spreading the Word," *Scholarly Publishing,* vol. 16, no. 2 (January 1985), pp. 99–107.

3. Edward H. Berman, "On Publishing, Probably Perishing, and Surely Paying," *Scholarly Publishing,* vol. 16, no. 4 (July 1985), pp. 307–12.

4. Jack Miles, "Intellectual Freedom and the University Press," *Scholarly Publishing,* vol. 15, no. 4 (July 1984), pp. 291–99.

5. Marsh Jeanneret, "God and Mammon: The University as Publisher," *Scholarly Publishing,* vol. 15, no. 3 (April 1984), pp. 197–204.

6. Herbert C. Morton, "A New Office to Strengthen Scholarly Communication," *Scholarly Publishing,* vol. 15, no. 2 (January 1984), pp. 99–145.

14. The Social Structure of Scholarly Communication

1. Judith S. Duke, *The Technical, Scientific and Medical Publishing Market* (White Plains and London: Knowledge Industry Publications, 1985), pp. 25–65.

2. Chandler B. Grannis, "Title Output and Average Prices: 1984 Final Figures," *Publishers Weekly* (August 23, 1985), pp. 41–44.

3. John P. Dessauer, *AAP Industry Sales Statistics: 1977* (New York: Association of American Publishers, 1978), especially pp. 18–19, 57, 126–27; also "Books Published by Selected Field: 1950–1975," in *Social Indicators* (Washington, D.C.: U.S. Department of Commerce, 1977), p. 516.

4. Paul DiMaggio, "Market Structure, the Creative Process, and Popular

Culture: Toward an Organizational Reinterpretation of Mass Culture Theory," *Journal of Popular Culture,* vol. 11, no. 2 (Fall 1977), pp. 436–48.

5. Irving Louis Horowitz and Paul Barker, "Mediating Journals: Reaching Out to a Public Beyond the Scientific Community," *International Social Science Journal,* vol. 26, no. 3 (1974), pp. 393–410.

6. Fritz Machlup, "They Don't Know They Are Sick," *Publishers Weekly,* vol. 208, no. 13 (Sept. 29, 1975), pp. 30–31; also Fritz Machlup and Kenneth Leeson, et al. *Information Through the Printed Word: The Dissemination of Scholarly Scientific and Intellectual Knowledge,* vol. 2: Journals (New York: Praeger/CBS, 1978).

7. Paul Doebler, "New Computerized Services Provide Speedy (But Not Free) Copies 'On Demand'," *Publishers Weekly,* pp. 34–66.

8. Staff Report, "The Book Boom: Action in Paperbacks," *Business Week,* no. 2490 (July 4, 1977), pp. 50–52.

9. Alan U. Schwartz, "The Threat of the One-Medium Market," *Publishers Weekly,* vol. 213, no. 14 (April 3, 1978), pp. 40–41.

10. William Chapman, "Report on Bureau of Labor Statistics Findings," *Washington Post* (May 14, 1977).

11. George P. Bush, ed., *Technology and Copyright: Annotated Bibliography and Source Materials* (Mt. Airy, Md.: Lamond Publishers, 1972).

12. John P. Dessauer, *Library Acquisitions: A Look into the Future* (Darien, CT: Book Industry Study Group, Research Report Number 3, 1976).

13. Susan K. Martin, *Library Networks, 1976–1977* (New York: Knowledge Industry Publications, 1977).

14. Marjorie McManus, report cited in *Authors Guild Bulletin* (March-May 1977), p. 26.

15. Prepared by the Association of American Publishers Education Committee, *The Accidental Profession: Education, Training and the People of Publishing* (New York: Association of American Publishers, 1977), pp. 101–2.

15. Social Science as Scholarly Communication

1. Carol H. Weiss, "Media Report Card for Social Science," *Society,* vol. 22, no. 3 (March-April 1985), pp. 39–47.

2. Reinhard Bendix, *Embattled Reason* (New York and London: Oxford University Press, 1970); new edition (New Brunswick and Oxford: Transaction Publishers, 1985). This work neatly expresses the fault lines in the struggle of social science against obscurantism of all types.

3. Irving Louis Horowitz, *The Rise and Fall of Project Camelot: Studies in the Relationship between Social Science and Practical Politics.* (Cambridge and London: MIT Press, 1967).

4. Even within the United States, pilot programs in optical disk technology are just getting under way. In addition to problems of service and applicability, there are issues of payments to copyright holders. Thus far, these reader stations for digital systems permit the option of reading *or* printing—but not of payment to publishers and authors. It will probably be well into the new century before this issue is resolved or even implemented at the international level.

See, Victoria Ann Reich and Melissa Ann Betcher, "Optical Disk System: An Evaluation," Washington, D.C.: The Deputy Librarian of Congress (October 1985). Mimeograph. 23 pp. Also see, Lois Lunin, "Perspective on Videodisc and Optical Disk: Technology, Research, and Applications," *Journal of the American Society of Information Science,* vol. 34, no. 4 (Nov. 1983).

Index

Academic careers: influence of publishing on, 124–26, 164, 170, 185

Academic presses: commercial publishing and, 172–74, 178; definition/function of, 169–70, 174; professional organizations for, 178–79; regional concerns of, 177; relationship to university of, 164, 171–72, 173; specialization of, 177–78. *See also* Publishing business; Scholarly communication; Scholarly publishing; Science/scientific publishing; Social science publishing

Access to information/knowledge: agenda setting and, 135–36; denial of, 134, 135, 138; in Europe, 116–18; free, 9, 23, 57–58, 70, 139; gatekeeping function of publishing and, 23–24, 136–37; geographical issues and, 133; as a human right, 116; isolationism and, 138–39; language and, 134; Lorimer's view of, 119–20; military research and, 135–36, 139, 140; new technology and, 17–18, 26, 43–44, 117, 120, 132–33, 193; norms/values and, 134; science and, 132–40; social science and, 193; Soviet Union and, 117, 133, 134–35, 137, 138; Third World and, 116, 138. *See also* Copyright; Databases; Property rights

Advertising, 155–61. *See also* Marketing

American Association of University Publishers, 178–79

American Copyright Council, 81–82

American Council of Learned Societies, 92

American Library Association, 59–60, 63, 67. *See also* Libraries

Ancillary/subsidiary sales, 192

Annuals/serials, social science, 184

Anti-intellectualism in publishing, 89–95

Argentina, 116

Aron, Raymond, 153

Association of American Publishers, 59, 62, 68–69, 74, 79–80, 81, 111, 127, 176, 179, 187, 198–99. *See also* Copyright Clearance Center

Audience. *See* Marketing

Authors: as copyright holders, 31, 73, 77, 78, 81–82; publishing business and, 32–33, 38, 40, 108–9, 113–14, 183, 197–98; social science publishing and, 183, 197–98

Authors' Guild, 65, 190

Authors' League of America, 59

Bell, Daniel, 157

Benjamin, Curtis, 127

Berlin, Isaiah, 94

Berman, Edward H., 170

Bibliographic databases, 34, 36, 42–43, 211